YESTERDAY
WE WERE IN
AMERICA

BY THE SAME AUTHOR

Green Dust: Ireland's Unique Motor Racing History

Triumph of the Red Devil: The Irish Gordon Bennett Cup Race 1903

There Might be a Drop of Rain Yet: A Memoir

Parsons Bookshop: At the Heart of Bohemian Dublin, 1949–1989

Prodigals and Geniuses: The Writers and Artists of Dublin's Baggotonia

City of Writers: The Lives and Homes of Dublin Authors

Princess of the Orient: A Romantic Odyssey

www.brendanlynchbooks.com

YESTERDAY
WE WERE IN
AMERICA

ALCOCK AND BROWN, FIRST TO FLY
THE ATLANTIC NON-STOP

BRENDAN LYNCH

FOREWORDS BY LEN DEIGHTON AND GROUP CAPTAIN A.J.H. ALCOCK, MBE, RAF

The
History
Press

To the irrepressible Margie.

And to the memory of Alcock and Brown
and all the brave aviation pioneers.

*Man must rise above the Earth – to the top of the atmosphere and beyond –
for only thus will he fully understand the world in which he lives.*

Socrates

Cover Illustrations: *Front:* The Vimy takes off, next stop Europe.
(Author's Collection) *Back:* A monument on Ballinaboy Hill points to
the Vimy's 1919 landing site. (Smb1001 via WikimediaCommons)

First published in 2012 by Haynes Publishing
This edition published 2019

The History Press
The Mill, Brimscombe Port
Stroud, Gloucestershire, GL5 2QG
www.thehistorypress.co.uk

British Library Cataloguing in Publication Data.
A catalogue record for this book is available from the British Library.

ISBN 978 0 7509 9000 4

Typesetting and origination by The History Press
Printed in Turkey by Imak

CONTENTS

FOREWORD
TO PREVIOUS EDITION

Wars are studied by historians because wars hasten progress, whether it is political, technical or social. This is particularly true of the First World War. Literacy and adult education for women and men, government supervision of industry and the conscription of workers and soldiers transformed Europe. The development of weapons also played a part in what became a worldwide conflict. In 1914 armies went to war with horses and swords. By 1918 warfare had been transformed by tanks, flame-throwers, radio sets, motor transport, poison gas and machine pistols not unlike those in use today. The fighting had transformed tactics, and made intellectual demands upon generals that very few could adequately meet.

Nothing changed more than aircraft. It had been the lightweight flying machines that won prizes at pre-war aviation gatherings. France's single-seat Morane-Saulnier Type H monoplane with its 100hp engine had been the highlight of many air displays. By 1918 the strategic bomber was targeting German industrial towns.[1]

By war's end the Vickers Vimy bombers, one of which John Alcock and Arthur Whitten Brown took across the Atlantic, had big and heavy Rolls-Royce Eagle VIII engines. By this time the rotary engine had become obsolete and the air-cooled engine had not yet demonstrated its true potential. So despite the added weight of the plumbing and the water needed for cooling, the Eagle with the Vickers airframe was probably the best combination available.

The Eagle owed its birth to the Mercedes engine. At the start of hostilities Rolls-Royce had taken it from a motor car on display in a

---

1 Although, in Russia in 1913, Igor Sikorsky built and flew some remarkable four-engine aircraft, the 100hp Argus engines they typically used were virtually the same engines that the Berlin factory had been fitting into motor cars since 1902.

showroom on Shaftesbury Avenue in London's West End. The Rolls engineers examined it carefully and produced their V-12, which was rather like two Mercedes straight-six engines put together. But the Rolls engineers improved it. It had forged steel cylinders and Mercedes-style welded induction and exhaust ports. The overhead camshaft had two valves and two plugs for each cylinder. It had four Watford magnetos each supplying six cylinders, and four carburetors to distribute the fuel evenly. During the war the Eagle had been boosted from 225hp to over 360hp. This engine was used in flying boats, airships and bombers. It was a notable success story and brought Rolls-Royce a large proportion of its profits. The Vickers Vimy night bomber into which two Eagles were fitted had arrived just too late for operational service and everyone concerned with its production hoped to see it used for commercial aviation. An Atlantic crossing would bring exactly the sort of worldwide publicity that would promote the big aircraft into airline use.

However, Brendan Lynch's story is not just about machines. It is the story of two men. John Alcock, the 23-year-old pilot, was the younger of the two. He started flying before the war and by the time he joined the Royal Naval Air Service he had logged many hours and flown numerous aircraft of various types. On a bombing mission in 1917 he was shot down over Suvla Bay and became a prisoner of the Turks.

Arthur Whitten Brown was older and the more sober of the pair. He had served on the Somme as an infantry officer before becoming a Royal Flying Corps pilot. Shot down in France, the leg injuries he suffered in the crash (the British would not permit their pilots to use parachutes) permanently disabled him. His lame leg caused him to be repatriated from his POW camp before war's end. In Britain he worked on engine research for the Ministry of Munitions and then went to work for Vickers where, purely by chance, he met Alcock.

Both men knew the dangers and difficulties that the early aircraft brought, and both men had examined themselves and contemplated their future with the focus that imprisonment provides. And both men had given thought to transatlantic flight. It was a chance meeting but a perfect pairing:

Alcock the bold, methodical, accomplished and very experienced pilot; and Brown, who was not only a dedicated navigator, but also functioned as what was later to be called the 'flight engineer'. Brown's mechanical knowledge was important at a time when engines – in particular their fuel flow and temperature – needed ceaseless attention.

The story of this historic flight has been shamefully neglected. It marked a moment when British aviation might have led the world. Alcock and Brown showed the way but the lesson was not learned. Britain, like other European powers, was content with low-performance engines on passenger aircraft that could do no better than short hops to South Africa and Australia; while in the 1930s American aircraft and airliners conquered both the Atlantic and the Pacific. Even in the 1950s Britain's remarkable jet-engined Comet was forced to stop off at Gander, Newfoundland, because it could not make the full non-stop Atlantic crossing.

In these days of ruthless competition it is satisfying to record that Alcock and Brown were attractive and modest heroes who became close friends. They generously insisted that part of their monetary prize was distributed among Vickers support staff. Brendan Lynch, in this excellent book, tells their story with the skill of a dedicated researcher and the talent of a popular novelist. *Yesterday We Were in America* is a very fine book; I only wish I had written it.

Len Deighton
Copyright © Pluriform, 2008

FOREWORD TO NEW EDITION
GROUP CAPTAIN A.J.H. ALCOCK, MBE, RAF, NEPHEW OF JOHN ALCOCK

The first non-stop Atlantic flight by my uncle Captain John Alcock and navigator Arthur Whitten Brown is a feat that still amazes me.

To guide an open-cockpit plane across the previously unassailable Atlantic wastes was a rare triumph of both flying and navigational ability. One mishap, one error would have meant an unknown watery grave for both men. An inspirational saga of courage against the odds, it was also a resounding triumph for the British aviation industry, which had earlier lagged behind its continental rivals.

After swapping school for a Manchester engineering apprenticeship, my uncle's interest in aviation was sparked when he was allowed to work on a biplane. Shortly afterwards, he watched the end of the 1908 London-Manchester air race with my grandfather, whom he promptly informed that, one day, he also would fly.

Both my father and myself followed in his footsteps. One of the most poignant moments in my flying career was when I commemorated the 1919 flight's sixtieth anniversary by piloting a specially painted Phantom jet from Canada to England with Flight Lieutenant W.N. Browne. We replicated the original crossing by overflying Newfoundland and crossing the Irish coast at Clifden.

We flew this route in three and a half hours in an air-conditioned cockpit at 28,000ft in smooth air above the weather. This compared to the sixteen hours the original Alcock and Brown had endured in their flimsy open machine, flying mostly below 10,000 ft in rough air and cloudy conditions.

John Alcock and Arthur Whitten Brown were modest men. Their trail-blazing exploit was overshadowed by later more publicised flights. I agree with Len Deighton that the story of their great achievement has been shamefully neglected. Not only the first non-stop Atlantic flight, but also the first over any ocean and the longest distance ever covered by man up to that time.

This comprehensive centenary book will, I hope, help to redress the balance. And give Alcock and Brown their well-deserved proper place in the pantheon of aviation pioneers.

ALCOCK AND BROWN
– RARE AVIATORS

STEVE FOSSETT, FROM AN INTERVIEW WITH THE AUTHOR

I could not compare my 2005 re-enactment of Alcock and Brown's great flight to the ballooning or any of my other exploits.

This was a special project that always had a great fascination for me and a sense of historical purpose. It was in the context of trying to honour Alcock and Brown and to be aviators like them.

My recreation of the flight with Mark Rebholz was difficult. It was a long journey.

The greatest danger for us was the take-off at such high weight. Alcock and Brown had that danger plus the unknown of weather. Very little was known about wind and weather in 1919.

The Vimy fliers took a big risk of losing their lives. Like them, we had significant risk of engine failure that would require ditching. Today there is an excellent Rescue Control system, so our survival would not have been in doubt.

The Vimy proved a difficult aeroplane to fly. We learned the reality of aeronautics in those early days. And the full measure of Alcock and Brown's achievement.

During the flight they got only three usable sextant shots. Yet, they flew and navigated the longest distance flown by man up to then. And, after sixteen hours and almost 1,900 miles, they landed just a few miles off course.

The first to cross an ocean non-stop, Alcock and Brown were rare aviators and real heroes.

ACKNOWLEDGEMENTS

This book is based on contemporary newspaper reports and Alcock and Brown's first-hand accounts published in *Badminton Magazine* and the *Royal Air Force and Aviation Record*, and also on interviews with Steve Fossett and Harry Sullivan, the last surviving witness of the Vimy's arrival, and the reminiscences of people in St John's and also of Vickers' staff. Another interviewee was Anthony Kilmister OBE, who shared his memories of 'Uncle Teddy' Whitten Brown (and who so kindly presented Brown's flying boots and torch to Clifden Museum).

My task could not have been completed without the generous assistance of many other fine people on both sides of that ocean the fliers had spanned. I must thank Damian O'Brien and Maeve McKeever, Cultural Tourism & Heritage, Fáilte Ireland, who supported this project from day one, and Karen Ocana of Air Canada's Corporate Communications, who enabled me to visit Newfoundland, from where the transatlantic fliers started. Also Air Canada pilot Capt. Steve Allard, Fg Off. Ben Lavergne and colleagues at St John's Airport, who answered my many queries.

For allowing me the privilege of studying Arthur Whitten Brown's chart, log book and letters I must thank the extremely helpful curator of the RAF Museum, Gordon Leith, and his equally enthusiastic colleague Peter Elliott, also Nina Burls and Laureen Woodard. Wg Cdr Guy Griffiths granted permission to quote from the diary of his great uncle and Arthur Whitten Brown's former pilot, the gallant William Allcock.

Many thanks to the eminently knowledgeable Nick Forder, Air and Space Curator at Manchester Museum of Science and Industry; Jackie Tipping, Manchester City Council; Kath Lapsley and Richard Bond, Manchester Archives and Local Studies; Tony Lees, Greater Manchester County Record Office; Sarah Hartley, *Manchester Evening News* and Jo Abley, North West Film Archive. Few could match the patience and professionalism of the staff of many libraries, notably the British Library, the British Newspaper Library, London's Science Museum Library, Dublin's Trinity College, Gerry Lyne and his fantastic crew of Dublin's National Library, and John Wells and Michael L. Wilson of Cambridge University Library.

Also, the following at the Memorial University of Newfoundland: Erin Alcock, Deborah Andrews, Debbie Edgecombe, Colleen Field, Shannon Gordon, Jackie Hillier and Linda White. My thanks also to Cal Best and Melanie Tucker at The Rooms Provincial Archives; Neachel Keeping and Helen Miller, City of St John's Archives; John Griffin, Provincial Resource Library, and Alasdair Black, Admiralty House Museum, Mount Pearl. Also Lara Andrews, Canadian War Museum; Capt. B. Bond, Canadian Air Force Heritage and History; Ian Leslie, Canada Aviation Museum, and Daphne and Brian Williams of North Atlantic Aviation Museum.

A special thanks to Michelle Goodman, Andrew Nahum and Laura Singleton in the London Science Museum. 'Health and Safety Rules' precluded a close inspection of the historic Vimy's cockpit. (Good job they did not rule in Alcock and Brown's time!) All the more reason to thank pilots John Dodd and Clive Edwards of Edwards Brothers Aviation for inviting me into the cockpit of Steve Fossett's Vimy, which enabled a true appreciation of the confined space from which the great Atlantic flight was directed.

Thanks to all those enthusiasts at the Vimy's Weybridge birthplace, notably Brooklands Museum's Julian Temple, John Pulford, Tony Hutchings, and Gerry Forristal. And Melvyn Hiscock for his invaluable first-hand experience of flying a replica Vimy. Also, Brian Riddle, Librarian, Royal Aeronautical Society; Mrs Diana King, Royal Aero Club; Emma Warren, Chertsey Museum; and Peter Collins, Peter Murton and Philippa Evans of the Imperial War Museum. And, for the memories of W.J. Richards, to Mrs Lyn Smith, Betty Wainwright and John Richards.

A sad and special thank you to the late Steve Fossett, who not only patiently answered my questions but also emailed me a few weeks before he disappeared. What an inspiration he was to so many! Also to Sir Richard Branson for his time, and his assistants Nicola Duguid and Helen Clarke.

In the USA I must thank David R. Holbrooke, a key figure in the Vimy recreation project. Also, Theo Elbert and Roger Mott, National

Aviation Museum, Pensacola; Peter Jakab and Claire Brown of the Smithsonian Institution; the *Washington Post*'s Alex Remington; Alain Delaqueriere of the *New York Times*; and Barbara Whitener of the University of Louisville Library. And a descendant of Ernest Archdeacon who put Europe on the aviation map, the equally imaginative artist and photographer, Evelyn Archdeacon.

In St John's, special thanks to Tourism & Cultures Donna Bishop; Brian Jones of *The Telegram*; aviation historian Nelson Sherren, who kindly drove me to see places associated with Alcock and Brown; ace photographer and Vimy flight enthusiast, Gary J. Hebbard; Lynn Robinson and Carla Foot of VOCM Radio; Mike Power, Jackie Bryant Cumby, Olga McWilliam Benson, John McWilliam and Robert Symonds, who supplied photographs and invaluable maps. Also Joe Bennett, St John's International Airport Authority, and Don Tate, Grand Banks Genealogical Site.

As an old Ban the Bomb lag I must record particular thanks for their enthusiastic co-operation to the following Ministry of Defence and RAF personnel: Steve Willmot, Steve Lloyd, Seb Ritchie, Lt Col Nick Richardson, Wg Cdr Andy McGill, Capt. Roy Wilcockson, Steve Williams, Capt. Norry Wilson and Philip of RAF Lincolnshire. Also Glynn Griffith, RAF Millom Aviation & Military Museum Group; Clare Carr, RAF Museum, Cosford; Tim Pierce, RAF College, Cranwell; John Benjamin, Shuttleworth Collection and the curator of Bournemouth Aviation Museum. And, finally to another ace flier, Gp Capt. Tony Alcock, MBE, nephew of the great John Alcock.

Many thanks, too, for their encouragement and assistance to *Aeroplane Monthly* editor Michael Oakey; Phil Groves and Lisa O'Brien, BAA; historian Alan Gallop; Barry Guess, BAE Systems Heritage; and Robert Gardner of *Circadian* (does anyone know more about propellers?). Also Gary Carr of Buyout Footage; Olive Guest, Jonathan Clowes Ltd; Steve Hynard, Hampshire Record Office; Carol Linton, Hampshire County Council Archives; Gill Arnott, Hampshire Museums Service; Doreen Netherton and Hilary Brenton, Dover Library; Michael Carter, Centre for Kentish Studies; Christel Pobgee, Kent Libraries; David Bristow, Fordingbridge; Rev Mike Bissett, St Margaret's Church, Penn;

Iain MacFarlaine, Francois Prins and David Hodgkinson. And Alan Flint and Bill Croydon of historic Eastchurch on the Isle of Sheppey, which, in July 2009, celebrated the centenary of Moore Brabazon's historic first flight by a British pilot in Britain.

In Swansea, thanks to Flt Lt Phillip Flowers, Harold Hughes, William George Sutton, Phil Treseder, Jacqueline Taylor, Jayne Watts, Mrs Gwen Williams and Emma Jones of the *South Wales Evening Post*. In Glasgow, Norry Wilson and Heather Stuckert, *Evening Times*; Lyn Morgan, Henry Sullivan and Maureen Wilbraham of the Mitchell Library. Also Helen Watson of the Scottish National Portrait Gallery, Edinburgh, and C. Pinchen of Tyne & Wear Archives Service.

In Dublin I particularly appreciate the help and advice of biographer Peter Costello and Joe Collins of Hodges Figgis bookshop. Also publisher Antony Farrell of Lilliput Press and colleague Carolyn Strobel, who allowed me to quote from Alannah Heather's wonderful *Errislannan* memoir. Thanks also to David Givens of Liffey Press, John McMahon, and Noel Lewis who read the manuscript, Colman and Dympna McMahon and Dympna O'Halloran for their consistent support, and the equally helpful Tony Byrne and Brian O'Neill of *Bygone Days*. And the late unforgettable Peter Stevens, with whom I often discussed the Vimy flight in the old Horsehoe Bar.

Thanks, too, to Denis McCormack at Multitech Computers, and to Chris, Conri, Gary, Sean, Stefan, and Nohema of Reads. Also to Brian Lynch of RTE, Nigel Leeming in Cork and Paolo, Matteo, Andrea and all at Bar Italia for sunshine replenishment at low moments.

In Connemara, thanks to Clifden Chamber of Commerce president Gerry Keane, Aidan O'Halloran, Michele Hehir, Aine O'Neill, the Station House Museum, Clare Hickey and Sorcha O'Sullivan of Connemara Flowers and, particularly, to James and the late Harry and Peggy Sullivan of Sullivan's Supermarket. Locals are to be commended for resurfacing the track to the Derrygimla landing site. Hopefully those entrepreneurs who considered concreting the historic bog will heed David Bellamy's words: 'The people of Ireland inherited this richness from the past. Please don't steal it from future generations.' A very special thanks to David and those environmentalists who helped to preserve one of the world's most important aviation sites.

I particularly appreciate the help of three Ballyconneely enthusiasts, Tom McWilliam, Gerry O'Malley, and historian Marty Conneely. Thanks to Marty, the Vimy landing cairn is now highlighted for aviation pilgrims. With its proximity to the Derrygimla landing site, perhaps Ballyconneely would be the ideal place for an Alcock and Brown Museum?

Thanks also to those museums who assisted in my vain search for the missing Vimy propeller. Made by Dashwood Lang (G1184.NG/ Series 273A/ DRG.A54/ 330H.PRollsRoyce) and presented by Arthur Whitten Brown to Cranwell College, it was allegedly displayed in the RAF Holborn Careers Centre up to 1990. One can only hope that it awaits identification in some store or mess.

A final thank you to Margie for sowing the idea for this book, and for her dinner-time patience while I wrestled a recalcitrant paragraph. Also to my late parents, Patrick and Siobhan, who first told me of the legend of Alcock and Brown. And to an old motor racing pal, Mark Hughes, and his equally indefatigable colleague and multiple author, Jonathan Falconer, who oversaw the book's production. Their ardour (not to mention impeccable taste!) was a considerable encouragement.

Sincere apologies to anyone whom I may have missed. And a hearty *Slainte* to all who helped me in what I consider was a good cause and to which I earnestly hope I have done justice, the incredible achievement of John Alcock and Arthur Whitten Brown. What an inspiration they provide in these days when man seems to have been reduced to a compliant cipher on a balance sheet.

I hope that their story stirs you as much as it still does me!

Brendan Lynch

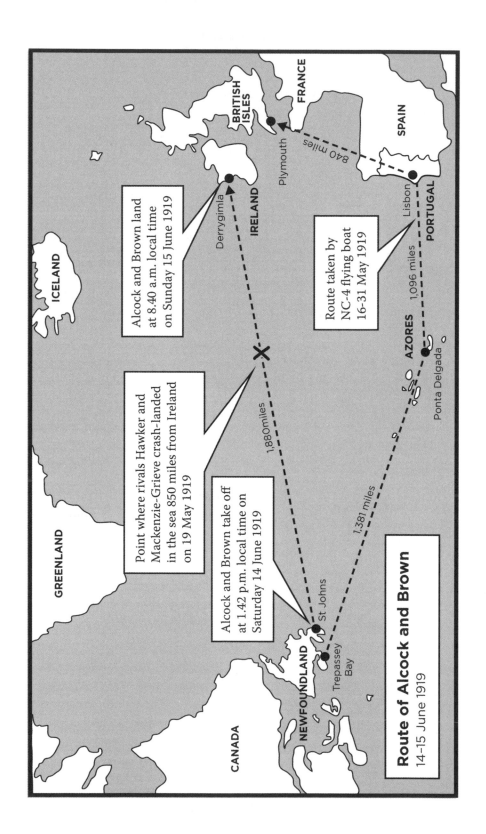

Route of Alcock and Brown
14–15 June 1919

ICELAND

GREENLAND

CANADA

NEWFOUNDLAND

St Johns

Trepassey Bay

BRITISH ISLES

FRANCE

IRELAND

Derrygimla

Plymouth

SPAIN

PORTUGAL

Lisbon

AZORES

Ponta Delgada

840 miles

1,880 miles

1,381 miles

1,096 miles

Alcock and Brown land at 8.40 a.m. local time on Sunday 15 June 1919

Route taken by NC-4 flying boat 16–31 May 1919

Point where rivals Hawker and Mackenzie-Grieve crash-landed in the sea 850 miles from Ireland on 19 May 1919

Alcock and Brown take off at 1.42 p.m. local time on Saturday 14 June 1919

INTRODUCTION TO PREVIOUS EDITION

One of the most moving experiences of my life was to witness the arrival in Ireland of Steve Fossett and Mark Rebholz on 3 July 2005 after their re-enactment of Alcock and Brown's first non-stop Atlantic flight of June 1919.

Huge crowds had assembled at Ballyconneely golf course from mid-afternoon on that Sunday. Irish, British, Canadian, and US flags flapped in the fitful breeze. Shrieking gulls dived and wheeled as if in winged celebration.

A cheer spread across the dunes as the replica open-cockpit Vimy was spotted fluttering in from the ocean. An even mightier roar reached up as it finally passed directly overhead at 200ft. Its grey wings assumed gigantic proportions; one worried about its pilot's ability to combat the wayward gusts.

Arms waved, scarves flew; it was a moment of drama and history that none present would ever forget. 'Imagine that flew all the way across the Atlantic,' an incredulous youngster said as he doffed his baseball cap, a comment that had also greeted the original 1919 fliers.

As the aeroplane lined up for landing, it seemed to lurch and stand in the air. Then it began its descent. The breeze clutched at those broad wings. The pilot fought for control. Spectators held their breaths.

Dropping rather than gliding, the four forward wheels on each side bounced gently on the ground. The wheels touched again, the Vimy stopped within yards.

Steve Fossett, his head just visible over the port side of the cockpit, cut the twin engines. Three or four minutes later both men rose stiffly from the cockpit. Avuncular in his yellow survival suit, Fossett smiled and shook hands with the towering figure of navigator and co-pilot Mark Rebholz. Spectators stared at the men who had crossed the mighty Atlantic in that flimsy machine. There was hardly a dry eye on the course.

'Alcock and Brown's story has never been properly related,' I turned to Margie, as we paid our respects to the tethered aeroplane before leaving.

'Why don't you do it, then?' she enquired.

That was where this book started. At Ballyconneely golf course, within sound of the Atlantic breakers, at seven on that momentous summer evening.

I envied Steve Fossett and Mark Rebholz as they headed for rest after their eighteen hours travail. My work was only starting, and it would take eighteen months!

INTRODUCTION
TO CENTENARY EDITION

Seventy years since I first heard the legend of Alcock and Brown around an Irish fireside, I am still as moved and uplifted by their incredible achievement. To bridge the wild Atlantic in an open-cockpit machine and with primitive instruments was, as Tony Alcock alludes in his foreword, a triumph of navigation, flying skill and rare courage.

My thanks to History Press for publishing this centenary edition of my book on the flight and, in particular, to commissioning editor Amy Rigg and equally lynx-eyed project editor Jezz Palmer. Thanks to Tony Alcock for his foreword, to Janet Hearn-Gillham and David for their help and enthusiasm and their friends, Virginia and Alan Payne, who supplied John Alcock's first Atlantic Airmail letter, which he carried with him in the Vimy.

Thanks also to Clifden's Shane Joyce for his invaluable information and efforts to pinpoint the Vimy's Connemara landing site, to Mary O'Connell of the town's Station House Museum and to Ann Evans of the Jonathan Clowes Agency. Also to Billy Foyle of Dolphin Beach Hotel and to Stephen Foyle of Foyle's Hotel, Clifden, where Alcock and Brown were treated to a reception by the local Council before their departure for London.

I must also extend thanks to Frances Mobbs and Vera Beames, who introduced me to Mary Rhodes and her Sweethope Cottage book, about the Kennedy family home. Mary deserves special thanks for rescuing Brown's diary and memorabilia. Sadly, Brown's father-in-law, Major David Kennedy, was killed during a daylight bomb attack on High Street Kensington on 19 November 1940. Four years later, the Brown's only child, 24-year-old Arthur Brown Junior, was shot down over Arnhem, a tragedy from which his parents never fully recovered.

In this special flight centenary year, 2019, I hope that Manchester authorities in particular will extend themselves – as Alcock and Brown did in 1919 – to celebrate the incredible achievement of their local aviation pioneers. Renaming the city's airport 'Alcock and Brown Airport, Manchester' in their honour would be a most appropriate tribute.

1

FREE OF THE PRISON OF GRAVITY

———————————◆◇◆———————————

Everyone who crosses between Europe and America owes them
a debt. But how did they do it in that flimsy machine?

Harry Sullivan

———————————◆◇◆———————————

Seven-year-old Harry Sullivan was in bed with measles in Clifden, on
the west coast of Ireland, on the damp morning of Sunday, 15 June 1919.
He recalls:

Because I was sick, I wasn't allowed to go to morning Mass with the rest of the
family. It wasn't long after the big flu epidemic which had killed more people
than the recently ended Great War. My parents weren't taking any chances.

They had hardly left when I heard this terrible noise. It seemed to be
coming from the sky. I was as curious as I was scared. Measles or not, I rushed
outside to investigate. I was just in time to see this greyish-coloured machine
swooping over the main street. Its two propellers were whizzing around and
its huge wings nearly touched the top of the church. I was amazed. I had
heard of flying 'planes but I had never seen one before. I watched as it roared
away towards the bog under the low cloud, its wings swaying up and down.

The noise was very loud, I could hear it for a long time. It must have been
awful for the men inside. Where had the machine come from, where was
it going? I would have something to tell my parents when they returned
– but how could I tell them without saying I had gone out in the street?

Harry did not know it, but he had witnessed the conclusion of one of the most significant and dramatic flights in aviation history. The pilot of the Vickers Vimy aeroplane was John Alcock, his navigator was Arthur Whitten Brown. Eight minutes after the youngster saw them, the two Englishmen landed beside the Marconi radio station in nearby Derrygimla bog. Deafened by a broken engine exhaust, they had lost their radio and endured iced-up controls and a near-fatal stall. Completely exposed to the elements in their open-cockpit biplane, they had survived fog, snow and virtually continuous cloud to become the first persons to fly the Atlantic ocean non-stop. Yet, navigating blind for most of the way, they landed just 20 miles off target after their 16hr marathon of 1,880 miles, the longest distance ever flown by man.

Staff from the Marconi station struggled across the swampy ground to rescue them. At first they did not believe that the fliers had crossed the Atlantic. 'Yesterday we were in America,' John Alcock vainly reiterated. It took a sealed mailbag from St John's, Newfoundland, to convince the Marconi men. Their cheers rang across the infinity of greeny scrub and boggy pools as they escorted the fliers to their warm station. But this was nothing to the acclaim that greeted Alcock and Brown on their triumphant return home via Galway, Dublin, and Holyhead. A quarter of a million people lined their train route and the streets of London, to welcome the men who a short time previously had languished in prisoner-of-war camps. Within a week of wading through Derrygimla, they braved the carpets of Windsor Castle to be knighted by King George V.

Alcock and Brown's achievement had a major psychological impact. It helped war-weary Britons turn a corner from the recent catastrophic conflict and the world's most devastating epidemic, the Spanish flu of 1918–19. Emerging triumphant from an Irish bog, the fliers had made a giant step out of the shadow of war and pestilence to reassert man's potential. Their success redirected attention to the future and opened a window to previously unconsidered possibilities. It inspired hope that man and technology could combine to build a brighter more secure world. That world had suddenly become a much smaller and, hopefully, safer place. Brown himself optimistically wrote: 'The aeroplane may well become a greater influence towards internationalisation than a signed covenant of the League of nations.'

Similar adulation greeted the epic solo ocean crossings by Charles Lindbergh in 1927 and Amelia Earhart in 1932. But, courageous as these aviators were, their flights were made in enclosed cockpits, with the advantage of superior navigational and meteorological aids. They had the benefit of lighter, more reliable and more efficient engines. Lindbergh carried little over half of Alcock and Brown's enormous handicap of 865gal of fuel.

Eschewing heroics and hype, Alcock and Brown had braved the unknown in a comparatively primitive machine wide open to the elements. Their success against the odds in completing the world's first epic aerial voyage was the most notable aviation feat after the Wright Brothers' earliest powered flights. First to bridge the Atlantic non-stop, the Vimy pair laid the foundations of worldwide travel for everyman a mere sixteen years after the Wrights first staggered into the air in a powered aeroplane. They are arguably two of the greatest and most unsung heroes of the early 20th century.

Alcock and Brown's unification of the continents was the logical outcome of man's obsession with transport, which dated from the invention of the wheel in Mesopotamia around 4000 BC. The chariot increased man's speed and his control of space and territory. Progression to four wheels relieved his shoulders of carrying burdens. The first dugout boat enabled him to navigate water; slowly in the beginning, until sail and then steam hastened his progress. The proliferation of the bicycle in the late nineteenth century provided a foretaste of the possibilities of individual long-distance transportation. After the railway revolution, the internal combustion engine and the automobile introduced the single most important development in transport and social mobility since the wheel. Only the air remained to be conquered.

The philosopher Socrates insisted, 'Man must rise above the Earth – to the top of the atmosphere and beyond – for only thus will he fully understand the world in which he lives.' Two thousand years later Arthur Whitten Brown reiterated the dream of flight:

I believe that ever since man, but recently conscious of his own existence, saw the birds, he has desired to emulate them. Among the myths and fables of every race are tales of human flight. The paradise of most religions is reached through the air, and through the air many gods and prophets have passed from earth to their respective heavens.

Man marvelled at the freedom of the birds and their power to go where he could not. He could catch birds and he could tame them, but he could only watch while they effortlessly soared to heights denied to him. In Greek mythology the Athenian craftsman Daedalus made wings of wax and feathers so that he and his son Icarus could escape from King Minos of Crete. They flew away, but Icarus rose too near the sun, which melted the wax of his wings. He fell into the sea and was drowned, and his father buried him on the Aegean island now known as Ikaria.

In real life, the early Chinese were the first to venture into the air, with unmanned kites. Made from bamboo and silk, these are said to have been flown in China 3,000 years ago. The devices were used to carry messages into the heavens to the gods. One was used for observation during a city siege in 200 BC. A man-carrying kite was allegedly flown in China in AD 559. On his return to Europe, Marco Polo described how kites were constructed and controlled.

Balloons provided man's earliest documented means of leaving the ground, and greatly stimulated interest in flight. Joseph and Etienne Montgolfier experimented with hot-air balloons in 1782. Pilatre de Rozier and the Marquis d'Arlandre made the first manned flight a year later from Versailles, but de Rozier became aviation's earliest casualty when he was killed while attempting to cross the English Channel. Italian embassy employee Vincent Lunardi made the first ascent in Britain in September 1784. The Channel was crossed the following year by Jean-Pierre Blanchard and his American passenger, Dr John Jefferies. Ballooning became popular with the aristocracy and the adventurous, but as time went by the limitations of balloons became tiresome. Without motive power there was no directional control, their operators were slaves to the winds. How could one achieve more controllable flight?

Thinkers and scientists such as Leonardo da Vinci long pondered the secret of heavier-than-air flight. Philip Hitti claims in his *History of the Arabs* that Ibn Firnas was the first man in history to make a scientific attempt at flying. Commemorated by a statue in Baghdad and the Ibn Firnas moon crater, the Cordoban inventor and poet allegedly flew the equivalent of a modern hang-glider in Andalusia in AD 877. Leonardo da Vinci made over 100 drawings illustrating his theories on bird and mechanical flight. His ornithopter (flapping-wing) flying machines were never built, and neither was the vertical-screw design that presaged the modern helicopter. Inspired by Leonardo, Hezarfen Ahmet Celebi is said to have glided across the Bosphorus from Istanbul's Galata Tower in 1638.

One of the earliest to begin to unlock the secret of heavier-than-air flight was a remarkable English Baronet, Sir George Cayley, Member of Parliament for Scarborough, who lived from 1773 to 1857. He prophesied:

> I am well convinced that 'Aerial Navigation' will form a most prominent feature in the progress of civilisation … and that we shall be able to transport ourselves and our families, and their goods and chattels, more securely by air than by water, and with a velocity of from 20 to 100 miles per hour.

The key to flight is lift, the ability to raise an object against the pull of gravity. To overcome an aeroplane's weight its wing must generate this opposing force, which is produced by the motion of the machine through the air. Cayley discovered that air passing over a curved surface travels faster than the air passing across its undersurface. The faster airflow over a cambered, bird-like wing creates an area of low pressure above the curved section (or aerofoil), which generates lift, supplemented to a small degree by increased pressure on the underside. Modern delinquents regularly demonstrate this when they put a hand, palm downward, out of a car window. The hand immediately and wondrously rises, thanks to the lift generated by the different speed of the air currents above and below it. Racing cars use aerofoils in reverse to create downthrust, which improves traction and enables them to corner at scarcely credible speeds.

In half a century of experimenting Cayley established the basic forces acting on an aeroplane: lift against weight, and thrust against drag.

He summarised the challenge as 'to make a surface support a given weight by the application of power to the resistance of the air'. He suggested the use of a cruciform tail as a means of obtaining longitudinal and lateral stability.

After experimenting with a kite modified into a glider, the first device to establish the basic format of an aeroplane, Cayley followed further models with the first gliders to carry a boy, and then man, successfully. Britain's earliest licensed pilot, J.T.C. Moore-Brabazon (later Lord Brabazon of Tara) insisted: 'It was with the glider that Sir George really laid his claim to fame, and it was because he worked along these lines that he was rightly named the father of aeronautics. The modern aeroplane is only a glider pushed along by a motor.'

Cayley never found a suitable power source. His gunpowder engine failed, and steam engines were much too heavy and cumbersome. The internal combustion engine, which powered the Wright brothers' aeroplanes, was not developed during his lifetime. But, fifty years before the brothers, his gliders accomplished the world's first manned heavier-than-air flights across Yorkshire's Brompton Dale. The passenger of his man-carrier, coachman John Appleby, protested: 'Please, Sir George, I wish to give notice. I was hired to drive, not to fly.'

Californian John Joseph Montgomery built a glider that was destroyed after its first take-off in 1883, and his subsequent machines were also unsuccessful. It was Germany's Otto Lilienthal who made a major contribution to heavier-than-air flight, making over 2,000 hang-glider flights. He was experimenting with a small compressed-gas engine of his own design when he was killed in a glider crash in 1896. Lilienthal influenced Bath-born engineer Percy Sinclair Pilcher. Had Pilcher procured some modest backing he could well have become the first person to make a powered flight in his new and untested triplane, though he would have faced difficult problems of control. But the 33-year-old Englishman died in a Leicestershire field in 1899, while making a towed demonstration flight in his Hawk glider. (A modern, powered reproduction of the triplane flew for nearly a minute and a half in 2003, longer than the Wright brothers' longest flight on 17 December 1903.)

Octave Chanute, a Chicago railroad engineer and bridge-builder, had also influenced Pilcher. He improved upon Otto Lilienthal's designs, evolving a biplane hang-glider. His example, plus Lilienthal's experiments and writings, in turn influenced the brothers Orville and Wilbur Wright of Dayton, Ohio, in the USA. Wilbur confessed in a letter to Chanute: 'For some years I have been afflicted with the belief that flight is possible to man. The disease has increased in severity and I feel it will soon cost me an increased amount of money, if not my life.'

Supporters of Gustave Whitehead claimed that the Bavarian-born builder of gliders and powered aeroplanes flew a bat-winged powered machine in Connecticut in 1901, but there is no documentary evidence or even photographs of the machine to confirm this. Thus the methodical Wright brothers have been recognised as the first to make successful powered, sustained and controlled flights. They became interested in aviation in 1878, when their father gave them a toy helicopter propelled by a rubber band. Orville was a successful cycle racer, and the brothers decided in 1896 to take advantage of the new cycling craze by manufacturing machines themselves. Their business flourished and ensured them sufficient income to indulge their passion for flight. They built their first glider in 1899. Fortuitously, a suitable power source was now available, the internal-combustion petrol engine that drove the fledgling automobile.

The Wrights' cycle manufacturing experience encouraged their constant search for lightness combined with strength, and enabled them to design and machine parts for their experimental gliders. Without financial backing or government support they spent years on patient gliding experiments, and even constructed a wind tunnel in which to test wing sections. Wilbur Wright noted:

> It was, in fact, the first wind tunnel in which small models of wings were tested and their lifting properties accurately noted. From all the data that Orville and I accumulated into tables, an accurate and reliable wing could finally be built.

Riding bicycles and observing birds had informed the Wrights on banking and turning. They focused on the crucial issue of flight control. A rear rudder managed left or right turns, while a horizontal rudder, or elevator, controlled pitch, nose up or down. Wilbur's implementation of wing warping, a twisting motion of the wings to produce lateral or roll control, was the final keystone. Having mastered the basics of control in their gliders, the brothers supplied the outstanding ingredient of power by building their own four-cylinder engine, designing their own efficient propellers, and incorporating both in a new biplane. On the morning of 17 December 1903 they soared into history with four short powered flights on the sandy Atlantic shores of Kitty Hawk, North Carolina. It was a monumental advance for the human species. For the first time in his long earth habitation, man had broken free from the prison of gravity.

The Wrights provided the *New York Herald* with the earliest first-hand description of flying:

Our most acute sensations are during the first minute of flight, while we are soaring into the air and gaining the levels at which we wish to sail. Then for the next five minutes, our concentration is fixed on the management of the levers to see that everything is working all right. But after that, the management of the flyer becomes almost automatic, with no more thought required than a bicycle rider gives to the control of his machine. But when you know, after the first few moments, that the whole mechanism is working perfectly, the sensation is so keenly delightful as to be almost beyond description. Nobody who has not experienced it for himself can realise it. It is the realisation of a dream so many persons have had of floating in the air. More than anything else, the sense is one of perfect peace, mingled with an excitement that strains every nerve to the utmost.

Officials of Washington's Smithsonian Institution claimed for many years that the first aeroplane capable of powered flight had been made by its third secretary, Samuel Pierpoint Langley. But his grant-aided Aerodrome had fallen, rather than flown, into the Potomac River in October 1903. (Orville Wright, in disgust, later presented the historic 1903 Wright aeroplane to London's Science Museum, where it remained for twenty years until the Smithsonian recanted.) By 1905 the Wrights were making flights of over half-an-hour's duration. Inexplicably, the sceptical US government declined their offer of a test machine, and America lost its lead in world aviation. Officialdom concurred with the opinion expressed in a 1906 comment in *The Times* newspaper of London: 'All attempts at artificial aviation are not only dangerous to life but doomed to failure from an engineering standpoint.'

A combination of French and Celtic flair soon ensured that the momentum of aeronautical development moved to Europe. Pioneer Brazilian aviator Alberto Santos-Dumont said of prime mover, Ernest Archdeacon: 'He was one of the most remarkable men I have ever met, his mind ever groping forward to discoveries and inventions, many of which have been fulfilled.'

Archdeacon was a wealthy lawyer whose forebears had come from Waterford in Ireland. He set numerous French balloon and motoring records, including a steam tricycle run of 286 miles with Leon Serpollet in 1890 and a class win for Delahaye in the 1896 Paris–Marseilles–Paris motor race. After hearing a lecture by Octave Chanute in Paris in April 1903, in which the work of the Wrights was described and illustrated, he immediately set about converting France to aviation. He exhorted readers of *La Locomotion*: 'Will the homeland of the Montgolfiers have the shame of allowing that ultimate discovery of aerial science, which is assuredly imminent, and which will constitute the highest scientific revolution that has been seen since the beginning of the world, to be realised abroad?'

The Parisian co-founded the Aero-Club de France in 1904 and launched an Aviation Committee, which concentrated on heavier-than-air flight, as distinct from balloons and dirigibles. He initiated a series of prizes to encourage aviation. In October 1906 Santos-Dumont became the hero of his adopted Paris when he won the prize for the first powered flight in Europe. Archdeacon also encouraged the efforts of aeroplane manufacturers and engine makers. Leon Levavasseur's compact 25 and 50hp motors soon played a major role in establishing European superiority.

Archdeacon worked with the Voisin brothers and former racing driver, Henry Farman, with whom he made France's first 1km flight in 1908. It was Farman who followed the lead of another French pioneer, Robert

Esnault-Pelterie, and adopted the ailerons that eventually replaced the Wright brothers' wing-warping system. Thousands flocked to see the Wrights demonstrate their latest machine at Le Mans that same year. But by 1909, thanks to Archdeacon's determination, Europe led the way with more stable and controllable aeroplanes. 'Remarkable in many ways and before its time in conception', was how Atlantic aviator John Alcock subsequently described the later-model Farman in which he learned to fly.

Luckily for Britain, Dublin-born media magnate Lord Northcliffe was among those who witnessed Santos-Dumont's historic 1906 flights in Paris. He immediately grasped the potential of the aeroplane, and its future defence implications for Britain. He insisted in a leading article in the *Daily Mail*: 'The success of M Santos-Dumont has an international significance. They are not mere dreamers who hold that the time is at hand when air power will be an even more important thing than sea power.'

He warned rising politician Winston Churchill:

A man with a heavier-than-air machine has flown. It does not matter how far he has flown. He has shown what can be done. In a year's time, mark my words, that fellow will be flying over here from France. Britain is no longer an island. Nothing so important has happened for a very long time. We must get hold of this thing, and make it our own.

Governments and the public continued to be sceptical of the strange men in their flying machines. The aero dreamers were subjects of derision for media such as the *London Opinion*, which published a limerick in 1907:

There was a young man of Mark Lane,
Who constructed an aeroplane.
It flew, so we heard,
Like a beautiful bird,
His tombstone is pretty but plain.

But the success of a week-long international aviation meeting at Reims in August 1909 marked a turning point and heralded the arrival of the aeroplane as a practical means of transport. Over 200,000 watched Louis Blériot demonstrate a machine that could carry two passengers. Louis Paulhan established a distance record of 82 miles in his Voisin. Two days later Henry Farman extended this to 112 miles. America's Glenn Curtiss set a new speed record of 47mph.

Lord Northcliffe attended the Reims meeting with Britain's Chancellor of the Exchequer, David Lloyd George. Replicating Archdeacon's zeal, Northcliffe began a crusade that was to prove a major influence on British aircraft development. Born Alfred Harmsworth in 1865, he had edited *Bicycling News* before founding the bestselling *Daily Mail* newspaper in 1896. Based on the style of US papers, it had banner headlines, shorter more readable stories, and a special section for women. Northcliffe increasingly used the *Mail* to propagate his interest in science and aeronautics. He met Wilbur Wright, and appointed Harry Harper to the *Daily Mail* as the world's first aeronautical correspondent. Alone among Britain's public figures, he cajoled the British government into matching French and German aviation progress.

Most significantly, Northcliffe launched a series of prizes that caught the public imagination and stimulated the fledgling aircraft industry. Although this was regarded by some observers as a circulation gimmick, he dramatically put aviation at the forefront of national discussion with the following announcement:

We desire to remove the impression that England is not in the van of progress in the new science, and we are anxious that the business of constructing aeroplanes, which will no doubt in the future be as large as that of motor-car making, shall be assisted as rapidly as possible.

The proprietors of the *Daily Mail* therefore hereby undertake to pay the sum of £10,000 to the first person, being the member of an established aero club, who flies in one day from a given spot within five miles of the London office of the *Daily Mail* to a given spot within five miles of the Manchester office of the *Daily Mail*. This offer is made without conditions or restrictions of any kind except those mentioned.

Northcliffe also offered £1,000 each to the first Briton to fly a circular mile in an all-British aeroplane, and to the first person to fly the English Channel. Aviation was still only in its infancy, but in July 1909 Blériot took the *Daily Mail's* Channel prize in his No. XI monoplane. He lyricised on landing near Dover Castle after the 35min flight: 'The most beautiful dream that has haunted the heart of man since Icarus is today reality.' In April 1910 the competition to win the prize for the first flight from London to Manchester excited national interest. The public became increasingly air conscious. Among the thousands who stayed up all night to see the dawn arrival of winner Louis Paulhan was young Manchester engineering apprentice John Alcock.

Despite its lack of industry, the remote island of Northcliffe's birth played an unlikely and enduring role in both early automobilism and aviation. Guglielmo Marconi built his first high-power, long-wave telegraphy station in Connemara, Galway, and the country's strategic position at the western tip of Europe established its potential for transatlantic flying. Irish-born designer and philosopher John William Dunne made a major contribution to early aircraft stability with his revolutionary aeroplanes' swept-back, V-form wings. In 1903 Ireland staged Britain's first motor race, the 327-mile Gordon Bennett Cup. Like the Wright brothers and most pioneer drivers, the winner, Camille Jenatzy, had progressed from bicycle to car racing. Many of these drivers in turn graduated from cars to flying. Third-placed finisher and former cycle racer Henry Farman, the son of an English journalist based in Paris, became one of Europe's leading aeroplane designers. Fellow-competitor Baron de Caters was Belgium's first flier. Baron de Forest, who broke the world speed record in Dublin, initiated the distance prize that launched young London racing driver Tommy Sopwith on his marathon aviation career.

Both J.T.C. Moore-Brabazon and former racing cyclist the Hon Charles Stewart Rolls won one of the Irish motor races before going on to distinguish themselves in aviation. Anglo-Irishman Moore-Brabazon first flew in France, after complaining in a letter to *Flight* magazine:

I have perhaps more than anyone, known the difficulties of constructing a machine in England where everyone is ready to discourage one, ridicule one, and look upon one as an amiable lunatic. My advice to anyone about to build a machine is to do it in France.

After experimenting with model gliders, which they tested from boxes in the Royal Albert Hall, Moore-Brabazon and Rolls progressed from balloons to aeroplanes. Flying on a French licence, the former in his Short biplane won the *Daily Mail* prize for the first circular mile in an all-British machine, in October 1909. Moore-Brabazon was awarded the honour of the first British flying licence in March 1910, while Charles Rolls held the second. A Cambridge engineering MA, Rolls co-founded the Aero Club of the United Kingdom (later the Royal Aero Club), which established a flying ground at Muswell Manor near Leysdown on the Isle of Sheppey. The pair played a pivotal role in British aviation history by launching the aeroplane manufacturing industry of the Short brothers, previously balloon manufacturers, with an order for the company's first two aeroplanes. Rolls became the first person to fly the Channel in both directions non-stop in 1910.

Public interest in flying flourished, thanks to Lord Northcliffe's enthusiasm and the daring of the pilots, who became a new brand of heroes. Up to 30,000 spectators flocked to see aerial displays at Hendon and Brooklands. In February 1911 Tommy Sopwith gave a special demonstration at Windsor Castle at the request of King George V, whose son, the future King George VI, later took lessons at Waddon Aerodrome. Flying schools and cross-country meetings mushroomed. Claude Grahame-White staged a series of nationwide shows and flew passengers in his nine-seater aerial charabanc. Many women took to the skies after America's Harriet Quimby became the first lady to fly the English Channel, in 1912. She advised: 'Flying is a fine, dignified sport for women, it is healthy and stimulates the mind. You don't know what a fine thing for the complexion a dew bath is.' Roland Garros made the first non-stop flight across the Mediterranean, from St Raphael to Bizerta, and Tryggve Gran flew the North Sea in 1914, before the declaration of war put an end to this first phase of aviation's development.

Most Britons acknowledged the importance of Lord Northcliffe's prizes in popularising aeronautics. But there was general astonishment at the new award that he offered on 1 April 1913. Shocked by Germany's huge military aviation budget, and reiterating that the French were now as far ahead in aeroplane development as they had been fifteen years previously in automobile construction, Northcliffe proclaimed in bold *Daily Mail* headlines:

We offer £10,000 to the first person who crosses the Atlantic from any point in the United States, Canada, or Newfoundland to any point in Great Britain or Ireland in 72 continuous hours. The flight may be made, of course, either way across the Atlantic. This prize is open to pilots of any nationality and machines of foreign as well as of British construction.

Many *Mail* readers noted the date. The announcement was either an April Fool's Day joke or a gimmick to boost circulation. Or perhaps the science fiction books of Jules Verne and H.G. Wells had gone to Lord Northcliffe's head; £10,000 was a lot of money (the equivalent of almost £1 million in 2019). The humorous magazine *Punch* offered a similar prize for the first flight to Mars. However, Germany's *Deutche Tageszeitung* noted: 'That it will be possible at no distant date to build an aeroplane capable of remaining in the air for 24 hours is perfectly obvious. It is not at all in order to describe the *Daily Mail* competition as visionary.'

Gustav Hamel's death in the English Channel aborted the Martinsyde company's planned transatlantic attempt in a specially designed monoplane, while a Curtiss flying boat proved greatly underpowered during tests. The First World War soon distracted the public from aviation feats. But, just before the conflict ended, the indefatigable Lord Northcliffe repeated his Atlantic prize offer. Within a year the mighty ocean was conquered, and John Alcock and Arthur Whitten Brown rudely interrupted Harry Sullivan's convalescence. Four short decades later, aeroplanes surpassed ocean liners as the predominant mode of travelling the Atlantic. Among those who made frequent crossings was the same Harry Sullivan, now a successful supermarket proprietor. Harry insisted:

Alcock and Brown may have scared me that morning in 1919, but I never fly the Atlantic without toasting them. They were the men who first opened up the ocean to flight. Everyone who crosses between Europe and America owes them a debt. But how did they do it in that flimsy machine?

2

THE APPRENTICESHIP OF JOHN ALCOCK

The idea of flying the Atlantic was first put to Capt. Alcock by Mr Percy Muller, the works superintendent for Messrs Vickers. The captain promptly replied: 'I am on it any old time.'

The Daily Sketch

The crew of the transatlantic Vickers Vimy were a contrasting pair. W.J. Richards, who worked closely with John Alcock and Arthur Whitten Brown during the aeroplane's assembly, remembered in an interview with Mrs Lyn Smith: 'Alcock was daring beyond all estimation. With no thought of danger whatsoever. He was hard-headed. Obstinate. Not always the nicest person – a bit rough, put it that way. But fine fighting material.'

Though equally battle-hardened and fearless, Brown was more withdrawn and thoughtful. Richards recalled:

Arthur Whitten Brown could make a very nice Roman Catholic priest. He was that type. Very quiet. Gentlemanly, sensitive, almost emotional. Who accepted the responsibility of being a navigator with intense feelings of appreciation of the risks involved. It must have been almost agony for him to have to contemplate what it would mean in his case. And yet the two men formed a perfect combination. The one that had the strength of purpose and character, and the other one who had the natural reserves of caution and a clear understanding of what was involved. Brought together in a close human relationship, they formed, I'd say, a perfect combination.

English history already boasted a famous John Alcock, a Yorkshire divine who lived from 1430 to 1500. Architect, bishop, and statesman, he served as ambassador to Castile, founded Jesus College, Cambridge, and was also Lord Chancellor of England under Henry VII. Public life then was hazardous, and Alcock was imprisoned by Richard, Duke of Gloucester. His nineteenth-century namesake would, however, lead a life of even greater risk in his flirtation with the heavens.

The oldest boy in a family of four boys and one girl, John William Alcock was born on 5 November 1892 at Batsford House Cottage, Seymour Grove, Old Trafford, Manchester. His father was a coachman and horse dealer, and the family later moved to 6 Kingswood Road, Fallowfield. Signing his schoolbooks and known to his friends as Jack, the future aviator was educated at St Anne's Parish School and Manchester Central High School. He showed an aptitude for cooking long before he was interested in mechanical matters. His sister and brothers particularly appreciated his skill at making sweets. His younger brother, Edward, also called John, insisted: 'His Parkin and treacle toffee was the finest in the world!'

Alcock was obsessed with engineering and mechanics from the age of 13. He read every magazine he could find on the subject and built models of flying machines, like fellow-Mancunian Edwin Alliott Verdon Roe, who later progressed to aeroplane manufacture and founded the Avro company. Alcock's brother recalled:

> It was in 1909 that he first showed an interest in aviation. I can well remember his early attempts to fly balloons, which he had constructed of silk and bamboo. These experiments caused a great deal of amusement to the family, but he continued and went on to small model aeroplanes.

The future aviator left school in 1908 at the age of 16 and started an apprenticeship with Empress Engineering of Longsight, Manchester.

To his delight he discovered that the proprietor, Charles Fletcher, had designed and built an aeroplane. Impressed with his apprentice's enthusiasm, Fletcher allowed him to work on his newly acquired Avro-built Farman-type biplane. Alcock's aviation ardour was further stimulated by that year's London–Manchester air race. He went with his father and thousands of others to Didsbury to witness the early-morning arrival of the French winner, Louis Paulhan. As the crowd raced across the grass to greet Paulhan, Alcock marvelled that the Frenchman's Farman was just like the one on which he had been working. On their way home he informed his father: 'One day, I am going to fly!'

Two years later Alcock went to work for engineer and Manchester Aero Club co-founder Norman Crossland. Coincidentally, Crossland was a friend of Arthur Whitten Brown, but Alcock was not destined to meet the latter until nine years later. The major turning point in Alcock's life came in 1912. His aero-engine skills were so highly valued that Charles Fletcher asked him to return to Empress, to work on an engine that had been sent for repair by Brooklands flying-school operator Maurice Ducrocq. The 19-year-old mechanic was then dispatched to Brooklands with the engine. His enthusiasm and mechanical intuition so impressed Ducrocq that the Frenchman immediately offered him employment. Ducrocq later recalled: 'I found John Alcock a very capable and efficient engineer and pilot, besides being a very nice fellow.'

Delighted to find himself at the hub of British aviation and motor racing, Alcock had no hesitation in accepting. Situated in Weybridge, Surrey, tree-fringed Brooklands had been opened in 1907 by Hugh Locke-King as the world's first purpose-built motor-racing track. Percy Lambert and Selwyn Edge, who won the 1902 Gordon Bennett Cup race, were among the early drivers who set endurance records on its banked 2.5-mile concrete expanses. Other notable racers were world land-speed record-breakers Malcolm Campbell, John Cobb, Henry Segrave and Kenelm Lee Guinness.

According to Moore-Brabazon, fliers were at first unwelcome at Brooklands. Former cycle racer Alliott Verdon Roe erected a shed there late in 1907. Two years later, following Samuel Cowdery's ('Col Cody's') first British powered aeroplane flight at Aldershot in Hampshire on 16 October 1908, Roe, evicted from Brooklands, became the first Englishman to fly a powered all-British aeroplane of his own design, making tentative hops in a triplane at Lea Marshes in Essex. Then, after a change of heart, the Brooklands management decided to create an airfield in the unused centre of the track. This attracted Roe back to the site, plus other aviators, and Tommy Sopwith opened one of Britain's first flying schools. The wooded uplands of nearby St George's Hill and Weybridge Heath exercised the attention of trainee pilots, but not as much as the sewage farm in a corner of the circuit, which lured many a fearful newcomer and those with faltering engines to its unwholesome embrace.

From the start Brooklands boasted a formidable French presence. Adolphe Pégoud became the first man to loop-the-loop in Britain there, and Louis Blériot set up a flying school. Sopwith, the Martinsyde Aircraft Company and Vickers started to build aeroplanes, and Dashwood Lang manufactured propellers. Brooklands was soon established as a centre of British aviation. Eastchurch and Hendon were the other two focal points, the former attracting a wealthy clientele of Royal Aero Club members, while Hendon, established by Claude Grahame-White, concentrated on sport and competition. Brooklands was the equivalent of Abelard's Latin Quarter, a cauldron of ideas, improvisation and passionate debate in Mr Eardley Billings' Blue Bird cafe. John Alcock could not have dreamt of more stimulating surroundings. He could look up and see his flying heroes Gustav Hamel and Alliott Verdon Roe in action every day. And all around, the music of revving engines.

Alcock realised his greatest ambition when Ducrocq taught him to fly. On 26 November 1912, three weeks after his 20th birthday, the Mancunian was granted Royal Aero Club Aviator's Certificate No. 368. As well as meeting such well-known fliers as Harry Hawker and Freddie Raynham, who ran the Sopwith school, he made friends with another mechanic and motorcycle racer, Bob Dicker. Born in the shadow of the Brooklands banking, Dicker was to enjoy a longer association with the circuit than any other person. He was also to play a part in Alcock's transatlantic flight attempt. Dicker recalled the new pilot's interest in speed in an interview for the *Brooklands Gazette*:

At that time I was messing around the track with racing motorcycles. It was soon obvious that Jack was very interested in motorcycles, and he would borrow a bike to put in a fast lap or two, between 50 and 60mph. That was some going in those days – no steering dampers, no shock absorbers, no sprung forks, no sprung frames – and lots of bumps! Jack competed in a hill climb just before the war and finished fourth.

In March 1913 Alcock embarked on his first air race. He beat Harry Hawker in a 100-guinea handicap and was runner-up to the Australian in the subsequent Maher Cup. *The Aeroplane* magazine wrote of him: 'He has suddenly developed into a biplane pilot of the very first class. On a really up-to-date machine, Mr Alcock would soon make a big name for himself.'

Maurice Ducrocq also raced motorcycles and cars. His Sunbeam was fitted with an engine designed by Breton Louis Coatalen, whose post-war creations would propel Henry Segrave to world land-speed records. In October 1913 Coatalen engaged Alcock to fly a Farman fitted with Sunbeam's first experimental V8 Crusader aero engine. Here, according to *The Aeroplane*: 'Alcock's skill as an engineer, his diligence and perseverance and his soundness as pilot found full compass.'

In June 1914, only four years after witnessing Louis Paulhan's aerial arrival from London, Alcock returned to Manchester as a racing pilot himself. He took third place overall in the London–Manchester–London air race behind the American winner, Walter Brock. Like most of his contemporaries, Alcock took the dangers of flying in his stride. Progress demanded many sacrifices; ballooning had claimed over fifty lives. Although Alcock would escape two wartime crashes, early aviation was a perilous business and accidents killed several high-profile pioneers. A gust of wind, a faulty valve, a control breakage was too often the difference between making headlines or a footnote. Moore-Brabazon recorded sadly:

They were my friends, I lived with them, I knew them as brothers. I have seen too many of them with their poor bodies burnt to ashes or crumpled into pulp to allow all their great sacrifices to pass without paying them the respect and homage that is their due.

American Lt Thomas Selfridge, flying as a passenger with Orville Wright, became the first powered-flight fatality in September 1908, when a broken propeller sent their biplane into the ground at Fort Meyer, Virginia. Three prominent pilots were killed in France the following year, Ferdinand Ferber, Eugene Lefebvre and Antonio Fernandez. No fewer than twenty fliers perished in 1910, including Charles Rolls and former president of the Aero Club de France Leon Delagrange. Peruvian Georges Chavez was killed two months later in Italy as he completed the first crossing of the Alps. Eugene Ely heralded the aircraft-carrier age by landing his Curtiss biplane on the USS *Pennsylvania* in January 1911, but perished shortly afterwards in Georgia. Calbraith Perry Rodgers, first to fly across the USA from New York to California, crashed fatally in 1912. Beautiful 37-year-old Harriet Quimby, America's first licensed woman pilot, was killed during a Massachusetts air show the same year.

Charles Rolls' death at the age of 33 was a major blow for British aviation. The training of early pilots by the Royal Aero Club, which he had co-founded, would help to ensure Britain's aerial success in the First World War. The conflict's outbreak in August 1914 ended the first stage of John Alcock's flying career. Both he and his Sunbeam-engined Farman were pressed into service at Eastchurch, on the Isle of Sheppey, where Winston Churchill had first flown the previous year. Alcock trained pilots for the Royal Naval Air Service (RNAS), and his graduates included Reginald Warneford, the first flier to shoot down a German airship, and Flt Lt Raymond Collishaw, DSC, one of Canada's most famous wartime pilots.

But the Mancunian soon tired of being a teacher. As he told *Badminton Magazine*:

> It was useful work, and very necessary also, but we chafed at the limitations. The desire to be out and in it was always with us. To get a taste of the real thing obsessed everyone, so I was frankly pleased on receiving orders to proceed to Romania for active service.

Alcock's commanding officer recommended him for a commission and in December 1916 he was posted as a flight lieutenant to No. 2 Wing, RNAS, in the Dardanelles.

The base for Allied operations in the eastern Mediterranean was the port of Mudros, on the island of Lemnos between Greece and Turkey. Appropriately, this was the legendary home of Aphrodite's husband, Hephaestus, the Greek god of technology, who made the chariot which the sun god Helios rode across the sky. In March 1917 Alcock was lucky to escape injury when he crashed and overturned a Sopwith Triplane in a ditch at Salonika. Later that same year he and his friends incorporated some Sopwith components in a small biplane they began to build, christened the Alcock A.1. However, he was destined never to fly it himself.

During his ten months at Mudros the Mancunian flew on anti-U-boat patrols and on long-distance bombing raids to Adrianople and Constantinople. Many of these flights took up to eight hours. Alcock recorded afterwards:

> Of necessity, we took chances in those days – or rather nights. It is easy to land a machine in the daytime, and with plenty of ground a squadron may be assembled; but to take a squadron over water and land them safely in the dark is hazardous, to say the least. It was in these circumstances that our Mudros machine was crashed and ruined. We had no time to grieve, however; accidents were part of the day's work, and we paid but little heed to our loss.

Shortly after setting a record 600-mile raiding flight in a Handley Page O/100, Alcock himself became a war casualty. The day of 30 September 1917 was to be the most exciting in his life until his transatlantic flight. All was quiet at the base that morning until, suddenly, three planes appeared high overhead. Startled crews scrambled and Alcock was the first to engage the German machines in his Sopwith Camel. After a brief exchange, he shot down two of the interlopers, an action that later gained him a Distinguished Service Cross citation. Later that night he departed with a crew of two on another long-range bombing raid. But this time he was on the receiving end. Anti-aircraft fire behind enemy lines knocked off his port propeller and caused the port auxiliary fuel tank to leak. Alcock immediately set about nursing his crippled plane home. He managed to fly on the remaining engine for 60 miles before he finally had to ditch off Suvla Bay. Turkish snipers opened fire on the three men and they decided that it would be safer to swim for shore. They hid among the rocks until the following noon, when they were forced to hand themselves over: 'Three burly Turks pounced upon us with little ceremony, stripping us of everything as a preliminary precaution. They took everything, and in somewhat embarrassing circumstances we were ruthlessly prodded towards the Turkish camp.'

Alcock and his crew were presumed dead until his colleagues heard that their bomber had come down in the sea and that its crew had been captured. He wryly informed fellow Mancunian Fred Mosely: 'Here I am doing time all through a burst propeller.' After a month in a stifling and verminous prison the men were transferred to a detention camp at Kedos, which housed several hundred prisoners of war from Scottish regiments. Despite contracting malaria, Alcock threw himself into camp activities, helping to build a theatre as well as indulging in his first hobby of cooking. A fellow prisoner recalled:

> Alcock was known as 'Honest John' when he was a prisoner of war. If there was any work to be done, he was always on the spot. He helped to build the stage for our 'revues', the sun shelter and the bandstand. He made reed mats and the open-air bathroom. He was caterer and Mess Superintendent for the large Mess of twenty-four officers. With his careful management, we were able to keep our health and strength. I remember old John sitting on his bed, beating up the white of eggs to make meringues! In between, he played a good game of hockey as full back, and he never missed a game of baseball.

Six months after he had arrived there, Kedos provided its own real-life drama. Alcock recorded:

> It was the evening of September 27 and the bill was *Theodore*, a new piece prepared by our own repertory company. The theatre was crowded and the Turks were in their accustomed place, when about halfway through the

piece a cry of 'Fire!' was raised. It was not the theatre, but the town itself that was alight. The subsequent conflagration beggared description, none of us will ever forget the sight. The entire town was burned to the ground.

Alcock was no correspondent, but in one letter home he wrote: 'Tell Coatalen I shall be ready for any big stunt after the war.' More than most of his fellow prisoners, he missed the freedom of the air and the joy of controlling an aeroplane. He resented each wasteful day that could have been better spent on fine-tuning a promising engine. After spending their last months living in the open, he and the other prisoners were finally released on 18 November 1918. He was luckier than many pilots he had trained, and Brooklands acrobatic hero Adolphe Pégoud, who, ironically, had been killed by one of his German students.

Alcock arrived back in England on 16 December, 'in good time for a Christmas which some of us had never expected to see again in our native land'. Having endured thirteen months of enforced idleness, the restless flier did not waste any time. He had often thought of the *Daily Mail*'s pre-war announcement of the £10,000 prize for the first non-stop Atlantic crossing. 'As soon as it was possible for me to do so, I saw General Scarlett and I was demobilised on March 10. At last I was free to attack the big problem of crossing the Atlantic. I approached Messrs Vickers.'

British interest in a transatlantic flight was renewed when Lord Northcliffe resurrected the *Daily Mail* offer. The prize was not the first to stimulate technological progress. In 1714 the British parliament offered £20,000 to whoever could devise an accurate method of determining longitude at sea. Clockmaker John Harrison designed an accurate and durable chronometer, which Capt. James Cook used to circumnavigate the globe and transform the nature of navigation. In 1795 Napoleon's Society for the Encouragement of Industry offered 12,000 francs for a method of food preservation for the French Army, which eventually led to canned food. During John Alcock's life, Ernest Archdeacon's prizes had propelled France to the forefront of European aviation.

The war had stimulated European as well as US aircraft development. Unlike 1913, when the *Daily Mail* prize was first announced, there were now several British machines that boasted both the power and the range to cross the ocean. One wartime flight in particular, a 2,000-mile trip in stages from England to Turkey, clearly demonstrated that long-distance flight was now practicable. John Alcock had been among those who had welcomed the Handley Page aeroplane to Lemnos.

Although he was only 26, the man who so boldly contacted Vickers had experience and confidence beyond his years. Thanks to his Brooklands apprenticeship, his flying instruction at Eastchurch and his service on the Eastern Front, he already had 4,500 flying hours to his credit. He was popular among his contemporaries, who were struck by his commitment to flying. A friend wrote:

Jack Alcock, as he was always called, was a short, stocky, young man with an engaging smile and a shock of fair ginger hair that was forever falling in his eyes. His was a wild and boisterous humour, given to practical jokes at the expense of others. For him, nothing need be taken seriously except flying and that he held sacred. A man only happy and at ease when flying or talking 'shop' with mechanics and pilots. He had little time for social niceties or intellectual pursuits; a technical journal was more important to him than a novel. Clothing never interested him. Even when in uniform, he managed to have a slightly dishevelled air!

Another man impressed with Alcock's qualities was author, MP and aviation observer Col Arthur Lynch. He described him as:

A typical Lancashire lad, a fresh-faced, clean-shaven, sandy-haired jolly Englishman, well made and active, not too tall or bulky, ready to laugh and ready to face any danger. And to keep his head till he had fought his corner. 'I like him,' a friend said, 'because there is no side to him.'

It was a much more sober Brooklands to which the battle-matured Mancunian returned early in 1919. But while the war had taken many of his friends, the various manufacturers were in their old familiar places; Vickers, Sopwith and Martinsyde. Alcock knew that the latter two, plus

Handley Page, had declared their interest in the Atlantic competition. At Vickers he was delighted to meet his old friend, Bob Dicker and two Ducrocq acquaintances, former flying instructor Archie Knight and Percy Maxwell Muller, now respectively the company's works manager and aviation superintendent. They were impressed with the seasoned version of the enthusiast they had known in pre-war years. And, as Knight later told the *Daily Sketch*, Alcock had added canniness to his repertoire. He let the Vickers men show their cards first. 'The idea of flying the Atlantic was first put to Captain Alcock by Mr Percy Muller, the works superintendent for Messrs Vickers. The captain promptly replied; 'I am on it any old time'!'

With no ceremony but a shaking of hands, that short exchange set in motion one of the greatest aviation feats of all time. For the next two months, until he embarked for Newfoundland, Alcock hardly ever left the Brooklands factory. Spurred on by his rivals' Atlantic preparations, his enthusiasm in turn stimulated designer Reginald Kirshaw Pierson and the mechanics and riggers, who worked all hours on the emerging Vimy.

To the British general public in 1919 the idea of flying across the Atlantic still seemed absurd, even suicidal. First of all there was the immensity of the distance. Measuring 2,000 miles wide at its narrowest point, between Newfoundland and Ireland, the Atlantic is the second largest of the world's oceans. Deriving its name from Greek mythology, it was originally known as 'The Sea of Atlas' and was first mentioned in the *Histories of Herodotus* in 450 BC. Following in the footsteps of the legendary St Brendan, its earliest explorers were the Vikings, the Portuguese and Christopher Columbus. Transatlantic crossings by sailing ships were time-consuming and perilous. In the nineteenth century steamships ushered in safer, speedier and more luxurious travel, but the loss of the *Titanic* in 1912 underlined the north Atlantic's hazards and violent weather aberrations. Apart from the winds and treacherous storms, few areas are as uninviting as the coast of north-east America, the closest point to Europe. The Labrador Current conveys a flow of deadly icebergs. The Gulf Stream bears welcome warmth to north-western Europe, but its collision with the cold currents off Newfoundland produces dense, clinging fogs. Ranging from sea level to 3,000ft, these have long bedevilled both shipping and aviation.

Despite the perils, the idea of flying the Atlantic exerted a romantic and commercial attraction on aviators and airlines from the earliest days. But the unknown hazards of the air far outdid the unpredictability of those at sea. Before weather ships and satellites there was virtually no meteorological information available. Apart from the Grand Banks fogs, aviators would face violent winds, regular cloud and rain, and electrical storms whose accompanying vertical currents would impose additional strain on the structure of a heavily laden aeroplane. Freezing temperatures added the risk of ice forming on the leading edges of the wings and tailplane, causing both a fatal weight increase and lack of control. Sparsely travelled shipping lanes meant that anyone involved in an enforced ditching was likely to perish by drowning or exposure. The extreme winter weather ruled out any air attempts for many months. The desirability of a full moon further reduced the window of opportunity to six days per month.

Apart from the weather, the capriciousness of early aero engines was infamous. They were far more stressed than later units, which would operate at only a fraction of their available power. The weight of the fuel necessary for a 2,000-mile crossing compounded the problem. Equally importantly, traversing the featureless Atlantic or any other ocean imposed a high premium on navigational skills. With no landmarks such as railway lines or mountain ranges to follow, it would be easy to stray off course. A good pilot always had half an eye on the ground for an emergency landing spot. The ocean would provide no such security. Navigation instruments were basic and sometimes as unreliable as the infant radio. But, undaunted by all these obstacles, John Alcock and Vickers pressed on with their transatlantic preparations. The only problem they acknowledged was that of finding a navigator. Where would they get someone capable of accurately directing their aeroplane across the uncharted vastness from Newfoundland to Ireland?

3

ALCOCK MEETS BROWN

I liked him from the first because he is so quiet, and from
the beginning he impressed me with his reliability.
I had the greatest faith in him right through.

John Alcock

The names of John Alcock and Arthur Whitten Brown are permanently linked in aviation history since they formed their Atlantic partnership at the Vickers works in late March 1919. Remarkably, they had not encountered each other before that meeting, though they lived within a few miles of each other in Manchester.

Outshone by London, Manchester was by no means a backwater. A leading player in the Industrial Revolution, the city had established itself from the 18th century as the financial and industrial hub of northern England. Its factories and teeming mills later inspired one of Britain's best-loved artists, L.S. Lowry. Known principally for its textile industry and described as 'Cottonopolis', Manchester produced such eminent scientists as James Prescott Joule and John Dancer, who developed microphotography. The atomic scientist Ernest Rutherford lectured at its university from 1907. Suffragette leaders Emmeline and Christabel Pankhurst were born there, as was birth-control pioneer Marie Stopes, who married a brother of early aviator Alliott Verdon Roe. The city made a rich contribution to the arts with writers such as Thomas de Quincey and William Harriet

Ainsworth, and conductors Sir Thomas Beecham and Sir John Barbirolli. The *Manchester Guardian* was founded in 1821 by industrialist and social reformer Joseph Brotherton, and soon became one of the world's most influential newspapers.

Thanks to its burgeoning industries the city had established itself in transport history long before Alcock and Brown put it on the aviation map. The world's first passenger railway was opened between Manchester and Liverpool in 1830. Sixty-four years later the Manchester Ship Canal provided direct access to the sea. Noted for its engineering expertise, the city featured many foundries and machine-tool companies. It was also the birthplace of one of the world's most famous car companies. Former newspaper vendor turned engineer Frederick Henry Royce opened a company making dynamos and electric cranes in 1884 at Cooke Street in Hulme. Twenty years later he produced his first engine, and then a car of his own design. The machine so impressed wealthy London engineer the Hon Charles Stewart Rolls that he sought out its inventor. Their meeting in Manchester's Midland Hotel led to the establishment in 1906 of the Rolls-Royce company, whose engines, designed by Royce himself, would power John Alcock and Arthur Whitten Brown to transatlantic success.

Whitten Brown's parents were Arthur George Brown and Emma Whitten, both Americans of English origin. The father, an engineer, was sent by the Westinghouse Electric & Manufacturing Company to Glasgow, where the future transatlantic navigator was born on 23 July 1886 at 42 Annette Street, Govanhill. Shortly after his son's birth, Brown senior was sent to build a new factory in Manchester. The family settled in 'Ellerslie', 6 Oswald Road, Chorlton-cum-Hardy, a more salubrious neighbourhood than Jack Alcock's, and just outside the city. Adventure was in the family blood. Arthur Whitten Brown's great-grandmother had been head nurse at the Battle of Pittsburgh Landing during the American Civil War. His grandfather was a pioneering railway constructor who was killed in the same conflict.

Though an only child, Arthur Whitten Brown was not spoiled. Self-reliant, he earned early pocket money by such tasks as grinding mica. He developed an interest in aviation after constructing and flying a box kite from plans in a magazine (he carried a photo of the airborne kite with him to Newfoundland). Stimulated by John Dancer's pioneering work, he took up colour photography while pursuing his studies at Manchester's Central High School and university. His schoolmates remembered 'Ted' as a thoughtful and exceptionally studious youth with a slight American accent, which dated from many childhood trips with his father to the USA. On one train trip in New York, after giving Brown junior a half-fare ticket, the conductor remarked: 'I ought to charge full fare for him. Look at what he is reading!' Brown was studying an advanced technical manual.

With his family engineering background it was no surprise that Brown went on to serve an apprenticeship with Westinghouse from 1903 to 1906. Despite his eventual engineering qualifications he never had any difficulty in mixing with those who had not enjoyed the privilege of his education. He recalled in his *Royal Air Force and Civil Aviation Record* memoir:

> In the works, I was for a time a workman among workmen – a condition of life which is the best possible beginning for an embryo engineer. I found my associates good companions, useful instructors and incorrigible jokers. My father's warnings, however, saved me from hours of waiting in the forge at their direction while a 'straight hook' was made, or from hunting the shops for the 'spare short circuit'!

Brown's interest in engineering and mathematics was balanced by his love for the arts. He became a member of the local operatic society and regularly attended plays and musicals. Like Wilbur Wright and Amelia Earhart, he was also an avid reader. He enjoyed novels and poetry, and studied French and German. He was intrigued by science-fiction author Jules Verne, who had written:

> In spite of the opinions of certain narrow-minded people who would shut up the human race upon this globe, we shall one day travel to the Moon, the planets, and the stars with the same facility, rapidity and certainty as we now make the ocean voyage from Liverpool to New York.

Brown may have been studious but, like Alcock, he was thorough and a man of action. By the time he was 17 he was a proficient mechanic and had learned to drive. He made many excursions across Lancashire on a motorcycle owned by Norman Crossland, who, eight years later, would employ John Alcock. Brown worked in the Westinghouse control department for two years before being sent to the company's Johannesburg office in 1908. On his return, in 1910, he was appointed a general engineer in Manchester. Three years later he revisited his parents' country to study streetcar lighting and starting sets in St Louis, Missouri.

As well as extending his experience, Brown wrote on engineering for various technical journals. Like millions of his generation, however, his budding career was rudely interrupted by the First World War. Unlike John Alcock, Brown was in his late twenties before he had any physical contact with aeroplanes. The war provided his introduction to flying, as well as shattering his previously comfortable lifestyle. He enlisted in the University and Public Schools Battalion at the outbreak of war in August 1914, and was gazetted a second lieutenant in the Manchester Regiment the following January. He was immediately catapulted into the horror of trench warfare at Ypres and the mud and blood-soaked necropolis of the Somme, where 1 million died in months for minuscule territorial gain.

Almost a century after the war it is difficult for armchair readers to comprehend the reality of the thunderous and relentless shelling, and the gas attacks, which permanently marked Brown and all those who witnessed the devastation. The first to conquer the Atlantic by air in an east–west direction, Capt. James Fitzmaurice, recorded: 'Long before I was 21, I had gazed into the glassy upturned eyes of broken soldiers, trodden a field wet with blood and still shuddering from the blows of a world conflict.' Fellow Irishman Henry Segrave, one of Brown's Ypres companion infantry officers and a future world land-speed record-breaker, wrote:

I was peacefully walking home to bed when, about 350 yards away, there was a blinding flash that lit up the whole place, and a great roaring sort of cough that made the very earth tremble, and a thing went across the sky swishing like a huge rocket. I have never known such a terrible sound.

There was no other word for it; it was terrible. It made me feel empty in the stomach. It was like Dante's *Inferno* let loose.

Gen. Haig was reported as saying in July 1914: 'I hope none of you gentlemen is so foolish as to think that aeroplanes will be usefully employed for reconnaissance purposes in war,' but army thinking quickly changed as the war progressed. The necessity of aeroplanes for observation led to a demand for pilots and observers. Both Brown and Segrave were happy to swap the squalor of the trenches for aerial risk-taking, even though there were no parachutes to save them in those early days, Royal Flying Corps (RFC) top brass opposing their issue on the grounds that a pilot might abandon his aircraft in an emergency, rather than fight. Brown gratefully recorded: 'Then came the second step towards the transatlantic flight. I had always longed to be in the air, and I obtained a transfer to the Royal Flying Corps as an observer.'

As warfare became more dependent on atmospheric conditions, knowledge of wind direction and navigation assumed vital importance. The increasing use of aircraft and the Germans' employment of deadly gas led to the setting up of the Meteorology Unit of the Royal Engineers in September 1915. Its function was to advise the General Staff, both at General Headquarters and in the field; to furnish the regular reports required for the correction of range in artillery operations, and all meteorological information required by the RFC.

A flying observer's duties included photography, checking enemy trench and artillery positions and also assisting his own artillery's range-finders. Despite the technological limitations of their aircraft, observers saved many lives by confirming or contradicting previous intelligence. But flying at optimum low altitude and in straight lines while undertaking aerial photography made them easy targets for anti-aircraft shells, known as 'Archie'. The roar of the engine made it impossible for crews to hear the sound of ground fire.

Posted to No. 2 Squadron at Hesdigneul on the French Western Front, Brown had an early experience of the dangers when he went on a mission with Cecil Lewis. Their aeroplane was rocked by Archie and enveloped in puffs of smoke while flying at 5,800ft. Luckily the machine was undamaged and they made it safely to the ground. But they were never short of reminders that their turn would come. They regularly sat down to dinner opposite the empty chairs of those with whom they had lunched.

Brown had his closest brush with death on 5 October 1915. By a curious coincidence, the man he flew with was 19-year-old Lt William Allcock, unrelated to his subsequent Atlantic pilot, John Alcock. Hailing from Knighton, Radnorshire, Allcock was an adventurous young man who had previously travelled as far afield as Calgary and St John's, which would also feature in Brown's life. It was their third flight together. The pair were flying a lumbering Royal Aircraft Factory B.E.2C reconnaissance biplane at 8,000ft over Hulluch, near Lens, when a burst of shrapnel knocked out their engine. Allcock recorded in his diary:

I turned for our lines, when just crossing them the machine caught fire at 6,300ft. I immediately put her nose down; the flames burst out and spread along the fuselage behind the pilot's seat. Brown threw the ammunition overboard and climbed back nearly into my cockpit, as the whole front of the machine was a blazing mass. In the meantime we were speeding to earth at 120mph. Brown was trying to keep the fire down from burning his clothes while I kept my eye on the pitot tube [through which the air speed registered on an instrument in the cockpit], the ground and the flames, pushing the joy stick further forward until we were nearly nose diving.

Every minute I thought would be the last for I expected the whole machine to collapse from strain as a number of wires were broken. Eventually I saw the ground not far below and found myself going straight at a village so I turned to the right and, spying a ploughed field, decided to land there, cutting through telephone wires and a tall hedge. A few feet from the ground I levelled out and the machine took the ground at 70mph. A perfect landing but the undercarriage being burnt, the machine ran a few yards and collapsed, digging her nose into the plough, and turned over.

Both men were lucky to escape with burns and bruises. Allcock concluded:

I was thrown right out 10 yards ahead, putting out my hands saved me but I lay dazed a little, in the meantime the tail came down and hit me on the head. Staggering round to find Brown, I found him hunting for me. He had fallen under the engine and just managed to crawl out a few seconds before the bearings broke and the engine fell on the spot. Looking on the wreckage we saw a mass of flame with every few seconds shots going off from the revolvers.

For the RFC this was just a routine incident, and a communiqué succinctly noted:

A B.E.2C, pilot, Lt Allcock, observer, 2 Lt Brown, when on artillery regis-tration was hit when over Hulluch and was forced to descend. The machine was found to be on fire over the lines and came down near Vaudricourt. The machine was in flames and totally destroyed.

Incredibly, Allcock flew the following day, and he and Brown resumed their partnership on 21 October. Life expectancy was short in the RFC, and the hapless Allcock was killed shortly afterwards in another crash. Brown's luck finally ran out on 10 November, while on a photographic reconnaissance with Lt Henry Medlicott over rain-swept Valenciennes, south-east of Lille. While other aircraft headed for home, they defied the stormy weather to complete their mission. Their aeroplane was hit, and Brown's left leg was shattered by a bullet. Medlicott tried to return to base but a ruptured petrol tank forced them down behind enemy lines. In the crash-landing Brown suffered severe injuries. He broke a leg, dislocated his hip and both knees, and lost several teeth. Despite their injuries, he and Medlicott managed to destroy all their notes before they were captured.

Brown spent several months in hospital at Aix-la-Chapelle before being transferred to a prison camp in Germany. Like Henry Segrave, who was also shot down, his injuries left him with a permanent limp. Regular pain ensured that he could not take as active a part as he wished in camp activi-ties, but he was luckier than Medlicott, whom the Germans shot when he attempted to escape. Like Alcock, Brown also became a proficient cook. He informed his father: 'We can do all our own cooking on the stove in cold weather – or on spirit stoves in warm. That is my job as I can make coffee, fry bacon, or boil eggs (when there are any).'

The recovering observer ameliorated the frustration of imprisonment by reading books and articles on navigation sent to him via the Red Cross. He later recorded: 'My two years of captivity involved, strange to say, the third step towards transatlantic flight. For it was as a prisoner of war that I first found time to begin a careful study of the possibilities of aerial navigation.'

Brown endured over a year's confinement before being transferred to a camp at Grand Chalet Rossinierre in Switzerland. This was close to Montreux, where one of his poetic heroes, Byron, had written *The Prisoner of Chillon.* As the months dragged on, Brown could empathise with that other frustrated captive:

It might be months, or years, or days,
I kept no count, I took no note,
I had no hope my eyes to raise,
And clear them of their dreary mote.

Finally, after a further nine months, Brown was repatriated to England. In the spring of 1918 he was seconded to the Aircraft Production Department of the Ministry of Munitions in London's Kingsway. Henry Segrave's father, Charles, worked here, and, more importantly, 22-year-old Marguerite Kathleen Kennedy, daughter of the Irish-born head of the department in which Brown was engaged on aero-engine design. Brown and Kathleen fell in love. They celebrated his new Pilot's Certificate by becoming engaged in October to get married the following April.

While the November Armistice was wonderful news for war-weary Europe, it meant that Brown and most of his colleagues were now out of a job. Cecil Lewis recorded the dilemma of the newly demobbed:

We walked off the playing fields into the lines. We lived supremely in the moment. Our preoccupation was the next patrol, our horizon the next leave. We were trained with one object – to kill. We had one hope – to live. When it was over, we had to start again.

While awaiting his demobilisation, Brown returned to his parents in Manchester for Christmas. Only a few miles away, newly returned Capt. John Alcock celebrated the holiday with his family. They were but two of the thousands of redundant Royal Air Force (RAF, formed on 1 April 1918) personnel who were competing for scarce work. They had risked their lives for their country, which now had little to offer them.

Handicapped by his lameness and never without a walking stick, Brown thought his prospects none too bright. A few days after Christmas he wrote to Kathleen Kennedy:

> I must have a long chat with your Daddy. I expect when discharged to have about £250 in cash, and I can get £500 a year in Manchester? The question is – shall we spend the £250 on furniture and build a little nest – or shall we take a chance and spend the money in going to New York and hunting for a job. We might live in a couple of rooms in my aunt Molly's house in Brooklyn – and we might get a reduction in rent.

Brown used the holiday to catch up with his reading and the Christmas shows. He had also developed an interest in the literature of the Kennedy country. He wrote to Kathleen: 'Yesterday, we did two theatres. *Yeoman of the Guard* in the afternoon and another at night. Have you ever read any of Yeats's Irish plays? I'll bring a copy down with me when I come next time.' He ended the letter on his usual romantic note: 'There is no beauty in the world, save when you are with me to share it.'

Before returning to London, Brown spent time on the RAF station at Scopwick, Lincolnshire, where he indulged his new skills as a fully fledged pilot. He apologised to his fiancée for losing a special pencil she gave him: 'I lost it overboard from an aeroplane one day while trying to make a note on a map – I was wild about it.' He wrote a more distressing note about a dog he had to put down: 'He tried to take a bite out of an Avro propeller. Poor little beggar – I had to shoot him. I haven't got over it yet – it is such a pity.'

In between flying, Brown had an encounter with a fortune-teller. He wrote to Kathleen on 22 January 1919: 'It is a wonderful business – just generalities which might apply to anyone! If it's good we'll believe it, but if it's bad, we will assert our superior intelligence, what?'

But the sceptical navigator still recounted the lady's forecasts:

> She told me that I should take a long journey across water soon, and that I wouldn't go alone, but that it would not be as soon as I had expected. Gee! I knew all that before. She also said that the future was very bright, but that I should have to work to make it so. She might have known that I hate work. Also I am to have a settlement of some kind – no doubt, my gratuity!

Back in London, Brown little knew how quickly that forecasted trip across water would materialise. Although Maj. Kennedy provided introductions to various companies, no one was interested in his services until he visited the Vickers works one morning in late March 1919. He noted sadly:

> When the ban on attempts to fly the Atlantic was lifted, I hoped that my studies of aerial navigation might be useful to one of the firms preparing for such a flight. Each one I approached, however, refused my proposals, and for the moment I gave up the idea.

There could hardly be any greater contrast than that between weaponry of destruction and that most quintessential English Sunday anthem, the peal of village church bells. Yet, far from its warplanes and other paraphernalia of death, Vickers first made its name as a maker of church bells, in the steel foundry launched in Sheffield in 1828 by George Naylor and Edward Vickers, the first president of the town's Chamber of Commerce. The company went public in 1867 as Vickers, Sons & Company and, after acquiring more businesses, began casting marine propellers in 1872 and artillery pieces in 1890. It bought out the Barrow Shipbuilding company seven years later, and in 1901 built the Royal Navy's first submarine, *Holland 1*. After taking over Wolseley Cars and the Whitehead torpedo manufacturers, Vickers Ltd (Aviation Department) started manufacturing aeroplanes at Bexleyheath, Crayford, Dartford and Erith in 1911. The Vickers Flying School was established the following year at Brooklands.

Vickers produced seven different types of monoplane before it began constructing pusher biplanes in 1912. In 1913 one such machine, optimistically named *Destroyer* (and retrospectively designated Experimental Fighting Biplane 1), was built to meet an Admiralty requirement and was one of the first purpose-built aeroplanes to mount a machine gun. Unfortunately it crashed on its first attempted take-off, but its successors proved more successful, evolving into the 'Gunbus' series. With the outbreak of war in 1914 the works at Crayford, Kent, took over the production of Vickers aircraft. Three years later the company produced a twin-engine long-range bomber designed by former flier Reginald Kirshaw Pierson. The machine took only four months to build after Pierson made the first sketch on a piece of foolscap paper at the Air Board in London's Hotel Cecil.

The well-proportioned biplane was christened Vimy, after the Canadian Army's success in the 1917 battle for Vimy Ridge north of Arras, which had previously cost 150,000 British and French lives. The Vimy first flew at Joyce Green, near Dartford, on 30 November 1917. The Vimy went into production in April 1918 and the majority were given Rolls-Royce power, but the type never saw action in Europe because the war ended shortly afterwards. The RAF bought some to re-equip units in the Middle East and to fly mail from Cairo to Baghdad. Others were based in Northern Ireland or used for flying and parachute training.

Pierson immediately designed a civilian version of the Vimy with a rotund, larger-capacity fuselage built of spruce plywood, which could carry either ten passengers or 2,500lb of cargo. The Vimy Commercial, as it was named, first flew early in 1919, at the same time as the company transferred its aircraft operation to Brooklands. From spring 1919 Vickers used the Vimy as part of a flying circus to popularise flying and to assess the potential passenger market. Fifty-five military transport versions of the Vimy Commercial were built for the RAF, and the Chinese government ordered forty-three.

Although John Alcock's brother claimed that Arthur Whitten Brown had been given an introductory letter to Vickers, it seems that the navigator's involvement with the Vimy transatlantic attempt was a monumental accident. Brown informed an American journalist that, like most people, he had no idea that Vickers were considering such a project. At a loose end, he simply travelled to Weybridge that March morning to accompany another RAF officer, who wanted to discuss radiators with Percy Maxwell Muller.

As he entered the Brooklands works, Brown's chances of the navigation opportunity of a lifetime seemed as far-fetched as the landing at nearby Addlestone golf course of a Martian ship, as recounted in H.G. Wells's *The War of the Worlds.* He recalled later:

> It was entirely by chance that I became involved in the transatlantic competition. While I was talking with the superintendent, Capt. Alcock walked into the office. We were introduced, and, in the course of conversation, the competition was mentioned.
>
> I then learned for the first time that Messrs Vickers were considering an entry, although not courting publicity until they should have attempted it. I sat up and began to take notice, and ventured to put forward my views on the navigation of aircraft for long flights over the sea. These were received favourably, and the outcome of the fortunate meeting was that Messrs Vickers retained me to act as aerial navigator.

John Alcock told a journalist about aviation's equivalent of the meeting between David Livingstone and Henry Stanley:

> Brown was having tea with Mr Muller, our superintendent. I had just been demobbed and I looked in about getting instruments for the machine. I had not decided on a navigator and I was looking for one. He started there and then going into navigation, and soon got beyond me. I concluded that he knew a good deal about it. I was struck with him right away and I asked him if he would care to fly the Atlantic, and he said he would be delighted to. From that time, a month or so before we left England, we worked together, getting gear, navigation instruments, and other things. We did the trials together, too.
>
> Brown turned out to be even a finer and cleverer chap than I had thought he would. He is excellent company, very jovial, and a splendid chap altogether. I liked him from the first because he is so quiet, and from the beginning he impressed me with his reliability. I had the greatest faith

in him right through. I didn't worry at all about navigation, and left it entirely to him. We are now great friends; indeed friends for life.

Neither inheritance nor privileged connections had brought Alcock and Brown to the verge of transatlantic glory. Their assets were self-acquired. Their courage and sense of adventure, their passion for aviation, and the skill and confidence they had built during their arduous flying apprenticeships. John Alcock was 26. Although toughened by the war, for him the future stretched to infinity. The 33-year-old Arthur Whitten Brown's horizons were comparatively foreshortened. But their shared enthusiasm negated this difference in perspective.

After their fortuitous meeting, Alcock brought Brown out to see the Vimy on its assembly trestles. It is unlikely that either of the men guessed that the three of them would be united for all time in the annals of aviation history. Brown had more immediate and mundane preoccupations. Generalities or not, that fortune-teller's forecast of a long journey was certainly going to be realised. His wedding would have to be postponed. Walton-on-Thames, Esher, Surbiton, Wimbledon; as his train clattered along the rails to Waterloo terminus the unemployed engineer turned Atlantic navigator considered how he would break the news to Kathleen Kennedy; and to the formidable Maj. Kennedy.

4

CONSTRUCTION OF THE ATLANTIC VIMY

◆◇◆

I saw it take off for the first time; it looked beautiful, like a bird. I can still see as it looked then. It looked beautiful, all silver.

Anne Boultwood

◆◇◆

Devastated by the twin catastrophes of war and Spanish flu, Britain and the rest of the world badly needed some cheering in 1919. 'It will be over by Christmas' was the general consensus when war broke out in August 1914. That turned out to be Christmas 1918. Not even the economies of the most advanced nations could withstand the conflict's social and economic consequences. An entire generation had been wiped off the face of the Earth. There was hardly a family in western Europe that was not in mourning. Over 8 million had perished, including ¾ million British breadwinners. The funding of the war mainly by borrowing bequeathed a massive national debt. With 5 million demobilised British soldiers and an equal number released from government war work, widespread unemployment created much official and general unease. People were hungry. Every train and underground forecourt featured limbless and maimed buskers. There was fear of social unrest. The only growth industries seemed to be the carving of sombre monuments and the composition of such ballads as 'Roses of Picardy' for confused and guilty couch survivors:

And the roses will die with the summer time
And our roads may be far apart
But there's one rose that dies not in Picardy,
'Tis the rose that I keep in my heart.

Politically, post-war Europe was much altered. Germany was now power-less, but seething under the punitive conditions of the Treaty of Versailles. The capitalist countries fretted about the establishment of the Bolshevik revolution in Russia. Britain was wrong-footed by the increasing clamour for independence in many of its colonies. As if all this was not enough, nature reminded destructive man of his molecular insignificance. The world was rocked by the Spanish flu, which raged from 1918 to 1919. It eclipsed the casualties of the war, with a death total of over 50 million. Among its victims were Maj. Herbert Wood, the creator of Vickers Aviation, and engineer Thomas Keppel North from Rougham, Norfolk, each of whom had made a major contribution to the production of the Vimy.

The new economic forces at work compounded Britain's general insecurity. The great export reliables of coal, cotton goods and shipbuilding would never regain their pre-war economical predominance. Gratefully removed from Europe's implosion, the USA now dominated the international economy. Social change was on the way. The Labour Party had committed itself to the ideal of public ownership of the means of production, distribution and exchange. The days of inept landed gentry officers sending legions of workers to certain slaughter had sunk with Kitchener.

The war also liberated women from the kitchen sink. They celebrated the election of Lady Astor, the first woman to take her seat in the Houses of Parliament. Religious leaders had less to cheer about. The conflict had sorely tested people's belief in the love of a universal God. Twenty-year-old veteran pilot Cecil Lewis, the son of a clergyman, concluded:

We are, collectively, the most evil and destructive of human creatures. We back up our greeds and jealousies with religion and patriotism. Our Christian priests bless the launching of battleships, our youth is urged to die gloriously 'for King and Country'. We even write on the tomb of our

Unknown Warrior that he died 'for God'. What a piece of impudent and blasphemous nonsense to write in the House of Him whose greatest saying was: 'This is my commandment, that ye love one another.'

With so much disillusionment, so many questions and doubts, people needed some distraction, some hope for the future, some encouragement. Something to make them live again and believe in themselves. The race to be first to fly the Atlantic provided one welcome diversion, a vehicle for inspiration. The success of the Vickers Vimy and its crew, Capt. John Alcock and Lt Arthur Whitten Brown, would greatly boost British pride and confidence. Being airmen had already given them a head start in the race for role models. Airmen were considered among the bravest, most gallant and glamorous of the war heroes. Their aerial feats had placed them apart from their ground-anchored comrades. But Alcock and Brown's Atlantic achievement was to lift spirits not only in Britain, but all around the world.

The Atlantic race offered beleaguered aircraft manufacturers an opportunity to advertise their products. During the war, Sopwith employed a staff of up to 5,000, who built 16,000 aeroplanes. The cessation of hostilities meant the end of such large-scale production. The government no longer panicked for immediate deliveries, but actually cancelled many outstanding orders. Aeroplane manufacturers had to adapt or go out of business. Tommy Sopwith recalled in an interview with Kenneth W. Leish:

> The bottom dropped out of everything. There was literally no work. We tried to keep the factory going by building motorbicycles and all sorts of odd jobs, but it was quite impossible to keep a number of people employed, or even any reasonable proportion of them, on aviation.

The world was not yet air-minded. But Britain's Air Ministry set up a civil aviation department in February 1919. It was organised into four branches. These dealt with the survey and preparation of air routes for the British Empire and the organisation of meteorological and wireless telegraphy services; publicity; the transmission of general information; and the licensing of civilian pilots, aerodromes and machines for both passenger and cargo carriage. A special Act of Parliament, The Air Navigation Acts, 1911–1919, was passed on 27 February, and commercial flying was officially permitted from 1 May 1919.

The first continental air passenger service started in February, from Berlin to Leipzig and Weimar. British aviation experts were soon planning air routes as far afield as Egypt and India, itineraries being tentatively mapped via Pisa, Taranto and Crete. But crossing the Atlantic with no such intermediate stops was considered a step too far for the time being. The British Army Chief of Staff, Maj. Gen. F.H. Sykes, told the London Chamber of Commerce that an Atlantic crossing should probably be a matter of navigation, meteorology and wireless, rather than of the endurance of machine and personnel. He warned:

> Even a small error in bearing might be sufficient to miss entirely so small a point in the Atlantic as the Azores. As yet, we know nothing of upper air conditions in the mid-Atlantic. The accomplishment of transatlantic flight demands an organisation capable of centralising at the starting point all information about the immediate conditions all along the route, in order that the rare opportunities when suitable conditions exist might be seized. It should not be undertaken lightly.

With the end of war demand, the survival of the aircraft companies depended on bold initiatives and the opening of completely new markets. One of the first to create a commercial demand for its products, Vickers employed its converted Vimy bomber to outstanding effect. The aircraft's fame would be built on three monumental achievements: Alcock and Brown's transatlantic epic, Keith and Ross Smith's December 1919 flight to Australia, and the first England to South Africa flight in 1920 by Pierre van Rynveld and Christopher Quintin-Brand. Vickers historian J.D. Scott reiterated:

> It was these flights which gave body to the possibilities of long-range passenger and mail communications, and so gave to the aircraft industry, and to what were to become the operating companies, definite aims for which to strive. Perhaps even more important was the way in which, at the

end of the war, when the aerial adventure (one of the few parts of the First World War which had not left behind a bitter disillusionment) seemed to be over, the long-distance flight rekindled the adventurous imagination.

According to Scott, Alcock and Brown's transatlantic Vimy had an inauspicious eviction early in 1919 from its Crayford manufacturing site, where the stock of forty machines occupied space urgently needed for the peacetime manufacture of sewing machines. And the pilot who claimed to have flown the Vimy from the production hangar at Upavon to its new home at Brooklands was none other than Cecil Lewis, author of the classic account of First World War flying, *Sagittarius Rising*, who at that time was general manager of the newly formed Civil Aviation Vickers Ltd. Lewis considered Alcock a leading pilot and Brown an equally professional navigator, and he insisted: 'The Vimy was a good choice for such a flight. She was fast, as such machines went then, compact, could carry the necessary petrol, and was fitted with Rolls-Royce engines. Probably she was the only machine in existence at that time to make the crossing.'

John A. Bagley of London's Science Museum and Hugh Scrope of Vickers, however, disputed these claims of the Atlantic Vimy's origin. After examining all the relevant documents and speaking to staff such as Archie Knight, who had worked on the aircraft, they concluded that it was assembled at Weybridge, in part from components transferred from Crayford. It was extra to a production batch for the RAF and had no constructor's number or military serial, being always referred to as the Atlantic Vimy in surviving paperwork. Most contemporary accounts agreed that the Vimy was built at Weybridge, as did a survivor of the construction team, Bob Dicker, who insisted that it was assembled and test-flown there. If it had been built at Crayford it would have been tested at Joyce Green.

John Bagley concluded:

The fact that part of it – probably a substantial part – derived from the Crayford production line explained why it was always regarded as Vickers property. They would have reached a settlement with the Air Ministry about the value of unfinished work at Crayford when that factory closed. If it really had been an RAF machine as C. Lewis suggested – then Vickers would have had to buy it or borrow it from the RAF for the flight. In neither case would they have been able to present it freely to the Science Museum. Certainly I would expect more records of the transaction to have survived, if this were an ex-RAF machine. The very absence of records tends to convince me that this was a purely internal affair within the company.

The aircraft was officially designated Vickers F.B.27 Vimy Mk IV, as were most of the Eagle-engined versions, but its origin hardly bothered John Alcock and Arthur Whitten Brown as they threw themselves into the preparation of their Atlantic attempt at Brooklands. Despite their contrasting characters, the pair complemented each other like the Wright brothers. Although they argued over limited cockpit space for various instruments, they thoroughly discussed every aspect of the Vimy's construction and the flight planning.

Alcock proved an efficient organiser but he had little time for meetings. It was Brown who had to go up to London to beg for Air Ministry support with navigation instruments. Ministry officials, who believed that the future lay with airships rather than aeroplanes, were unenthusiastic but eventually lent him a compass and a wireless transmitter and receiver. Brown also did the rounds of the fuel companies for petrol and oil. Despite Alcock's unfamiliarity with tailoring concerns, both men made repeat visits to try their electrically heated flying suits at Burberry's, the London company that had supplied clothes to Roald Amundsen and Robert Falcon Scott for their Antarctic expeditions.

Although temporarily disappointed with the wedding postponement, the Kennedy clan was also supportive. Despite being Irish, Maj. Kennedy was more attuned to military manuals than he was to the poetry of compatriot W.B. Yeats. He put loyalty above personal feelings and, seeing the transatlantic attempt as a patriotic exercise, he used his influence wherever possible to help the fliers. In between all the hard work Brown managed to appease Kathleen with the odd dance and West End show. She in turn presented him with a small black cat mascot, Twinkletoes, for the Atlantic attempt. Alcock, not to be outdone, produced a companion mascot, which they christened Lucky Jim.

Their late entry ensured that the Vickers fliers were rank outsiders for the *Daily Mail* transatlantic prize. Australian Harry Hawker had extensively tested his Sopwith Atlantic long before the Vimy was even assembled. Frederick P. Raynham and Capt. C.W.F. Morgan had completed a twenty-four-hour incarceration in their Martinsyde Raymor while it consumed its full load of fuel. These aeroplanes and teams arrived in St John's, Newfoundland, a whole month before Alcock and Brown had even completed testing their Vimy.

As soon as Vickers entered the Atlantic race Reginald Pierson set about modifying the basic aeroplane. The nosewheel and tailplane skids were removed and the gunner's position in the nose was faired over. The pilot and navigator would sit side-by-side in the main cockpit, as normal. Additional tanks, partly accommodated by doing away with the mid-fuselage gunner's position, increased the Vimy's fuel capacity to 865gal, giving it a range of 2,440 miles. With other companies so far ahead there was little time to be lost. Pierson operated at speed, noting in his diary on 21 February 1919: 'At present I am getting out drawings of (1) New oil tanks, (2) New water tank of increased capacity, (3) Petrol system, and I hope to let Muller have these by tomorrow morning.'

Hired by Vickers as a wireless officer, 25-year-old W.J. Richards was among those involved in the aeroplane's assembly:

I was sent to Brooklands to assist Arthur Whitten Brown install the wireless in this Vimy. Things were happening almost hourly, you might say. Since Vickers had been rather later than others in getting ready to prepare for this flight, everything was in a tizzy. People rushing here and there to get started in time. Each one had a job. Anything to do with whether the lift was correct would be a rigger's job. And then the Rolls-Royce engines, together with the petrol feed and that kind of thing. And then you had John Alcock and Brown battling with each other for the little bit of space there was to accommodate the gadgetry they must take with them.

When it came to preparing the machine, it was a completely typical British ham-fisted approach. The main thing was to get there safely. I had the experience on more than one occasion that they would take the Vimy out for a quick flight. There were all sorts of questions about fitting the extra tanks, where the weight would be distributed, centres of gravity, and also the connections between tanks and filters and all that sort of thing. The machine would come back and off would come the wings and engines. Turn the fuselage upside down, and on to the trestles, and work with the thing upside down.

Speed and team spirit were the essence of the Vickers endeavour. Richards reiterated:

> How to fit anything in, so that it was done in a suitable way, was almost out of the question in circumstances where the mechanics, engineers, riggers were climbing over the aircraft at all times, everyone rushing around. We hadn't got a minute to spare. It was a crash job. In the sense that there was no minute to spare because there were other people already on their way out to Newfoundland. The teamwork was wonderful. Everyone was full of eagerness. Pride, as a matter of fact. And hopeful of success.

Works superintendent Percy Maxwell Muller and works manager Archie Knight oversaw the Vimy's preparation in a cauldron of hammering and colourful exhortations. Taller at the upper wing than at its biplane tail, it was 15ft 7in high and 43ft 6in long, with a wingspan of 68ft. The wing chord (width from leading to trailing edge) was 10ft 6in, and wing area a substantial 1,330sq ft. As well as the redesigned fuselage, a new fuel system was installed using a total of seven tanks and a service tank. The pilot and navigator had 97gal ahead of them in a nose tank, and 64gal immediately behind their seat. The other five fuselage tanks held 704gal. The petrol supply was maintained by an impeller-driven petrol pump with regulating valves, to maintain a constant flow to a service tank in the upper wing that had an overflow return to the main tanks. The aeroplane would also carry 50gal of lubricating oil and 64gal of water. Fully laden, it weighed 13,000lb. The Vimy would have enough fuel, but would it be sufficiently robust to withstand the undoubtedly arduous weather conditions of such a long flight?

The *Empire News* detailed the machine's construction:

> The spars are of box section spruce, except in the engine bay, where the struts are of round steel tube, reinforced where necessary, and with wooden fairings; the ribs are of spruce. The engine mounts are carried on four struts on each side, and the chassis is attached below the engine mountings, thus minimising the stress on the anti-lift wires. The front of the fuselage, being constructed of steel tube, is very rigid, and this construction is carried back as far as the rear spars. To the rear of this point, a special wooden tube is used for the longerons.
>
> The petrol tanks are supported on steel tubes. The fuselage is braced with swaged steel tie rods. Throughout the machine, streamline steel tie rods are used in external bracing, and round steel tie rods in all internal bracing. The engine controls are operated by concentric shafts with short cable connections. The main controls are of cable and follow standard practice. All flying controls are remarkably light in operation, due to the provision of balancing surfaces where necessary. In no part, has strength and solidity of construction been sacrificed to lightness.

The Atlantic Vimy was powered by two water-cooled twelve-cylinder Rolls-Royce Eagle VIII engines, which normally turned over at 1,080rpm. Their big advantage was reliability. It was estimated that the 360bhp units could run for 100 hours before needing a service, compared to thirty hours for most other engines. Fuel consumption was calculated at 70 litres per hour, and cruising speed at 90mph, while the landing speed was 45mph. John Alcock spent two days at Derby checking and collecting the engines. His mechanical knowledge impressed both engineer Bob Lyons, who would accompany the team to Newfoundland, and the managing director of Rolls-Royce, Claude Johnson, a friend of Lord Northcliffe.

Some 9ft off the ground and 4ft behind the tip of the nose, the Vimy cockpit was to be the discordant nerve centre of the Atlantic attempt. The four-bladed wooden Lang propellers, each of 10ft 5in diameter, would create a gale less than an arm's length from the fliers' shoulders. The open exhausts would bellow a further 6ft away and 2ft in front of the crew, a sloping windscreen, approximately 8in high, protected them from the slipstream. With space at a premium, Alcock and Brown would be jammed together in their bulky flying suits on a thin leather-cushioned wooden shelf barely 4ft wide.

Fitting two men into the narrow cockpit was a problem. W.J. Richards recalled:

> Both Alcock and Brown had all sorts of things they wanted to take. In the case of Brown, navigational equipment. Maps, sextants and all that kind of thing had to be squeezed into this space. So when it came to fitting the wireless set, which was a rather bulky outfit, where to put it and how to make it operational was quite a problem. In one instance, where Alcock wanted room for something he must take with him, he took a carpenter's saw and took a lump out of the fascia board. Just like that! As far as John was concerned, he didn't need a fascia board. All he wanted was a place to put the particular gadget that was essential to the job. When Richards was introduced to Alcock, the Lancastrian informed him: 'I don't want any bloody wireless. All I want is a pair of wings and a couple of engines. That's all there is to it!' Richards recalled that Alcock was not the only one who had doubts about the value of a wireless at that time.
>
> Wireless was regarded as a gimmick, it certainly wasn't a science. It was just something that clever little boys were playing around with and amusing themselves, it wasn't taken seriously at all. Even in the RAF, wireless had not by that time made a place for itself, it was still experimental. But for those fliers it could have been a life-saver, allowing them to send an SOS and keep in touch with shipping along the route, so that they could have been picked up.

The Vimy's cockpit looked more like a 1920s domestic hallway than the flight deck of a transatlantic aeroplane. Instead of a maze of dials and gauges, it featured an array of functional brass switches and ivorine-labelled levers mounted on a varnished wooden fascia. The four engine switches were line abreast under the windscreen cowling on the port (left-hand) side, facing the navigator. In the centre panel underneath were the two pump control handles for regulating the flow of fuel to the engines and, beside them, the black-faced petrol pressure gauge. Below them were two small levers for the main petrol pumps, port and starboard, plus a hand-operated petrol pump and cock for priming the gravity tanks from the main tanks.

The ungainly hand-starter magneto, with port and starboard selector switches, projected from the fascia opposite the navigator. Underneath this was the wireless, with its aerial lowering reel by his left side. Here there were two more switches, one for illuminating the instruments set in the sides of the engine nacelles, and the other for the petrol-overflow gauge, which was situated 3ft up one of the vertical struts behind the cockpit. The instruments on each engine nacelle casing, which could be read from the cockpit, recorded the engines' rpm and their oil pressure.

The navigator's sextant was clipped to the dashboard in front of him, and the course and drift calculator to the fuselage by his side. His charts, log and the Baker navigational machine were stored under his seat. The Very signal pistol and the torch, which he would use for inspecting the engine gauges by night, were in a small cupboard behind him. The battery for heating their flying suits rested on the floor between the two men.

The air-speed indicator (ASI) faced the pilot on the opposite starboard side of the cockpit, to the right of the two engine temperature gauges and the clock. A large liquid-damped bowl compass was mounted underneath the ASI. The throttle control, with an indicating arrow for operating the engines independently or together, was on the pilot's right. There were also two radiator shutter controls indicating 'OPEN' and 'SHUT' positions, and two magneto 'ADVANCE' and 'RETARD' control levers. The black-rimmed four-spoke control wheel projected outwards towards the pilot's lap, while the metal rudder bar was at his feet. He would not let go of these controls for the duration of the flight.

The Vimy was assembled in record time. According to Arthur Whitten Brown, Vickers only started work on it on 13 February. It was barely a month later, after his 10 March demobilisation, that John Alcock convinced the company that he was the man for the pilot's job. It was not until the end of that month that he met Brown at Brooklands and ensured the perfect navigator for the voyage. Yet, with everyone from designer and pilot to the humblest rigger working around the clock, the aeroplane was ready for its first test flight on Good Friday, 18 April.

The *Empire News* congratulated the Vickers team on the speed and quality of their work:

> The excellence of their construction, the satisfactory installation of the engines, the arrangement of the petrol pipes to prevent air locks, the efficiency of the lubricating and water systems, the general stability of the machine, and the ease of control, are alike highly praiseworthy. The satisfactory solutions of all these problems were of the highest value, for they saved the navigators unnecessary physical effort during their long flight, the arduous nature of which, as it was, made an immense demand upon their bodily and mental endurance.

The first test flight went perfectly. After subsequent trials lasting up to ten hours Alcock declared the Vimy ready for the Atlantic attempt. Only a fortnight after the death of Italian ace Capt. Palli near Mount Blanc, the Vimy fliers had a salutary reminder of the dangers they faced when news arrived that one transatlantic contender had crashed. Major Wood and navigator Wylie narrowly escaped drowning after engine trouble downed their Short Shamrock biplane off Holyhead. The mishap was equally disappointing for the crowds that had gathered in Bawnmore, Limerick, where a 70-acre field had been prepared for the aircraft's final departure. A bare fortnight after its first test, the Vimy was disassembled and packed for its long journey to Newfoundland. The following day's *Evening Standard* broke the news; 'NEW ENTRY FOR ATLANTIC FLIGHT –VIMY!'

Vickers workers were excited about their aeroplane's participation in the great air race. Among those who lined up to see the Vimy depart was Mrs Anne Boultwood, the forewoman of the team of ladies in the erecting and doping shop who sewed the fabric on to the wings and tailplanes:

> I can remember working eighteen hours a day for a whole week before the test flight. We worked on it up to the last minute. I saw it take off for

the first time; it looked beautiful, like a bird. I can still see as it looked then. It looked beautiful, all silver. There was shellac on the ribs, on the wings and on the tailplane elevator. All the dope was silver. I always felt confident that the fliers would succeed because I knew that they were the sort of men to do or die.

But the Vimy did not leave the factory without last-minute drama. W.J. Richards recalled:

The wings were put in packing cases and the fuselage had protective material and boxes. As the lorries went through the gate, one of the wings fell off its truck and there was panic as to whether it should be held up. Everything was examined. Should they carry on and hopefully repair any damage when they got to the other end? It was quickly decided 'Don't lose a minute. Get the machine away and deal with it in Newfoundland.' And that's what happened. It was an unpropitious start.

Many Vickers staff turned out at Waterloo railway station as their team departed for the *Mauretania*, which was to leave Southampton on Sunday, 4 May. Alcock found time to post photographs of the aeroplane to his friend, Fred Moseley. He and Brown were accompanied by the former's friend, Bob Dicker, head erector Gordon 'Monty' Montgomery, foreman carpenter Ernie Pitman, and Rolls-Royce engineer Bob Lyons. The crated Vimy and its team of eight mechanics and riggers would sail separately on the SS *Glendevon*. Brown kissed his fiancée goodbye. 'I've got a hunch we're going to win,' he reassured her. But there were many among the gathering who wondered how on earth he and Alcock could overhaul their rivals, who were already well established in Newfoundland.

5

ALL ROADS LEAD TO NEWFOUNDLAND

---◆◇◆---

They will soon be hitching giant dirigibles to New York City
skyscrapers to take on and off passengers.

Augustus Post

---◆◇◆---

On the opposite side of the ocean, US aeronauts and aviators had also
long pondered the conquest of the Atlantic. Benjamin Franklin and
Thomas Jefferson were the first to bring news of European ballooning to
America. Eight years after conquering the English Channel, Frenchman
Jean-Pierre Blanchard made the continent's first untethered balloon
flight in Philadelphia in January 1793. The audience included George
Washington and the French ambassador. Charles Ferson Durant became
the first successful American balloonist in September 1830. Ascending
from New York's Castle Garden, he dropped copies of poems he had written about the joys of flight.

It was not long before more ambitious Americans discussed a transatlantic attempt, surmising that the prevailing winds could sweep them
across to Europe. On 13 April 1844 they were startled by the *New York
Sun* announcement that Irish musician and balloonist Thomas Monck
Mason had beaten them to the honour; in the opposite direction.

The *Sun's* banner headline proclaimed:

ASTOUNDING NEWS BY EXPRESS, VIA NORFOLK! THE ATLANTIC CROSSED IN THREE DAYS! ARRIVAL AT SULLIVAN'S ISLAND, NEAR CHARLESTON, S C, OF MR MASON, AND FOUR OTHERS, IN THE STEERING BALLOON, VICTORIA.

Mason had indeed made a famous flight to Germany, but the Atlantic crossing story proved to be a hoax perpetrated by Edgar Allan Poe. It was not the *Sun*'s first attempt to boost circulation by directing readers' attention skywards. Nine years earlier it had published a series of equally fanciful articles about life being observed on the moon through an immense new telescope.

Reality inevitably caught up with fiction. In 1859 New Hampshire's Thaddeus Lowe constructed the world's biggest balloon for the first American attempt to fly the Atlantic. With a diameter of over 100ft, it featured a rattan woven basket and a small steam-powered launch suspended underneath. Repeated mishaps forced Lowe to abort his plans, leaving John Wise to make the next attempt. Wise fell out with his newspaper sponsors, but not before achieving a record-breaking flight of 800 miles in July 1859 from St Louis to Henderson in Jefferson County. A month later he made the world's first airmail delivery when he flew letters from Lafayette to Crawfordsville, Indiana.

Washington Donaldson's 1873 Atlantic attempt failed when he crashed in the Catskill mountains. Underlining the hazards of early ballooning, both he and Wise later perished in separate accidents in Lake Michigan. Veteran balloonist Samuel King made the final Atlantic attempt in September 1881. He confidently ascended from Minneapolis, Minnesota, but the wind suddenly changed direction and blew him back to land. In October 1910, journalist Walter Wellman attempted the earliest Atlantic crossing by a powered airship. He made a successful ascent from Atlantic City and flew almost 400 miles out to sea, but both engines failed and Wellman and his crew of five were lucky to be rescued by a ship.

American ballooning expertise may have lagged behind that of the French, but the country hosted the first successful manned flight in a powered heavier-than-air aeroplane, when Orville and Wilbur Wright took to the air in December 1903. Ironically, despite the Ohio brothers' achievement it was Britain's Claude Grahame-White who brought aviation to the heart of the US administration. In October 1910, the former cycle racer demonstrated his Farman biplane above the streets of Washington before circling the Capitol building several times. Onlookers were astounded by his control and by the aeroplane's manoeuvrability. The first long-distance flight in the USA was made the following year, when Calbraith Perry Rodgers overcame the handicap of deafness to cross the continent in a Wright biplane from Sheepshead Bay, New York, to Pasadena. He took forty-nine days and sixty-nine stops, hardly a good augury for a transatlantic attempt.

Lord Northcliffe's 1913 offer of a £10,000 prize for the first non-stop Atlantic crossing exercised American as much as European minds. Two US entrants signalled their intention to compete. French-domiciled Paris Singer of the sewing machine family (the lover of dancer Isadora Duncan, and whose mother had been the model for the Statue of Liberty) announced that he would enter an aeroplane that would be piloted by Auguste Maicon. Fellow philanthropist Rodman Wanamaker sponsored a large multi-engined flying boat, the *America*, which Glenn Curtiss completed in July 1914. Co-designed by Englishman John Cyril Porte, whose fellow pilots were to be Americans John Henry Towers and George Hallett, the aircraft performed well in initial tests but its engines lacked power. The *America*'s flight was also to be used to commemorate the centennial of the ending of hostilities between Britain and the USA in 1814. But the outbreak of the bigger 1914–18 war on 4 August scuppered the optimistic hopes of scooping the *Daily Mail* prize.

Thanks to the same conflict, however, the Americans were well equipped by 1918 to return to the Atlantic fray. During the final years of the war they had developed large anti-submarine flying boats powered by four 400hp twelve-cylinder Liberty engines which were capable of long-distance flight. The US Navy lost little time in planning a transatlantic attempt and, early in 1919, organised a team of four Curtiss NC biplanes to fly from Long Island to Plymouth. These, however, would not be eligible for the *Daily Mail* non-stop prize. Their attempt was to be in stages via Newfoundland's Trepassey Bay and the Azores to Lisbon.

The announcement on 18 March 1919 that Londoner Tommy Sopwith had entered an aeroplane for the Atlantic race, and that it was already on the high seas, shocked the US Navy. Some officers feared that the British might beat them to Atlantic honours. Others countered that the navy enjoyed a healthy head start over the British, who would first have to travel and then assemble and test their aeroplanes. While the navy worried about Sopwith, members of the Royal Aero Club were equally concerned that the Americans were themselves secretly preparing aircraft for the *Daily Mail* non-stop competition.

Atlantic flying fever was in the air. At the conclusion of a business conference in New York on 31 March, US Aero Club secretary Augustus Post confidently predicted that the ocean would be flown within thirty days: 'They will soon be hitching giant dirigibles to New York City skyscrapers to take on and off passengers. Within a few years, there will be established mail and passenger routes between America and Europe.'

In fact, a lighter-than-air aircraft almost made the first-ever transatlantic flight. After Britain's Air Ministry decided to test the R-34 airship's suitability as a passenger carrier, it made a successful nineteen-hour test flight around the Irish Sea at the end of March 1919. The Ministry accepted the Aero Club of America's invitation to send an airship to Atlantic City for a forthcoming gathering of aviation groups. Public interest in Britain and the USA grew. *The Times* correspondent in New York reported: 'The flight has put the city in a flutter of excitement. Discussion has entirely superseded Prohibition as the preoccupation of the bulk of the citizens.'

The Air Ministry's intention was to use the trip to study flying conditions over the Atlantic and to demonstrate the airship's capability on long voyages. The battlecruisers HMS *Renown* and *Tiger* were dispatched to provide weather forecasts along the route from East Fortune in Scotland to New York. Despite the preparations, however, the flight was postponed until July, but not before focusing renewed attention both on flying the Atlantic and on its commercial implications. The *New*

York Times cautioned: 'John Bull is hard-headed and business-like. He is set on being master of the air. What is Uncle Sam going to do about it?'

The US Navy's flying boat plans became public knowledge when an astute journalist noticed in naval orders that Cdr John H. Towers, who had been involved in the pre-war attempt with John Cyril Porte, had been given additional duties. The scoop should have appealed to Naval Secretary Josephus Daniels, who combined newspaper publishing with politics. The journalist discovered that Towers's responsibilities entailed preparing naval material and personnel for a transatlantic flight. The disclosure, and the news of the Sopwith and other competitors, accelerated the American test programme at Rockwall Point, Long Island. The Americans were still confident that none of the British crews could take off before mid-May. Secretary Daniels estimated that the NC flying- boats would be ready to fly the Atlantic at the end of April. He confirmed: 'The American Navy's trial will be made with the NC-1, or with a large naval seaplane of the same type. We are bending every effort and want to have the credit of being the first to cross.'

One of the pilots, Lt Cdr Albert C. Read, described the significance of their attempt:

> If the flight were successful, not only would an immense amount of valuable information be obtained concerning long-distance overseas flying, but Naval Aviation, the Navy Department, and the whole country would receive the plaudits of the entire world for accomplishing a notable feat in the progress of science. The mass of the people would be made to realise the importance of aviation as a valuable arm of the naval service, and the way would be blazed for others to follow and thus act to promote commercial trans-Atlantic service.

The government-backed venture was planned like a military operation. A flotilla of navy ships equipped with searchlights was stationed along the route to provide emergency support and radio and direction communications. Twenty-one vessels covered the first stage from the departure point at Trepassey Bay to the Azores. Fourteen patrolled between the Azores and

Lisbon, and another ten patrolled the final leg to Plymouth. The entire operation was said to have cost $2 million, the equivalent of £400,000.

The calamities suffered by even such a well-organised effort underlined the hazards of early long-distance flight. One aircraft caught fire before the start on 16 May, while bad weather sank another after its crew was rescued. A third came down but managed to reach port after taxiing for 200 miles. But despite the weather and engine problems, the NC-4 finally reached Lisbon on 27 May to complete the first crossing of the Atlantic by air. It was piloted by Albert Read, Walter Hinton and Elmer Stone, with crewmen James Breese, Eugene Rhoades and Herbert Rodd. The 2,450-mile marathon crossing had taken a total of twenty-seven flying hours since leaving Trepassey Bay eleven days earlier. Four days later the NC-4 landed beside the *Mayflower* monument in Plymouth. The *New York Times* noted that its British arrival was almost one hundred years to the day after the American ship *Savannah* had started the first steam-powered Atlantic crossing from Savannah to Liverpool.

The American success was acclaimed in Britain, Read and his companions being fêted at the House of Commons by the Prince of Wales, Winston Churchill and other dignitaries. The British media congratulated all the flying boat crews and the aeroplane's designer, Glenn Curtiss. But, while praising the American initiative and organisation, Claude Grahame-White pointed out that the Atlantic flight would be a life or death matter for the non-stop *Daily Mail* contenders. They would have no chain of destroyers to support them. Muriel, the wife of Sopwith Atlantic pilot Harry Hawker, agreed:

> There is no doubt the American boys are great sportsmen, but they have been admirably backed by their government, while our government has done practically nothing. I must say I feel sore about this. Our boys have had no help at all. Even the weather reports have been far from satisfactory.

Harry Hawker himself became a subject of controversy in the USA when he jokingly articulated what many of his stiff-upper-lip English hosts were shy to say:

It's hardly a serious attempt with a ship every twenty yards! If you put a ship every fifty miles, you have no faith in your motors.

But in a statement to the *New York Times* he explained:

We didn't want ships and I may also say that I think that Raynham, Admiral Kerr and all the other pilots entered for the *Daily Mail* competition who are now in Newfoundland would thoroughly agree with me. They are confident an aeroplane can do the trip entirely on its own power. I should not expect the British public would cheerfully pay to have scores of ships out in the Atlantic for possibly a month or two while we waited for suitable weather.

Following Hawker's later abortive attempt, the Americans had the last words on the matter. Though woefully underestimating the Australian's task, the *New York Times* pointed out that many useful results were gathered from the wireless and other tests that the destroyers had conducted:

It is these lessons which, in the view of the naval officers, make the difference in the feats of Hawker and of Read and Towers. They express the fullest admiration for Hawker's pluck but ask what would have been learned if he had got across, whereas the American flight has provided much information of the greatest value. Moreover, in that all the American pilots aimed for small definitive objectives and obtained them, the task set for them was infinitely more difficult than Hawker's. He had only to land somewhere in the British Isles.

Praiseworthy as the US achievement was, however, it lacked the romance and prestige of the non-stop competition for which *Daily Mail* contenders were assembling in Newfoundland from March 1919. The fact that only one of the four flying boats completed the journey was a stark reminder of the difficulty of crossing the ocean, even in stages. Moreover, the non-stop hopefuls would fly alone in landplanes and without any official back-up. They would also have to negotiate the much more hostile weather of the colder northern route. Compared with the high-neck-uniformed

Americans, the casually dressed British crews such as Alcock and Brown looked like freebooters, true products of Brooklands' Abelard academy, and fearless descendants of the privateers who had once roamed the seas they were now hoping to conquer by air. One of the *Daily Mail* navigators, Charles W.F. Morgan, was actually a descendant of the greatest buccaneer of all, Sir Henry Morgan.

Although they lacked support ships, the non-stop fliers were encouraged when the Air Ministry finally offered instruments and established a special meteorological bureau in Newfoundland. The Admiralty Wireless Station at Mount Pearl, near St John's, would co-ordinate special weather reports from the US Weather Bureau, the Canadian Meteorological Office and from stations in the Azores and Lisbon, and make these available to the fliers. The Ministry's Sqn Ldr Gendle underlined the need for future professional international co-operation:

> Any organisation that is set up for future flights must be clearly established both technically and financially, and not dependent only on the kindness and goodwill of those concerned. In other words, the Governments on both sides of the Atlantic must be prepared to meet very considerable expenditure. Any organisation set up for Atlantic flights will also be a great help to weather forecasting for the British Isles.

Newfoundland experienced an aviation invasion in the spring of 1919. Its eastern coast boasted no fewer than five projected take-off sites for transatlantic attempts: Trepassey Bay, Cape Broyle, Harbour Grace, Mount Pearl and St John's. John Alcock and Arthur Whitten Brown were only one of seventeen crews who declared their interest in the non-stop *Daily Mail* challenge. Five prospective American entrants included 32-year-old Ruth Law, the first woman to fly at night and among America's most colourful pilots. She announced that she would fly a new twin-engine Curtiss biplane: 'I am going to show these men a few things. I'm not afraid. Take my word for it, I don't want to commit suicide. There'll be plenty of boats out there. I'm going to fly straight across and not get my feet wet.'

However, her new aeroplane and a replacement Martin bomber failed to materialise and, like US endurance record holder Katherine Stinson and Howard Rinehart of the Dayton-Wright Aeroplane Company, she abandoned her plans. As did Capt. Lipsner, former Chief of the Aerial Service, who had hoped to pilot a new Martin flying boat financed by the Aviation Club of Chicago. The American challenge faded completely when the giant Sunrise seaplane entered by Swedish American Capt. Hugo Sunstedt crashed at Bayonne in March.

Norwich aircraft manufacturer Boulton and Paul announced that it would compete with a converted twin-engined Bourges bomber. The Alliance Aeroplane Company of London entered a single-engined Seabird biplane to be crewed by J.A. Peters and Capt. W.R. Curtiss. Former naval flier Australian Sidney Pickles and navigator A.G. West were to fly a Fairey biplane. Captain Arthur Payze entered a Liberty-engined Whitehead biplane. Fellow wartime pilot Leth Jensen proposed flying from Newfoundland to Paris, where three French fliers also announced their interest: Lt Roget and the team of Capt. Coli and Lt Ria.

The fancied Cyril Porte resumed his pre-war attempt, planning to use a five-engined Felixstowe Fury triplane flying boat. But according to the *Daily Mail*, Winston Churchill denied him promised funding on cost grounds and Maj. Arthur Partridge, who had inspected a take-off site at Cape Broyle, was ordered home by the Air Ministry. Sadly, Porte succumbed shortly afterwards to tuberculosis. Jensen, the Americans and the other prospective entrants eventually failed to materialise, leaving only Alcock and Brown and three fellow British teams to converge on remote and windswept Newfoundland in the cold spring of 1919.

For the emissaries of the latest technological revolution, Newfoundland was like stepping back in time. Nobody hurried; everyone had time for a friendly greeting in the first North American country to greet the sun each day. The transatlantic competitors were equally surprised by the accents of their hosts. Reflecting their immigrant origins, their speech seemed more English or Irish than American. The most easterly part of North America, Newfoundland had a long experience of European visitors and adventurers. Vikings settled there in 1001. Five hundred years later Bristol adventurer John Cabot made it the first British overseas colony. The capital city, St John's, derives its title from Cabot's alleged landing on 24 June, the feast day of St John the Baptist.

Because of its harbour and proximity to rich fishing grounds, the city gained prominence as a commercial trading outpost for the French, Spanish, Portuguese, and English from the late 16th century. Its wharves and warehouses were connected across many streams by a path that became known as Water Street and is now recognised as the oldest commercial street in North America. The port's importance made it a prime military target. The English and French frequently used St John's as a battleground until the British finally recaptured it in 1762.

By the early 20th century the country's immigrants had begun to see themselves as Newfoundlanders, rather than as Europeans. Their participation in the First World War encouraged the growing sense of national identity. In 1919 Newfoundland was an independent dominion within the British Empire, responsible for its own internal affairs (thirty years later it became the tenth province of Canada). It even had its own time, which would cause confusion in later reports of the 1919 flights. It was the first in North America to adopt Daylight Saving Time in 1917, known locally as John Anderson's Time, after the Legislative Council member who introduced it. The time in summer 1919 was two hours thirty-one minutes behind GMT.

Like the transatlantic contenders, Newfoundland in 1919 was also emerging painfully from the shadow of the First World War, which had cost the country dearly. At least twenty-one Newfoundlanders had flown with the RFC, including Joseph Daymond and Capts Ronald Ayre and Victor Bennett, who were decorated. As the first *Daily Mail* fliers arrived in the country, the last of those who had served in Europe returned home in the SS *Corsican*. They were the lucky ones. The opening day of the Battle of the Somme on Saturday, 1 July 1916 had resulted in the country's biggest disaster. That morning, 801 members of the 1st Newfoundland Regiment left their trenches near Beaumont-Hamel, which the soldiers had named St John's Road. Within seventy-five minutes more than 700 were killed, missing or seriously wounded.

The country's dependence on the sea exerted a heavy toll. An anonymous poem, 'Harbour Grace', expressed its people's hardships:

Here wife, sweethearts, sister and mother
Watched the disappearing sails
Bearing away husband, son, or brother.
And some who sailed beyond the bar
And rest on a foreign shore
And many rest beneath the sea and return to home no more
No loved ones near to shed a tear
Or breathe a parting prayer.

Large numbers of Irish immigrants settled in Newfoundland, but there was a much earlier legendary connection between the two countries. St Brendan, the patron saint of sailors and navigators, is said to have reached America in the 6th century, long before Columbus and Cabot. The medieval text *Navigatio Sancti Brendan Abbatis* (The Voyage of St Brendan the Abbot) is regarded by some as a factual account of a sailing from Europe to North America. Explorer Tim Severin underlined the feasibility of Brendan's voyage when he replicated the journey in a similar leather boat in 1977, landing at Peckford Island, 150 miles north-west of St John's. A stone found near L'Anse aux Meadows bears an inscription that resembles Ogham, the earliest Irish writing style, which died out in the seventh century.

Whatever the veracity of the legend, geography ensured that both Newfoundland and Ireland played a significant role in the earliest attempts to bridge the Atlantic. In 1850 far-seeing local bishop J.T. Bullock suggested running a cable between the two countries: 'I hope the day is not far distant when St John's will be the first link in the electric chain which will unite the Old World and the New.'

Eight years later his hopes were realised when the first transatlantic cable was laid from Newfoundland to Ireland's Valentia Island by American financier Cyrus Field. Then, on 12 December 1901, Guglielmo Marconi received the earliest wireless signals to cross the Atlantic from Cornwall to Cabot Tower on Signal Hill, St John's. Four years later the

Italian built the high-powered station at Derrygimla in County Galway that established the first point-to-point fixed wireless service between Europe and America.

With its tradition of regular contact with maritime communities throughout the Atlantic basin, outward-looking Newfoundland took the influx of transatlantic aviators in its stride. The hard lives of the locals meant that only the essentials mattered, but flying soon rivalled the weather and shipping disasters as the main topic of conversation. Sceptical crowds flocked to see the arrival of the crated aeroplanes and watch their assembly. Flying to Europe in a day? A likely story. Many asked the same questions. What did the aviators know of the treacherous ocean weather? Could these flimsy machines really tame the mighty Atlantic, which had claimed so many of their citizens and fishermen? And, if they succeeded in flying, which team would win the race to Britain? Most importantly, who would make the first flight ever seen in Newfoundland?

6

FINAL FOUR ATLANTIC CONTESTANTS

---◆◇◆---

The family man associates St John's with cod liver oil and wood-pulp.
Now we know that the staple product is fog.

Harry Hawker

---◆◇◆---

In the aftermath of the well-supported NC team's one-in-four success, many observers regarded the non-stop Atlantic attempts as suicidal. *The New York Times* protested:

> Public opinion would like to issue an injunction against their setting out over the Atlantic, but the law against attempted suicide is not technically applicable. The Atlantic may be flown without a stop, possibly in June when halcyon weather prevails, but the odds against the success of a small plane with one engine should be a deterrent. To stake all on its limited motive power, not to speak of the frailty of wings of narrow spread, seems like courting death. If the Atlantic passage is to be achieved, it must be by a big biplane powerfully engined. That seems to be the best professional opinion.

Not one of the non-stop transatlantic entrants had any doubts about the risks of his intended voyage into the unknown. Each of them was a war veteran, with the exception of Harry Hawker, who had been rejected on health grounds and perhaps had more to prove than most. Alcock and Brown had been prisoners of war, as had future east–west Atlantic flier Col James Fitzmaurice. The fliers were a breed apart from those who had not looked death in the eye. Some 6,000 of their RFC comrades had perished in the war, as well as over 5,000 German pilots. They possessed a higher appreciation of life than most but, as survivors, they were also self-reliant, fearless and confident. War had inured them to danger; the Atlantic race provided a rare opportunity for adventure in an unfamiliar and uneasy post-war world. They were eager for its challenge.

The competition Vickers finally faced were the three aeroplanes entered by Martinsyde, Handley Page and Sopwith. Like Vickers, these companies had thrived during the war but now faced a very uncertain peacetime future. Formed at Brooklands in 1908 as a partnership between H.P. Martin and George Handasyde, Martinsyde had originally planned a transatlantic attempt in 1914 before its pilot, Gustav Hamel, was drowned during a cross-Channel flight. During the war it moved to Woking and manufactured fighters and bombers for the RFC, and later supplied the fledgling Irish Air Corps with its first aeroplane.

In 1916 Martinsyde introduced the ungainly G.100 biplane, which was a capable ground-attack aircraft but, known as the Elephant, was an easy target in a dogfight. Produced at the end of the war, the company's F.4 Buzzard single-seat biplane powered by a Hispano-Suiza engine was alleged to be faster than any of its rivals. Earlier in the war, a small Martinsyde S.1 scout had featured in one of the conflict's most bizarre aerial incidents. Piloted by Capt. Louis Strange, it flipped over as he stood up in the cockpit to change the ammunition drum of the machine-gun mounted on the centre-section of the upper wing. He was left hanging by the magazine he was trying to remove. Strange managed to re-enter the cockpit and right his aeroplane just before he reached the ground (and survived to face further punishment in the Second World War).

After the war Martinsyde focused on long-range designs for the civilian mail market. The company's transatlantic machine was a two-seat biplane, 25ft long with a span of 41ft and a fuel capacity of 370gal, giving it a range of 2,500 miles at an average speed of 100mph. Powered by a single

Rolls-Royce Falcon engine, it was slimmer than its wider-bodied Sopwith rival. Named the Raymor, it was to be flown by 26-year-old pilot Freddy Raynham, who would sit behind 29-year-old navigator Capt. Charles William Fairfax 'Fax' Morgan. Born in Dover, the latter was a qualified pilot and RNAS veteran who had lost his right leg during the war.

As reticent as Morgan was voluble, Raynham, from Honington in Suffolk, was a former racing pilot and British altitude record-holder. He gained his pilot's licence before he was 18, but not without a confrontation in April 1911 with Brooklands' most malodorous hazard: 'Today the machine has landed in the sewage farm with a new pupil. We got in a frightful mess. I have just got back and had a bath and changed and Mrs Winmill is tackling the clothes.' A friend and rival of Sopwith's Harry Hawker, Raynham became an Avro flying instructor when still only 19. Shortly afterwards he was appointed Martinsyde's chief test pilot. Test flying was dangerous in those early days. Raynham was lucky to escape when an Avro Pike bomber he was piloting crashed in 1916. Later the tail broke off a Martinsyde in which he was looping the loop over Brooklands, and he once more plummeted to hard earth.

The biggest British bomber of the war and the largest *Daily Mail* Atlantic challenger was built by Frederick Handley Page. Born in Cheltenham in 1885, Page became an electrical engineer and worked briefly for Westinghouse, who had also employed Arthur Whitten Brown. He designed and built his first experimental glider in 1909. This led to his Bluebird monoplane and the founding of Handley Page Ltd, Britain's first publicly traded aircraft manufacturing company.

After building a succession of monoplanes and biplanes, Page moved from Barking to Cricklewood, where he constructed the long-range O/100 and O/400 bombers, one of which flew a record 440 miles to attack Constantinople. The four-engine 'Super Handley' V/1500 bomber, which weighed 15 tons fully loaded, just reached operational service when the war ended. As well as making long-distance flights, one of his aeroplanes carried a record forty passengers over London in 1918. A modified O/400 inaugurated a London–Paris passenger service the following year.

Frederick Handley Page had a strong commitment to research and safety. Between the wars he developed wing slats or slots, which reduced an aeroplane's stalling speed and allowed it to land in a shorter distance. He adapted one of the now-redundant V/1500 bombers for the transatlantic competition. Powered by four Rolls-Royce engines, the machine dwarfed its fellow competitors with its length of 46ft and span of 126ft. It was to be piloted by Maj. Herbert George Brackley and Tryggve Gran, and commanded by Rear-Adm. Mark Kerr, the first flag officer to gain a pilot's licence and, at 55, the oldest person involved in the *Daily Mail* race. Former Norwegian national footballer Gran was an accomplished skier who had participated in Robert Falcon Scott's Terra Nova expedition and was the first to find the bodies of the explorer and his companions in the Antarctic in 1912. Brackley, aged 25, was a former Reuters journalist who had been taught by John Alcock at Eastchurch.

Tommy Sopwith became one of Britain's most influential aeroplane manufacturers after taking up flying in 1910. He crashed on his first flight after only 300yd, but at the end of that year he won the £4,000 prize offered by fellow racing driver Baron de Forest for the longest flight from England to the continent in a British aeroplane. He immediately founded the Sopwith School of Flying at Brooklands and, two years later, set up the Sopwith Aviation Company. In 1913 one of his aeroplanes raised the British altitude record to 13,000ft, and the following year his seaplane won the second Schneider Trophy contest at Monaco. The Londoner produced many different models during the First World War, the most famous of which was the ultra-manoeuvrable Sopwith Camel. Along with the earlier Sopwith Pup it achieved later fictional fame as the machine flown by Biggles, the character created by RFC pilot Capt. W.E. Johns. The Camel also featured in Charles M. Schulz's *Peanuts* cartoon strips, as the dream mount of the beagle Snoopy.

Sopwith built the 32ft-long, two-bay Atlantic biplane for the transatlantic attempt. Based on the company's Cuckoo torpedo bomber and powered by a single Rolls-Royce Eagle, it would be crewed by 30-year-old Harry Hawker and Lt-Cdr Kenneth Mackenzie-Grieve, 39, from Fir Hill, Droxford, Hampshire. A former acting commander of the aircraft carrier

Campania, and holder of a Humane Society life-saving medal, Mackenzie-Grieve was an experienced Royal Navy navigator who took special leave for the Atlantic attempt. Although he was a teetotal non-smoker, the diminutive Hawker was a boisterous and sometimes temperamental character, and the best known of the transatlantic pilots. A blacksmith's son born in Melbourne, he had worked as a mechanic from the age of 12 until he saved sufficient money to emigrate to England in 1912. He learned to fly after joining the Sopwith Aviation Company as a mechanic, and his natural aptitude soon gained him the position of chief test pilot.

During the war the Australian had flown as many as twelve aeroplanes each day, before they were handed over to the RNAS or RFC. He also set altitude and endurance records, and earned a reputation as one of Britain's most resourceful and fearless pilots. Mackenzie-Grieve said:

> To my mind, he is an ideal pilot, with unlimited pluck, unfailingly good judgment, and what is equally to the point, an inexhaustible supply of good spirits. In his handling of an aeroplane, I am tempted to believe that he takes advantage of some sixth sense which allows him to become an integral part of the machine.

Hawker and Mackenzie-Grieve's Sopwith was the first of the transatlantic entries to be prepared, and perhaps the most deserving of success. Tommy Sopwith told an interviewer: 'In those days, we literally thought of and designed and flew an airplane in a space of about six to eight weeks!' Sopwith had decided to take part as early as July 1918 and, true to form, he designed and built the Atlantic in less than two months. At Hawker's insistence it boasted two unusual features: a detachable undercarriage that would be jettisoned after take-off to reduce weight and drag, and a top section of fuselage shaped like a boat that could be detached in the event of a ditching. Before Alcock and Brown's Vimy had been constructed, the Sopwith had flown a test distance of 900 miles in nine hours, equivalent to half the distance between Newfoundland and Ireland. Sopwith estimated that the transatlantic crossing would take nineteen and a half hours, and claimed that his aeroplane was capable of flying for twenty-five hours at 100mph on its fuel load.

The crated Sopwith Atlantic was the first *Daily Mail* contestant to be unloaded in Newfoundland, on 29 March. Freddie Raynham and Charles Morgan arrived on 11 April with their Martinsyde Raymor. Comparable in size and range, both the Raymor and the Atlantic were considered by some experts to be too small for an Atlantic attempt. This could hardly be said for the 10 May arrival, the Handley Page V/1500 biplane, which was packed in no fewer than 109 crates, one of them 45ft long. The last team to arrive, in late May, would be the least-fancied John Alcock and Arthur Whitten Brown with their Vickers Vimy.

The enthusiasm of the Atlantic aviators was matched by their surprising ignorance of the local weather and terrain. Winter bids a reluctant annual farewell to Newfoundland. The Sopwith crew were taken aback when they arrived to find St John's harbour blocked by pack ice, and newpapers reporting the deaths of those who had fallen through ice. Their ship had to be diverted to the port of Placentia, from where a train eventually brought the fliers and their aeroplane to St John's. Harry Hawker noted an additional hazard: 'The family man associates St John's with cod liver oil and wood-pulp. Now we know that the staple product is fog.'

Newfoundland is not Constable country. Instead of inviting green fields, the fliers found woods, ditches and undulating boulder-strewn slopes. Only a light layer of soil covered the rock stratum. Martinsyde's Morgan was the first flier to arrive in St John's, in February 1919, and also almost the competition's first casualty. He was extremely lucky to survive Spanish flu, which he contracted on the SS *Corsican*. On his recovery, and on the advice of future politician Joey Smallwood, he choose a field that was still under snow by the side of Quidi Vidi lake, half a mile from St John's. Extremely narrow, it was only suitable for take-off in a south-westerly or westerly wind.

The Handley Page team found the most promising land, 60 miles away by road at Harbour Grace, from where Amelia Earhart would later depart on her solo conquest of the Atlantic. The best-financed team, it was rumoured to have invested £4,000 in clearing a 1,200yd landing strip that sloped down to the sea, compared to the £100 Alcock and Brown would spend. Handley Page employed twelve mechanics overseen by Col E. W. Steadman, and even had a tracked tractor for towing its aeroplane.

Following a long search, Sopwith's Montague Fenn selected a take-off area at Glendenning's Farm, 6 miles from the city. When the snow melted, the 400yd-long tree-lined stretch proved to be far from flat, with a shallow depression traversing its centre. 'It's the best there is,' Fenn assured the sceptical Hawker and Mackenzie-Grieve, as teams of horses slithered through the slush with the heavy crates, and sixty men struggled to level the ground. But in the spirit of the original Newfoundland pioneers, the Sopwith team got to work clearing the ground and building a 55ft-long wooden hangar and workshops. The sound of hammering and sawing reverberated back from the slopes, except when interrupted by the all-too-frequent rain and sleet storms. Gradually the Atlantic took shape before the eyes of astonished locals. Hawker was acutely aware that the risk of a take-off or landing accident on such hostile terrain would severely inhibit their test flight programme. He also observed: 'The aerodrome was about 450 feet above sea-level and seemed to catch all the sorts of winds that we did not want.'

There was blissful ignorance in London of the conditions facing the *Daily Mail* competitors. When news did eventually percolate to the Royal Aero Club, some of its alleged experts were in no way unfazed. The Club secretary was reported as saying that there was no reason why Harry Hawker could not start, as long as he could get his aeroplane to the aerodrome! A newspaper quoted the secretary:

> It would be quite easy to clear away sufficient ground to give the airplanes room to take off. If it freezes next week, when other conditions will probably be propitious, the machines can be run over the frozen crust of snow. And if it thaws, they could lay down planks and so construct a platform large enough for a preliminary run.

Fittingly, the Sopwith team was the first to make a test flight, on the sunny evening of Thursday, 10 April. Hundreds of locals flocked to Glendenning's Farm to see the Atlantic taxi tentatively across the uneven snow-bordered ground. As it roared into the air, others rushed out of their homes to watch it circle St John's for half an hour. The streets were thronged as locals witnessed Hawker and Mackenzie-Grieve make history, the first to fly in Newfoundland. The earliest flight by a Newfoundlander would be made one month later by Lt Richard Janes over his native Trepassey, in a Curtiss flying boat from the US Navy vessel *Aroostook*. The air at altitude was colder than Hawker and Mackenzie-Grieve had experienced at home, but, apart from a problem with their wireless, the machine performed perfectly and the pair bounced happily back to earth, to cheers from appreciative spectators.

Having already thoroughly tested his aeroplane in England, Hawker was confident that he and Mackenzie-Grieve were ready to leave at short notice. Rather than waste time with further risky trials from their impromptu airfield, and spurred by the Martinsyde's Friday arrival, they ambitiously decided to take off on the following Saturday. Freddy Raynham and many dignitaries turned out to see them depart, but their final preparations took longer than expected and they postponed their departure for one day. Sadly, on that Sunday Newfoundland's infamous weather closed in. But for this the Sopwith could well have won both the *Daily Mail* prize and made the first-ever Atlantic crossing in stages or otherwise. The Australian noted in his book *Our Atlantic Attempt*:

> Our original intention was, if possible, to get away before any one else came on the scene. We were always ready to push off at a couple of hours' notice, just time enough to get the tanks filled up, the mail aboard, the Thermos flasks filled, and the engine nicely warmed up. But this scheme was quickly seen to be out of the question on account not only of unfavourable winds, but also on account of the softness of the aerodrome and heavy snowfalls.

Determined to be ready as soon as conditions improved, Hawker and Mackenzie-Grieve braved the piercing cold to test their life-saving suits and the 10ft-long boat forming a section of fuselage top decking behind the cockpit. They checked and rechecked every part of the Atlantic and regularly ran its engines. They replaced the faulty wireless and removed all the paint from the bracing wires, which Hawker estimated would increase their speed by half a mile per hour. Though he had tested a four-blade propeller at

Brooklands, Hawker decided to use a special two-blade version that would provide more thrust for a better take-off. And as an extra precaution to counter the bumps and soft ground conditions he fitted the Atlantic with larger wheels than normal, which he would jettison after take-off.

The Sopwith crew enjoyed the company of their old friends Raynham and Morgan, who also stayed in the Cochrane Hotel, but they had not reckoned with the Raymor team's determination and speed. The winds that prevented flying did not inhibit the Martinsyde crew, who worked around the clock to ready their aircraft. They saved additional days with their canvas hangar, which was erected in a fraction of the time it had taken the Sopwith team to construct theirs. Less than a week after its arrival, the red Raymor was ready to fly.

While the weather still precluded an Atlantic attempt, a brief respite allowed Raynham and Morgan to make their first test flight, on Wednesday, 16 April, from their well-drained Quidi Vidi field. Repaying Raynham's earlier visit to Glendenning's Farm, Hawker and Mackenzie-Grieve watched the test, aware that their time advantage had been lost. The Raymor performed faultlessly and no one was in doubt that the Atlantic race was now well and truly on. Raynham said that he hoped to leave the following Sunday, weather permitting. Neither gave any consideration to the Vickers Vimy, which was only now being flown for the first time at distant Brooklands, and neither team expected that the weather would ground them – for an interminable month.

While Hawker and Mackenzie-Grieve were away from their aeroplane one day, they heard that Raynham and Morgan were preparing to leave. They raced back to find that the Raymor pair were only testing their engine. With shared aviation and wartime experience, the fliers' rivalry was nevertheless a friendly one. Having earlier kept a close watch on each other's progress, they established a gentleman's agreement that neither team would take off without informing the other. Hawker explained:

> After all, we were there on the same errand, we had both got to do our best for British aviation. It was going to be no good being on tenterhooks the whole time, waiting was bad enough for all of us anyhow. So one day we

quickly arrived at a very simple mutual agreement. We would each give the other a couple of hours' notice before starting. And the same time to the wireless people, so as to enable them to get their warnings out broadcast to ships. And by that means the atmosphere was rendered a little less electrical.

But the Sopwith fliers' patience was sorely tested. The month's delay was the longest period that Hawker had ever been grounded since he began flying in 1911. The Australian was heard to remark that he wished he had never left his beloved Brooklands. As fog shrouded St John's, he learned that the Harbour Grace field was now ready for the Handley Page. Another formidable competitor just half-an-hour's flying time distant who would threaten both teams. Would they ever get away? *The Australian* recorded:

> The weather was uniformly rotten. Sometimes it would clear up a bit and look promising, but the reports from the meteorological station almost always continued to put a different complexion on it. The thick white fogs would, whenever the wind went into the east, roll in from the banks and smother us. One felt sometimes like having a go in spite of them, but our aerodrome was not the sort of ground one could negotiate blindfold.

Alcock and Brown and their team, meanwhile, were en route from Southampton and refining their Atlantic flight plans as they sailed. The four-funnelled *Mauretania* brought back war memories for Alcock. It also was a Mudros veteran, having transported 6,000 wounded soldiers in three voyages from there to Southampton. Alcock insisted that, having already thoroughly tested the Vimy, they were in a good position to be able to start the flight with the minimum delay. This prospect pleased Brown, who was eager to return to his fiancée as soon as possible. He spent much of his time discussing Atlantic navigation with the ship's officers and its commander, Capt. Rostron. Upbeat about his chances of transatlantic success, Brown wrote to Kathleen: 'I made friends with the *Mauretania* officers and spent most of my time on the bridge learning how to navigate properly! Many thanks for your wire. I am coming back soon to claim you – and to live happily ever after! All my love, Teddy.'

With their Vimy still on the high seas, the Vickers party arrived at Halifax on 9 May. After three exhausting days of ferry and train rides, Alcock and Brown finally reached St John's on the night of 13 May. In her forecast of his long voyage, Brown's fortune-teller had omitted to warn him of the weather conditions. Sunny England seemed a world away as they negotiated the wet and exposed muddy streets. Their spirits were revived, however, when they checked into the Cochrane and met their Brooklands mates, Hawker and Raynham, and their navigators, Mackenzie-Grieve and Morgan. The four-storeyed hotel, which had also sheltered Marconi, stood at the corner of Cochrane and Gower Streets, on the side of a steep hill leading down to the harbour. The rambling refuge, with its cut-glass mirrors, potted plants and nautical prints, was a convivial place. Local musicians regularly regaled its distinguished guests.

The fliers played practical jokes on each other. Some found that the air had been let out of their automobile tyres. Hawker refreshed unsuspecting visitors with a bowl of water balanced on his sitting-room door. Brown kept Kathleen informed: 'All the newspaper men are here too so it's rather jolly. We have been spending all our time looking for an aerodrome and have scoured the vicinity as far as 30 miles away, but have not been very successful to date.'

The Vickers team were confronted with an example of US determination when the cruiser *Chicago* arrived in St John's to act as a base for the C-5 airship, with which the US Navy hoped to make their Atlantic attempt. Powered by two Union engines, the 196ft-long dirigible had achieved a 1,000-mile flight from New York. Commander Lt E.W. Coll and his crew were confident of its ability to cross the Atlantic. But, like the European visitors, they underestimated the unpredictability of the Newfoundland weather. Despite the best efforts of the ground crew to deflate her, strong gales wrenched the airship from its moorings on Thursday, 15 May. Two crewmen jumped just in time as the C-5 was sent soaring through a gap in the hills and out over the ocean. Swallowed up by the racing clouds, it was never seen again. It was an expensive debacle, and a timely warning to the British aviators of the challenges they themselves would soon face. But not soon enough for Harry Hawker, whose patience was now at an end.

7

HAWKER AND GRIEVE
SURVIVE DITCHING

◆◇◆

Excitement and anxiety about the possible fate of Hawker and Grieve
spread all the world over; but nowhere was it more intense than
amongst us at the Cochrane Hotel.

Arthur Whitten Brown

◆◇◆

The Sopwith Atlantic and Martinsyde Raymor crews waited and waited,
while one day's gales were replaced by the next day's fog. They endured
the Newfoundland thaw, when ice melted and froze at the same time.
Reacting to ill-informed criticism from Britain about his delay in
taking off, Harry Hawker pointed out that he and Mackenzie-Grieve
consulted the meteorological experts each morning and that their deci-
sions to postpone the flight were made daily. Freddie Raynham and
Capt. Morgan were equally restive. Morgan was summoned for driving
without a licence. 'If the weather clears, the St John's police will have to
chase me through the skies,' he insisted. 'We'll get away if we have half
a chance.'

Harry Hawker's patience finally gave way when he heard of the arrival
of the US Navy's NC machines at nearby Trepassey Bay. His focus was
the non-stop transatlantic prize, but he was unhappy about the prospect
of an American aeroplane being first across the Atlantic, in easy stages or

otherwise. When he heard on Friday, 16 May that the flying boats had left for the Azores he decided to set off, whatever the weather.

The Australian's determination to do his bit for Britain might have owed something to the fact that the RFC had turned him down for war service on medical grounds. He wrote later:

> On the Saturday evening we got the unconfirmed report that all three seaplanes, the NC-2, the NC-3, and the NC-4 had safely arrived at the Azores. After that there was only one thing to do, namely, get as much sleep as we could, for we didn't intend to have any the following night. We meant having something more interesting on hand.

Although neither crew ever admitted it, it was strongly rumoured that Hawker and Raynham had even provisionally agreed to opt out of the *Daily Mail* challenge in order to scupper the US effort by flying themselves in stages to Europe via the Azores and Portugal. On the Saturday night before their Sunday attempts they were alleged to have decided that, if the wind permitted, they would head for the Azores. But the wind veered slightly during the night and the two teams resumed their non-stop flight plans on Sunday morning, 18 May. Hawker denied these rumours after-wards, pointing out that they had no supplies of fuel on the Azores.

By this time Alcock and Brown had been five days in Newfoundland. Their slim hopes of overhauling Hawker and Raynham then suffered another setback. Their Vimy had been delayed for a week by strikes at London docks and was still on the high seas. With neither aeroplane nor airfield it was obvious that they had sparse hopes of success against rivals who needed only a break in the weather to be off. Dismayed at the dif-ficulty in finding a suitable take-off site, Alcock and Brown devoted all their time to searching the countryside around St John's and beyond. They were returning from another fruitless journey on Sunday when they were told that Hawker and Mackenzie-Grieve had taken off just after three that afternoon from Glendenning's Farm.

It had been a busy day. True to their gentleman's agreement, the Atlantic's crew had briefed Raynham and Morgan, who took advantage of the same weather window and left shortly afterwards. Alcock and Brown acknowledged that one of the two teams would certainly succeed. But though apparently beaten to the *Daily Mail* prize, they decided that they would fly to Ireland anyhow, to demonstrate the potential of their Vickers Vimy.

An unusually cloudless sky, favourable wind and the prospect of a full moon that night encouraged Hawker and Mackenzie-Grieve as they climbed into the cockpit of the Sopwith Atlantic. Adm. Kerr and Maj. Brackley were among the last to wish them luck. 'Tell Raynham I'll greet him in Brooklands,' Hawker quipped before waving a final farewell to the few spectators who had travelled the 4 miles from St John's. The wind direction was perfect. The large wheels were a bonus, as the experienced Australian coaxed the Atlantic along the damp makeshift runway to a perfect take-off. As he and Mackenzie-Grieve flew over St John's they could see the large crowd assembled around the Raymor on the shore of Lake Quidi Vidi. Hawker was concerned about the effect of the wind on his rivals' aeroplane; the lakeside runway was at right angles to their Glendenning's Farm site.

If Raynham and Morgan were worried about the crosswind, they did not show it as they bade goodbye to their team barely an hour later. Raynham briefly considered Hawker's sporting suggestion to fly light to the Sopwith field and take off from there, but abandoned the idea when he realised it would be dark before they could transfer all the necessary petrol. Despite the wind he was confident of a safe take-off from the drier Quidi Vidi ground, after which his slightly faster Martinsyde should overhaul its rival on the long flight to Europe. Unlike Hawker, who was heading for Galway, Raynham's target was Dingle, further south, and then Brooklands, a journey of just over 2,000 miles. Allowing for changes of course to combat adverse weather, both fliers carried sufficient fuel for 2,400 miles.

The heavily laden Raymor made sluggish progress along the rough ground for 200yd. Gradually it gathered speed and, to everyone's relief, lifted slowly into the air. But it was no sooner airborne than a gust of wind suddenly sent it drifting sideways across its intended path. Helpless against the crosswind, the Raymor slammed into the ground with such force that the undercarriage was torn away. Spectators rushed to rescue the fliers. Raynham was cut and bruised, while Morgan sustained a severe eye injury and had to be helped down from the wreckage. Their only good fortune was that the petrol-laden aeroplane did not catch fire. If it had, both men would have perished.

Harry Hawker wrote afterwards:

What they did was a magnificent act of pluck. The east-north-east wind suited our aerodrome pretty much as well as any other, and better than most, but it was almost the worst possible wind for the Martinsyde aerodrome. But knowing this, Raynham and Morgan never hesitated to attempt the flight, and in doing so they displayed a spirit and a courage for which Grieve and I have nothing but the most intense admiration and respect. They were visited with cruel hard luck indeed.

Everything went well at first for Hawker and Mackenzie-Grieve as they headed out into the Atlantic. Once over the coast they ditched their undercarriage as planned and immediately gained another 7mph. Apart from the inevitable fogbanks, the weather was good for the first few hours. They sped steadily eastwards at a healthy 105mph into a full moonlit night. *Waltzing Matilda* composer Andrew 'Banjo' Patterson later celebrated *Hawker the Standard Bearer* and his effort to bring aviation honour to their native country:

Now who are these whose flag is the first
Of all the flags that fly
To dare the storm and the fog accurst
Of the great North Sea, where the bergs are nursed
And the Northern Lights ride high?

Shortly after 7.30 (10.00 GMT), however, the standard-bearer's luck began to change. The aircraft swung from side to side as it ran into heavy turbulent cloud. Soon afterwards the engine water temperature rose alarmingly. Surmising that loose ends of radiator solder were clogging the water pump filter, Hawker dropped the biplane's nose to clear the obstruction. The manoeuvre seemed to work, and they continued for a couple of untroubled hours. But at 12.30 GMT, having flown over 800 miles, the water temperature soared again. Fifty minutes later the Sopwith's red lights were spotted by the SS *Samnanger* at position 50.28N, 30.2W. Amazingly, this information was apparently relayed to no one except the *Glendevon*, whose master reported it on his arrival a week later in St John's.

Hawker throttled back the engine, and this once more seemed to cool the water. But at 6.00 GMT, and within 850 miles of Ireland, he and Mackenzie-Grieve accepted that they would very soon run out of both water and engine. They staggered on for a further hour and pursued a zigzag course in search of a possible rescue ship. Just before the remaining water boiled away, the hull of an old Danish tramp steamer, the SS *Mary*, loomed out of the fog. Mackenzie-Grieve fired a Very flare to alert the crew, and Hawker ditched the aeroplane only 200yd away from the vessel. Despite the heavy swell, the fliers unhooked their improvised boat. Second Mate Hoey and Seaman Schwartz of the *Mary* spotted the aeroplane off the bow of the ship. They launched a boat with some difficulty in water that was so rough that it washed Mackenzie-Grieve's flight log out of his pocket. After an anxious ninety minutes the fliers were hauled aboard the steamer at 8.30 a.m.

Captain Duhn of the *Mary* described the rescue as a fraught affair:

When I came on the bridge, the machine had already alighted in the water. The airmen told us that they had dropped rockets, but we did not see them. The work of saving them was pretty difficult because it was blowing very hard. Another hour and we might not have been able to launch the boat. Hawker and Mackenzie-Grieve were in water up to their waists but their water-tight suits kept them dry. It was rather a difficult hour before we succeeded in reaching them. All the airmen wanted to do was sleep. When they had had their sleep-out and got a good meal with a glass of Schnapps, they were all right.

Though thankful for their providential escape, Hawker and Mackenzie-Grieve bade a reluctant farewell to the still-floating Atlantic. Hawker was frustrated that they could not secure the aeroplane, so that he might determine the reason for its overheating. Had the Sopwith not suffered this problem, instead of being down in the sea they would now be within a few hundred miles of Ireland and much-deserved success. Not only would they have won the *Daily Mail* prize, they would also have been first across the Atlantic, in stages or otherwise. They were disappointed that their rescue ship, which was en route from Norfolk to Aarhuus, had no radio. Hawker worried about his wife and baby daughter, who might think he had drowned. But at least both men were safe and heading towards Europe, albeit painfully slowly for the pilot, who was seasick for most of the journey. But he knew that, had it not been for the *Mary*, like so many other pioneer aviators, no more would ever again have been heard of Mackenzie-Grieve or himself.

Alcock and Brown, Raynham and their journalist friends waited at the Cochrane for news. They expected to hear that the Sopwith pair had claimed the *Daily Mail* prize. But, hollow-eyed from lack of sleep, they prepared the following morning to accept the worst news. Their hopes were raised by the rumour that the fliers had been rescued in the mouth of the River Shannon off the Irish coast. 'Britannia Rules the Waves' exulted a local headline. But the story proved to be one of many hoaxes. A local journalist recalled how, a month previously, he had discussed the dangers of the flight with Hawker. The Australian had offered to make a large bet and leave the money behind him that, should he be forced down in the sea, he would still return safely to Brooklands.

The hours became days and, on the American side of the ocean, it was finally accepted that the Atlantic had claimed its first aviation victims, just as the English Channel had taken the great Gustave Hamel in 1913. Capt. Montague Fenn and the Sopwith team packed their belongings and prepared to return home. Some experts speculated that Hawker's use of a heavy gauze water filter might have led to his engine overheating. He had installed the additional filter after discovering sediment following his 10 April test flight and subsequent engine trials. Rolls-Royce mechanics insisted that there was absolutely no need for the extra filter, which could have led to clogging of the water system. As if to underline the dangers of flying, a crash at Farnborough took the life of another pilot, while five airmen perished within a week in separate accidents in the USA.

Distressed by the delay, Mrs Muriel Hawker and others waited forlornly outside the Sopwith hangars in Brooklands, hoping that her husband would still stagger in from the sky. As time passed with no news, observers in the UK began to accept the worst. There was not one sighting, or radio report, only a garbled message that sent eight ships on a fruitless search of the south-west coast of Ireland. In the House of Commons Josiah Wedgwood and other MPs criticised the British government for not having done more to assist Hawker and the transatlantic aviators. The popular Hawker was widely mourned. King George V sent a telegram of condolence to his presumed widow. Lord Northcliffe immediately offered £5,000 to help her and her baby daughter.

Mrs Hawker was one of the few who obstinately believed that her husband was still alive. She reminded sympathisers how he had survived his crash-landing off Portrane, Dublin, during the 1913 Round Britain race. Every bit as courageous as her husband, she wrote to the *Daily Mail*:

> With firm faith in the power of God to succour my husband and his companion, wherever they fell, but with lonely heart, I thank you for your most generous offer. Whenever the time comes for my trouble to be relieved, among my happiest duties will be that of teaching my little Pamela that her father did not hesitate to venture all for the honour and glory of his country. While appreciating this as a very noble offer, I can not and will not, as you know, believe that my husband is not alive.

While they waited in St John's with diminishing hope for some tidings of the Atlantic crew, Alcock and Brown renewed their efforts to find a suitable take-off site. They were painfully aware that the Handley Page was now nearing erection at Harbour Grace. One plan they considered was to assemble the Vimy at Mount Pearl and then fly it to Harbour Grace for final fitting and take-off. But Adm. Mark Kerr's generosity did not match his initiative in finding a congenial site. He agreed that the Vimy could use the ground, provided Vickers shared its cost and used it only *after* the Handley Page had begun its Atlantic attempt. Alcock and Brown faced further competition for scarce space. Capt. Sydney Bennett, son of the Newfoundland Minister of Militia, arrived to find a base for Boulton and Paul's aeroplane.

With the Atlantic's departure and the Raymor accident, Newfoundlanders were increasingly stirred by the great race to be first non-stop across the Atlantic. Many went daily to observe the progress of the Handley Page team at Harbour Grace. The *Evening Telegram* was moved to poetry:

> The world awaits. The hemispheres
> Are listening for the pulse that tells
> 'The flight is on', and such a flight
> Earth's all-consuming watch compels.
> And thou! Of powers of air the Prince!
> St Michael! Bear thy sword to shield
> Our fliers till they proudly land
> Triumphant in some Irish field.
> The world awaits, the millions list
> New tidings. And on many a strand
> On stranger lips in accents strange
> Is heard the name of Newfoundland.

But not all locals were enamoured with the aviation interlopers. One reader complained to the St John's *Daily News* that the aeroplanes would interfere with the supply of eggs:

> As one who protested against the bicycle nuisance twenty years ago, I also wish to voice a protest against airplanes being allowed to fly over the city, frightening our poultry and thereby interfering with the supply of eggs, so important during the present shortage of food. This nuisance is only just beginning, and now is the time to stop it before the airplane becomes as great a pest as the bicycle and the motor car.

Undeterred and still without a navigator, the bruised Freddie Raynham started repairing his aeroplane for another attempt. His mechanics built new wings from spares and repaired the engine, which had only been slightly damaged. Raynham joined Alcock and Brown as they waited in the Cochrane for news of the Atlantic. With Hawker's experience and the Sopwith's reliability, both Alcock and Brown felt that the Australian and his navigator should have succeeded. But, while admiring their courage, Brown thought that the Sopwith pair would have been wiser to have waited for more favourable weather. As their hopes for the fliers' survival faded, Brown noted sadly: 'Excitement and anxiety about the possible fate of Hawker and Mackenzie-Grieve spread all the world over; but nowhere was it more intense than amongst us at the Cochrane Hotel, who had shared their hopes and discussed their plans.'

During the recent war Alcock and Brown and their fellow fliers had come to accept fatalities as the norm, but the presumed deaths of Hawker and Grieve, with whom they had become so friendly, was a body blow and a reminder of their own mortality. Luckily they had the distraction of competition and the urgency of the continuing aerodrome search to occupy their minds. Hawker's disappearance brought the transatlantic competitors closer together. Both Raynham and Sopwith's Capt. Fenn offered the Vickers crew the use of their respective grounds to assemble the Vimy. Alcock and Brown accepted Raynham's offer of the Quidi Vidi field, while continuing their search for a suitable take-off site.

Although assured by locals that the best land had already been appropriated by the other teams, Alcock and Brown pursued their quest using hired cars. They then bought an old Buick in which they covered many more hilly and fruitless miles. Brown recorded their frustrations:

The best possibilities for an aerodrome were several level strips of meadow-land, about 100 yards wide by 300 yards long; whereas the Vickers Vimy, fully loaded, might need 500 yards of clear run into the wind. One day, a telegram arrived from a landowner in Harbour Grace, offering what he called an ideal aerodrome. Alcock raced off to inspect and secure it; but when he returned in the evening, his one-sided grin told me we were still out of luck. The 'ideal aerodrome' was a meadow 150 yards by 300 yards – and the price demanded for hire was £5,000, plus the cost of getting it ready and an indemnity for all damage. Land *sells* in Newfoundland at one shilling and fivepence an acre.

The Vimy and its assembly team finally arrived at St John's in the SS *Glendevon* on Monday, 26 May, its chances of success severely jeopardised by the London strike delay. But, thanks to Raynham, the assemblers and mechanics now had a place in which to work on the aircraft. Teams of horses owned by Charles Lester were hired to haul the twenty-two crates to the Quidi Vidi assembly site. These contained the Vimy's fuselage and wings, and also the Rolls-Royce engines, propellers and spare parts. It took a day and a half to complete the operation. Screens and scaffolding were erected, and everyone set to work to prepare for the machine's assembly. Bob Dicker recalled: 'What a grand lot of lads we had – never a moan or grumble despite the fact that conditions were far below home standards.'

Relieved to be at last united with their aeroplane, Alcock and Brown returned to the Cochrane to even more exciting tidings. Hawker and Mackenzie-Grieve had been found! Bearing in mind the previous false rescue rumours, they initially doubted the report, but the knowledge that the story had originated with Lloyd's finally convinced them. The news quickly spread throughout St John's, and flags that had previously mourned at half mast were now run up completely in celebration. The fliers themselves hoped that they might learn more about the reality of Atlantic flight once the Sopwith crew related their experiences.

Fred Memory of the *Daily Mail* arrived with further details of Hawker and Mackenzie-Grieve's safe arrival in western Scotland. The previous day, Sunday, 25 May, the SS *Mary* had reached the Butt of Lewis with siren blowing. She signalled to a shore station: 'All hands have been saved from the Sopwith aircraft.' The destroyer HMS *Woolston* picked up the airmen and took them to Scapa Flow. Mrs Hawker was informed as she was leaving a Sunday service in Kingston-upon-Thames, and King George sent his immediate congratulations. Post offices and town halls around the country displayed notices about the rescue. London cinemas interrupted their performances to break the news, and the audience of a Wagner concert at the Royal Albert Hall stood and cheered for several minutes. A group of Romans raised £980, which they cabled to the *Daily Mail* for the fliers. Newspapers said that there had not been such excitement on the streets of London since the war. Positive interest was rekindled in the Atlantic flight attempts.

Hawker and Mackenzie-Grieve were greeted by thousands when they finally arrived at London's Euston Station. The King awarded each of them the Air Force Cross. Lord Northcliffe presented them with a compensatory cheque for £5,000 at a Savoy banquet, while Capt. Duhn and his crew were awarded cash bonuses and a silver medal for Gallantry in Saving Life at Sea. Another ship, the SS *Lake Charlottesville*, retrieved the battered Atlantic, which had remained afloat and was later exhibited at London's Selfridges department store. While experts in St John's still blamed that extra fuel filter, Hawker explained that their misfortune was probably due to rust particles, which had accumulated when the radiator had been drained during the freezing Newfoundland nights. Perrott Phillips subsequently claimed in *Weekend* magazine that Hawker had privately confided that his problems had stemmed from incorrect use of the radiator-shutter lever. But Hawker did not waste too much time on inquests. A week after his arrival in Scotland the Australian was performing aerobatics at London's Hendon Aerodrome.

Despite prohibition, many toasts were drunk by both fliers and journalists at the Cochrane. The good news had a major psychological effect on the Atlantic contenders. Since the Sopwith's disappearance they had gone about their preparations with a fatalistic grimness. Confirmation of the rescue dissipated the tension and restored their original optimism and enthusiasm. Raynham and Morgan's recovery accelerated, practical jokes were renewed. Congratulatory telegrams were sent to Hawker and Mackenzie-Grieve, whom Raynham invited, without success, to be his new navigator.

Aviation and the non-stop Atlantic race were now big news in North America. The transatlantic competitors studied the first-ever air-map of the USA, which the director of the US Army Air Service issued on

26 May. It showed distances between all the major cities and towns, as well as describing the terrain, aviation fields and possible fields for emergency landings. Gen. Menoher said: 'Judging by the numerous flights now being made, the entire country will be aerially charted before the close of 1919 – and ready for a universal air service, which has been predicted so often for 1920.'

Elated by the news of Hawker and Mackenzie-Grieve's survival, the Vickers team started work the following morning. Their aeroplane gradually took shape until the weather broke on Friday, 30 May. Only the top section of fuselage remained to be assembled, but gales, rain and snow stopped work for four days. The gloom intensified with the news that a Canadian flier, Capt. Mansell T. James, had disappeared on a flight to Atlantic City. The Vimy crew derived some consolation from the fact that the storms would also delay the Handley Page programme, but worried at how far ahead their rivals were. They were also concerned about the rumoured impending arrival of the Alliance and Boulton and Paul aeroplanes, and the visit to St John's of Maj. Leth Jensen, who was involved with an alleged Atlantic attempt by the Gnome-Rhône engine company. Jensen inspected two possible take-off sites but found neither to his liking, and none of these aeroplanes materialised.

The Vickers crew had another surprise visitor. Adm. Kerr arrived from Harbour Grace and confirmed that the Handley Page should be ready for a test flight within a week. He hoped the machine would make its Atlantic attempt the week after that. As Alcock and Brown surveyed their half-erected Vimy they knew that they had little chance of beating Kerr's team, but they were encouraged that they had so substantially reduced their rival's head start.

As the Vimy fliers redoubled their quest for a take-off site, they had some good news. While they wondered why it had taken him so long, their carter, Charles Lester, offered them a field at Mundy Pond. A large meadow, half on a hill and with a swamp at the bottom, the ground boasted a reasonably level 300yd in the shadow of Mount Scio. Beside it were some other fields on Symonds's Farm, which they also managed to secure after much haggling. Alcock and Brown could have saved valuable time and energy had they found the site earlier, but at last they had a promising take-off area. Lester immediately organised a team of thirty workers who laboured twelve hours a day for a week, levelling hillocks, blasting boulders and demolishing walls and fences. The field sloped downwards from the west, and the hoped-for 400yd would permit an eastward or westward take-off, but would be even less level on its north–south axis. Secure with their take-off field, the Vimy team began to feel that they were at last on course for their Atlantic attempt.

8

THE VIMY'S
FINAL PREPARATIONS

◆◇◆

We hoped to make the journey safely, but it was only prudent
to take such precautions, for accidents will happen at times,
however careful one may be.

John Alcock

◆◇◆

Although the gales only occasionally abated, the weather improved and
expedited the Vimy's assembly at Quidi Vidi. Brown brewed tea for the
crew on an open fire. Bob Dicker, in charge of installing the flying and
engine controls, recalled:

> All the work was in the open and the weather made it hard going. Everyone
> worked up to fourteen hours a day. To save time travelling in and out to
> St John's, Montgomery and I lived in a couple of wing packing crates. But
> we were well looked after. John Alcock supplied and cooked our food when
> he brought the lads down each morning. We could have what we liked as
> long as it was bacon and egg. Midday meal was always sausages and fried toast.

Alcock had a gift for supervising and inspiring men. Each day brought
new problems, but he kept his head and organised the mechanics and
riggers to make the best use of their time. Like Brown, he worked from

early morning to nine each night, rolling gasoline barrels, tightening nuts and helping with the construction. Occasionally he press-ganged the journalists, most of whom were as enthusiastic about the enterprise as the workers themselves. Among those who regularly helped was former RFC officer Fred Memory, whom Northcliffe had sent over to cover the flight attempts for the *Daily Mail*.

Although the UK media would go into overdrive after Alcock and Brown's triumph, there was a noticeable lack of British journalists in Newfoundland to record the preparations of the nation's entrants. Fred Memory had arrived at the beginning of April, and *The Times* reporter a few weeks later. Despite the absence of American participants in the non-stop race there were no fewer than seven US newspaper and press-association journalists in St John's, including representatives of both *The New York Times* and *The World*. One possible explanation was that the London media was reluctant to report a *Daily Mail*-sponsored event. But, while pleased with the US attention, the British fliers were disappointed at the apparent media apathy in their own country. As a US journalist pointed out, St John's was almost as accessible from London as it was from his own city of New York. Among the local journalists covering the flights was self-educated Joseph Robert Smallwood, the future Prime Minister, destined to bring Newfoundland into the Canadian Confederation.

The American journalists were intrigued by the contrasting characters of the Vimy fliers. They admired Alcock's energy and unaffected humour, and were taken aback by his lack of commercialism. For a man of his achievements they found him to be as unassuming as he was composed and fearless. One wrote: 'Of all the pilots who have been at St John's, he is the least suggestive of a man who has had an exceedingly hazardous, nerve-straining occupation. He is good-natured, equable and apparently without the temperamental vagaries which some fliers have shown.'

Another remarked on his enthusiasm: 'Alcock is one of those who really loves the game and who is radiantly happy from the moment he begins to put on his flying clothes until he lands and takes them off.'

The journalists found Brown to be equally affable and approachable, but more reserved. One scribe recorded:

Light, wiry and shorter, his face is that of a student, the clear inquiring blue eyes dominating every feature. His eyes are younger and the lines about them – ineradicable souvenirs of his long period with the Germans – are emphasised by a liberal sprinkling of grey hair. His manner is that of a man of great nervous energy under good control.

It was difficult working so far from their home base and with so many interruptions because of the unpredictable weather. But the Vimy crew proved equal to the task and their aeroplane quickly took shape. Although they enjoyed the Newfoundland hospitality, the number of 'rubberneckers' created problems. One favourite pastime was testing the firmness of the wing fabric with the point of an umbrella. Alcock and Brown patiently answered many technical questions, but the former eloquently dispersed the idlers who leant against the Vimy's delicate wing trailing edges.

Although he was a fearless pilot, Alcock was a calculating risk-taker. In case of a ditching like Hawker and Mackenzie-Grieve he had one petrol tank constructed in the form of a boat-shaped raft. This tank would be the first to be emptied, and it was attached by a quick-release mechanism. He also had a small cupboard for emergency rations fitted in the aircraft's tail, which would be the last part to sink should they come down in the sea. 'We hoped to make the journey safely, but it was only prudent to take such precautions, for accidents will happen at times, however careful one may be.'

Alcock explained the Vimy's sturdy construction to journalists and how its multiple tanks offered more stability than a single tank, in which fuel would surge in turbulent conditions. While Bob Lyons of Rolls-Royce attended to the installation and checking of the Eagle engines, Alcock significantly took no chances with the radiator water. He improvised a still from a piece of copper fuel pipe and boiled the water in an old gasoline barrel. This distillation ensured that there would be no traces of alkali or sediment that might block the engine radiators. It was a precaution Harry Hawker might have employed to good effect, and also Adm. Kerr, whose programme would later be delayed by radiator problems.

While the assembly proceeded, Brown discussed navigation with Cdr Byrd of the US Navy. He tested his radio and navigational equipment. He rigged up a receiving station on the roof of the Cochrane and practised sending and receiving wireless messages. Luckily for him there was a station at nearby Mount Pearl, one of thirteen built by Marconi for the British Admiralty and opened in September 1915. With the assistance of Lt Clare from the station he learned how to tune the set into various stations.

The Atlantic fliers were soon beating a path to the door of RAF meteorologist Lt Lawrence Clements. Whereas a month previously it had taken ten hours for weather charts to reach St John's from England, these now took only half that time. Londoners still had no idea of the weather conditions on the east coast of North America. An unprecedented succession of cloudless days made them wonder why the fliers were not already winging their way from America, and a question was even asked in the House of Commons about the delay. Sweltering in the sun, they could not understand that summer came late to Newfoundland. Despite exhortations from the *Daily Mail* proprietor, the British public was tiring of the wait.

They were not half as frustrated as the aviators in Newfoundland. The Vimy team lost further valuable time when weather again interrupted work, just when their aeroplane was almost assembled. Although the Handley Page was ready to fly, the conditions also prevented Adm. Kerr's team from carrying out long-awaited tests. Despite his bad leg, Brown killed time by investigating St John's, a lively town with a population of over 30,000. He marvelled at its striking situation on the steep slope of its narrow landlocked harbour, which opened abruptly to the Atlantic under the Signal Hill and South Side Hills landmarks. Newly rebuilt after a disastrous fire in 1892, it was a wide-open place that offered no shelter from the arbitrary fog and gales. Roads wound up to the surrounding hills, and the streets and clapboard houses seemed vulnerable and temporary afterthoughts. Above the harbour, tiny square-frame fishing shacks of red and green and brown perched precariously on almost every available ledge.

The navigator was intrigued to find that the town's inhabitants pursued a way of life that had changed little over the centuries. The busy harbour was the focal point, and around it revolved such varied industries as shipbuilding, timber working, tanning and fish processing. The gossip was of arrivals and departures, drownings and the recent boiler explosion that had killed five on the SS *Cape Breton* off Cape Spear. And who had been seen going into Mr Pedigrew's pharmacy for something stronger than cough mixture. In the harbour's real-life theatre he heard descendants of English settlers use expressions that Shakespeare would have recognised. A profusion of frail platforms overhung the water and swayed under the weight of fish. The navigator recalled his most vivid impression: 'We explored the town pretty thoroughly and were soon able to recognise parts of it with our eyes closed, for its chief occupation seemed to be the drying of very dead cod!'

Brown tutored A.B. Ford, a flier who had arrived from San Diego and offered his services as a navigator to Freddie Raynham. Ford had no previous experience, and the Vimy navigator spent hours with him, going over books, charts and calculations. Brown also joined Alcock for visits to the Star Theater and the Nickel Theater cinemas. On other nights they played cards with Raynham's crew and the journalists who stayed at the Cochrane. But the aviators never lost sight of the real purpose of their visit to St John's. A relieved Alcock told *Badminton Magazine*: 'There is an end to most things, even to a Newfoundland storm. The rain clouds lifted and atmospheric conditions returned to normal. We seized our chance for a trial run on Monday, the 9th of June.'

Weather conditions at Harbour Grace had, however, improved before those at St John's, and the giant Handley Page beat its rival, staging the first all-important test flight on Sunday. To add insult to injury it flew over St John's before returning to base. 'That's about torn it,' Alcock ruefully exclaimed to Bob Dicker. The Vimy crew were, however, heartened that they were now only one day behind their early starting rivals. They were further cheered when rumours circulated next morning of the Handley Page's overheating problems.

Alcock and Brown preferred to keep news of their test quiet, but that was difficult in a place as small as St John's. Long before the engines had been warmed up, a throng of spectators had assembled at Quidi Vidi. Alcock could hardly wait for his first flight in six weeks. How wonderful to feel the machine come alive under his hands. And, all around, those familiar instruments, each as hungry as he for action. For a change, the weather was perfect and the sun shone benignly. The take-off area made distant Brooklands seem like a billiard table. The Vimy bobbed up and down like a wagtail before Alcock lifted it into the morning air and safely negotiated the gap between the low hills. Both aeroplane and engines performed perfectly, just as they had on their last test a world away in England. Alcock headed west past Signal Hill and flew over the sea for about fifteen minutes. In between admiring the dazzling icebergs, Brown tested his wireless equipment. He failed to raise a signal; it was the only problem they encountered during the forty-five minute flight.

Alcock turned back, and the noise of his return brought many people out to the streets. He flew over South Side Hills and beyond Cape Spear before circling the city and starting his descent. Alcock remembered to head for the Vimy's new home and not Quidi Vidi. Guided by a bonfire, he quickly found Lester's farm, whose clearing had been completed the previous evening. He made a perfect landing but, as he topped the brow of the slope, he saw that they were heading for a roadside fence. The exhaust beside him bellowed as he opened up the starboard engine and swung the machine away from the stone wall, which could have wrecked its undercarriage. Delighted with the Vimy's performance, Alcock remarked as he descended from the aircraft: 'I hope to be in London before the weekend!'

The Vickers personnel were as thrilled as their fliers finally to see their aeroplane in the air. They would give Adm. Kerr a run for his money yet. They pushed the machine down to the most sheltered part of the field, where mechanics immediately got to work. The area around the aircraft was roped off, a wise precaution as the noise of the Vimy had attracted additional spectators, most of whom were now backing Alcock and Brown to leave before the Handley Page. By 4 o'clock the mechanics had removed both propellers and were checking every moving part. Alcock and Brown were so encouraged with their progress that they planned to make a second flight at 6 o'clock the following morning, weather permitting.

Up to this point neither of them had entertained any serious hope of beating the Handley Page to the starting line. Now they realised they were in with a chance. Their optimism was very quickly disabused. Shortly after

5 o'clock they heard the roar of engines coming from the north-west. It was their rival, flying directly overhead with Maj. Brackley at the controls. So much for the alleged overheating problems. The giant wings of the four-engined V/1500 cast a shadow over both the ground and their hopes. It was obviously in the final stages of its transatlantic preparations and also ready to leave. Alcock commented on the irony that it was he who had taught its pilot to fly.

Confirmation came from Harbour Grace later that night of the Handley Page team's optimism following their successful test. Adm. Kerr was ready for an imminent take-off. He issued a statement:

> Everything worked most satisfactorily, including both receiving and transmitting wireless. The engines worked especially well. Requisite adjustments will be made and another test will follow. Weather reports indicate that the present favourable conditions are becoming disturbed, so that the date of the transatlantic flight is unsettled.

The admiral might have had the biggest aeroplane and the best chance of success, but the natives of St John's were firmly behind the Vimy crew. They had developed a proprietorial interest. They had come to know the fliers, Brown as he limped through the streets and harbour, and Alcock as he careered around in the battered Buick. Observing the team's hard work and seeing the aeroplane in flight had cemented their interest and loyalty. The Vimy became *their* aeroplane, their David that would take on the mighty Goliath in Harbour Grace. Many insisted that the Handley Page's size and complexity would delay its fine-tuning. Their aeroplane would get away first. The *New York Times* confirmed: 'The whole project of a transatlantic flight by landplane had come to be taken here as St John's own, and the interest has risen remarkably of late. Naturally, the Vimy men are the favourites here.'

The sight of the two aeroplanes in the air clearly demonstrated that the Atlantic race was now truly a reality. Spectators swarmed to Lester's farm. Local children dared the breeze from the propellers when Alcock tested his engines. Old men held their hats as the wind almost fanned them off their feet. Both the Vimy and Handley Page crews had agreed to carry a small number of letters to Europe, but so many now rushed to purchase special surcharged stamps that the post office declared that no more airmail would be accepted for either machine.

Media interest also mushroomed. Alcock and Brown had to answer the same questions from frequently uninformed reporters, who repeatedly referred to the dangers the fliers faced. The Vimy team spoke of their confidence in their twin-engined aeroplane. Alcock reminded journalists how, after its companion failed, he had flown over 60 miles on the remaining engine during the war. He assured *Daily Mail* readers:

> If any mishap should befall one engine when the journey is half completed, the other one will carry the plane safely to Ireland. But should an accident happen before the fuel load has been reduced by one half, the machine would have to come down.

The Vimy crew's duties were well defined. Alcock would pilot and control the aeroplane and its engines. Brown would look after navigation and communications, and also the instruments registering altitude, air speed, rpm, engine temperatures and oil pressure. Alcock would never be able to leave the control wheel nor remove his feet from the rudder bar, and Brown would also experience considerable discomfort. He would have to bend double to observe the motion of the waves through the floor-mounted eyepiece of the drift indicator. Monitoring external gauges would require painful contortions in the tight cockpit. The navigator would regularly monitor the vital exterior fuel overflow gauge and manage the return of excess fuel from the upper-wing supply tank by using the cockpit handpumps.

Peter R. Mann of London's Science Museum explained the importance of the gauge, which would later feature in one of the Vimy's Atlantic dramas:

> When the service tank is full, it overflows through the petrol overflow gauge into No. 2 fuel tank and then back again to the collecting tank. The main pump cocks are manipulated until surplus fuel is just trickling through the

petrol-overflow gauge. This ensures that the engines are supplied with a consistent head of fuel. If the petrol-overflow gauge is empty, the pumps are not supplying enough fuel and the main pump cocks must be opened slightly. If the petrol-overflow gauge is full, the pumps are supplying too much fuel. There is a danger that the engine carburettors will be supplied at too great a pressure, so the main pump cocks must be closed slightly.

Journalists were particularly eager to hear how Brown would find the tiny island of Ireland at the end of their 1,900-mile flight. The pilot had heretofore been the most important person in flying, but as aircraft ventured farther afield the navigator's role had become equally or even more crucial. Brown was asked by *The Aeroplane* magazine to write a feature on the subject. Satellite navigation and directional radio would later ensure that navigators could traverse the globe with pinpoint accuracy, but trailblazing Arthur Whitten Brown did not even have a serviceable radio. His navigation owed more to the early Phoenician traders – or to the philosopher Thales of Miletos, who taught Ionian sailors to navigate by the Little Bear constellation 600 years before the birth of Christ.

When early navigators ventured out of sight of land they determined their latitude – north or south direction – by observing the height of the sun during the day and the North Star at night. They had no way to determine longitude accurately and, once at sea, had no idea how far east or west they were. Estimates were made based upon the time it took to reach a certain point. This was a simple form of dead reckoning that Brown would also use: the process of estimating one's current position based upon a previously determined position or 'fix', and then advancing that position on to a chart, based upon known speed, elapsed time and course. The 16th-century invention of the Chip Log ensured a major advance in the accuracy of dead reckoning.

A weighted line containing knots at regular intervals was let out of a moving boat. Its progress could be calculated from the number of knots that went out over a specific period of time, hence the term 'knots' as a measurement of nautical speed. (A knot, or nautical mile per hour, is the equivalent of 1.15 statute miles per hour.)

The navigator's indispensable tools were the magnetic compass and the sextant, which provided a means of determining the angle between the horizon and the sun, moon or stars in order to calculate latitude. The Mercator Projection of 1569 allowed a compass bearing to be shown as a straight line, enabling navigators to sail the shortest distance between two points. Two hundred years later John Harrison's seagoing chronometer enabled sailors to determine longitude. The adoption in 1884 of the meridian of Greenwich as the Prime Zero Degrees Meridian established a universal system of its measurement. No longer would ships stray so easily or fall victim to hostile vessels or dwindling supplies.

The Vimy navigator explained how he was going to find his way across the featureless ocean:

It is my intention to rely upon a method of navigation similar to that employed by mariners, but modified for ease of application in the air. The position of the aeroplane is found at any time by observing the height of the Sun or some suitable star through a sextant – noting the Greenwich time of the observation and plotting the result by means of a special chart showing what are known as 'curves of equal altitude'.

Variable air currents and wind were the big bugbear of aerial dead reckoning:

The wind has a great effect upon the aeroplane, and the greatest care has to be used in noting drift, or how much the aeroplane is blown off her course. For observing this, I carry a drift-bearing plate which shows the angle between the course steered and the direction in which the machine moves. Knowing the errors which may arise, I shall be satisfied to reach any part of Ireland, although I shall shape our course for Galway Bay!

Following their test flight, Brown lost no time in dismantling the wireless generator and taking it to the Admiralty Wireless Station experts at Mount Pearl. There, he learned that the wheels and undercarriage of Hawker and Mackenzie-Grieve's machine had been recovered off Cape St Mary's. The wireless was as important to Brown as his navigation instruments.

The experience of Hawker and Mackenzie-Grieve had reinforced his belief that, though wireless might still be unproven, it could be a lifesaver. It would enable him to communicate and, hopefully, receive vital weather bulletins. Lt Clare remedied the generator problem and Brown refitted it on the Vimy's lower port wing, where it was driven by its own small independent impeller.

Back on Lester's farm the Vimy effort was threatened by a problem far greater than the recalcitrant wireless. Brown explained:

> The fuel we had intended to carry was a mixture of petrol and benzol, sent from England. On examination, we found in it a peculiar precipitate, like a very soft resin. It was sticky and had the consistency of India rubber wetted by petrol. When dry, it reduced to a powder. Naturally, we could not afford the risk of letting such a deposit clog our filters, and perhaps, owing to the stoppage of fuel supply, cause engine failure.

Although he was almost ready for another attempt, the sporting Freddy Raynham immediately offered his supply of petrol to the Vimy team. This eventually proved unnecessary, as the SS *Graciana* arrived from England with Percy Maxwell Muller and a fresh supply of 800gal of fuel. The energetic works superintendent's presence boosted team morale and also relieved the hard-pressed Alcock and Brown of time-consuming administrative chores. Muller quickly discovered that Newfoundland was more like his native Scotland and did not share England's sunshine. He was impressed by the team's progress in such a short time, when he saw at first hand the problems they had faced with both weather and terrain. The ship also brought a new engine for Freddy Raynham, which he was confident of installing in the Martinsyde within forty-eight hours.

Alcock and Brown were well aware that, should weather delay the Vimy, there would now be three aeroplanes jostling for take-off at the same time. The navigator was already looking forward to leaving for Ireland. He was amused to hear that a US couple had just wed at 2,000ft over Houston, Texas, in a Handley Page. He wrote to his fiancée: 'I wish I had brought you along now, it is lonely without you, my dearest little wife-to-be.

Tell you what! I'll try to time our arrival at Brooklands from Ireland so that we can drive straight from there by car to the Registry [*sic*] Office.'

Unlike Brown, Alcock preferred to unwind with a beer than with a letter. But the pilot found time to reply to 19-year-old May Kirtson of Erdenheim, Pennsylvania, who wrote asking if he could take her as a passenger. She had three brothers in the army but she was rejected by the air services because of her sex. She wanted to show that she was not afraid of crossing the Atlantic. Alcock thanked her but explained that the aeroplane had only room for two. He was as averse to correspondence as he was to meetings and publicity. His mother, Mary Alcock, explained to a reporter: 'He is of a retiring disposition and his last words were "I won't write to you. I want the whole affair keeping as quiet as possible. But I should like you to write to me as often as you can."'

Two days of gales prevented the Vimy team from a second test until Thursday, 12 June. Although he was aware that the fuel load was nothing compared with what they would carry on their eventual departure, Alcock was encouraged by the comparatively smooth take-off, their first from what they had christened 'Lester's Field'. They flew over the hills and nearby bays and tested the engines and all the controls. Apart from an oil leak that mechanics quickly cured, the aeroplane behaved faultlessly and the engines did everything asked of them. Brown made trial observations with his navigation instruments, but the wireless let him down once again. The transmitter worked for a brief spell before giving him a violent shock as he struggled to repair it.

Alcock delighted their St John's supporters with a final circle of the town before he landed the Vimy. He told Percy Muller that he was confident the aeroplane was now ready to fly the Atlantic. From being the last and least-fancied of the transatlantic entrants, the Vimy was now a leading contender for the *Daily Mail* prize. Their main rival might have a superior aeroplane and facilities, but the Vimy could triumph if it got a head start. Acutely aware of the apparent readiness of the Handley Page, Alcock and Brown decided that they would waste no more time on unnecessary trials: 'So pleased were we with the result of the test that we decided to set off as quickly as possible.'

Like all the previous *Daily Mail* challenges, the Atlantic race was also to be regulated by Britain's Royal Aero Club. Alcock and Brown immediately invited Lt Clements to affix the club's official seals and record the engine numbers to ensure that there would be no cheating. Inscribed 'H.M. Customs, Newfoundland – In Bond', the two seals were attached to a strut on the lower port wing. Brown wrote a final letter to Kathleen Kennedy on the Cochrane's headed notepaper: 'Just a line by aerial mail as a souvenir of the flight – which should take place at an early date now. Everything has gone well so far, with the exception of a little trouble with the wireless. Kindest regards to Major Kennedy and Eileen. Sincerely, Teddy.'

Alcock, the man who professed never to write letters, also found time for a brief note to his young sister, who had regularly sent him food parcels while he was a prisoner of war: 'My dear Elsie, Just a hurried line before we start. This letter will travel with me in the official mailbag, the first mail to be carried over the Atlantic. Love to all. Your loving brother, Jack.'

This letter joined the 196 others and one parcel in a small bag that the Newfoundland Postmaster General, Dr Robinson, entrusted to the Vimy pair. Some were from private individuals, others were letters of greetings from North America to the Old Country addressed to King George V, the British Prime Minister and leading London newspapers. As there were no airmail stamps, a limited number of red 15-cent Cabot stamps were overprinted for the Vimy flight: 'Air Post, 1919. One Dollar'.

With all preparations well on course, weather now became the outstanding issue. Brown besieged Lt Clements at Mount Pearl for meteorological reports. The available information was still meagre and slow in arriving owing to transmission delays. The reports indicated good weather, which further encouraged the Vimy pair to leave as soon as possible. While ignorance proved to be bliss, they might have been wise to heed the pre-aviation rule of thumb that suggested that, if the weather was good on one side of the Atlantic, it was bad on the other.

Fred Memory also moved up a gear with his dispatches to the *Daily Mail* in London. Although ill in France, Lord Northcliffe keenly followed the transatlantic flight activity and he impressed on his staff the importance of headlining the news from Newfoundland. He had reporters stationed in the west of Ireland to record the first arrival. When Memory queried Alcock's choice of Friday the thirteenth, the otherwise practical pilot, whose Empress Works number had been 13, replied:

> That's the very reason I wanted to get away. Number thirteen has a charm for the machine. It was the thirteenth of its type turned out from the Weybridge works, there are thirteen in our party, and we arrived here on the thirteenth of last month! Friday is my lucky day and Lieutenant Brown says that thirteen is a lucky number for him also.

An obstinate crosswind, however, forced Alcock and Brown to miss their lucky Friday. Fearful that the Handley Page might leave before them, both men were still in favour of risking a take-off. But after much discussion Percy Muller successfully dissuaded them. Brown recorded their final preparations and change of date:

> With all the hurry and bustle, we found that everything could not be ready by Friday, the thirteenth, and that a postponement until 4 a.m. on Saturday was essential. We worked at high speed on several last-minute jobs. The compasses were swung, the wireless apparatus repaired, more elastic shock-absorbers were wrapped around the axles, and the navigating instruments were taken on board, with food and emergency supplies. The last coat of wing-protective dope was dry and nothing had been overlooked. The only articles missing were some life-saving suits, which we were expecting from the United States. Alcock and I went to bed at 7 p.m., while the mechanics remained all night with the machine.

Observers of the Vimy attempt were struck by the precautions taken by the team. If they did not succeed, it would not be for their lack of diligence. During the war Alcock had witnessed many accidents caused by hastily prepared aeroplanes. Despite the urgency he insisted that:

> the mechanics were as meticulous with the petrol as they were with the water. Before the long and painstaking process of filling the tanks, all the

fuel was first hand-filtered from the barrels through specially designed double filters. These contained a layer of chamois and another of fine wire mesh, a process which also obviated the need for a filter anywhere in the aeroplane's fuel system.

Despite Alcock's best precautions, the Vimy's final fuelling was interrupted by unexpected drama. Bob Dicker explained:

Everything was going well but as we were loading the petrol, one of the axles' shock absorbers broke. This meant unloading all the petrol and carrying out repairs. This took us all night. In the meantime, the fliers went to the Cochrane hotel for a rest. Jack was a little sad at not being able to make the thirteenth – his lucky number!

Automobile headlamps and flares illuminated the cold early morning scene as the draining of the aeroplane was completed. The mechanics then repaired and strengthened the starboard shock absorber. Repeatedly rubbing their hands to keep warm and shouting to encourage each other, they rolled back the barrels and restarted the painstaking filtering and refuelling. Their corner of Lester's Field was the only patch of light in the immense darkness. A cold exterior Caravaggio tableau. While the planet slept, the flickering lights seemed to accentuate the fragility and the resourcefulness of both man and machine. How small was man. Yet how daring he had become, to challenge the heavens and the mighty oceans; and in such an unprepossessing assembly of fabric, wood and metal! Dawn was breaking as the mechanics transferred the last of almost 900gal. Although tired, they noticed that the wind was dying down. Would this be the long-awaited day when their aeroplane would finally head for Ireland?

9

DRAMATIC TAKE-OFF

◆◇◆

As they passed over at about 600 feet, they were waving
vigorously and heading out towards Cabot Tower and
they soon became lost from view.

Bob Dicker

◆◇◆

Despite Fred Memory's enthusiastic dispatches, most Britons were oblivi-
ous to the fact that aviation history was about to be made on the other side
of the Atlantic. Far from Newfoundland's fogs and gales, they rose on the
morning of Saturday, 14 June to the balmy embrace of the seemingly eternal sun. Not only did distant aviators not preoccupy them, the soporific
warmth dissipated any interest in the headlines on Bela Kun's revolution
in Hungary or the debate on the Treaty of Versailles between Germany
and the Allies. Crowds fanned themselves at King George's parade review.
Hyde Park's packed Serpentine resembled a piranha pool. Old Trafford
was crowded for the Australia versus Lancashire cricket match, the Ascot
races were looming, and all was well with the world. Only the fliers' fami-
lies, Kathleen Kennedy, Lord Northcliffe and Vickers personnel wondered
when Alcock and Brown would start their big adventure.

Warm in their fleece-lined soft leather knee boots, Alcock and Brown
arrived with the light of the 4 a.m. dawn at Lester's Field. A cool sun
unexpectedly followed them, throwing Signal Hill into sharp relief against
the sky. Would it also illuminate their long eastern voyage? The normally

uncoordinated pilot wore a navy-blue suit. Brown was smartly attired in his light blue RAF uniform and peaked cap, his stick by his side for the journey to Ireland. Both men exuded a jaunty but purposeful confidence, as if, after all their previous setbacks, they knew that this new day would finally see their departure.

The Vimy team had moved the aeroplane to its intended take-off position at the top of the slope. Alcock and Brown loaded their provisions: sandwiches, a vacuum flask of hot Oxo, Horlicks malted milk, water and many bars of Fry's chocolate. The mail had been stowed the previous evening. They placed additional food and a bottle of brandy high in the tailplane emergency box. They also brought cigarettes and matches. Alcock habitually smoked while flying, but this time he would not light up owing to their huge cargo of fuel. Charles Lester's horses were corralled, the countdown began.

The weather, however, had other ideas. A stubborn western cross-wind indicated that there could be no immediate take-off. Undaunted, Alcock continued his preparations. He ordered the rewinding of the damaged shock absorber's elastic cable. After checking every control and movable part of the Vimy he ran the engines. They roared into life at the first swing of the starting handle. It was almost as if they too could not wait to go to work.

The wind persisted, the engines coughed in complaint as they were shut down. Unknown to Alcock, Vickers rigger Harry Couch screwed a horse-shoe under his seat. Alcock had a secret of his own. He carried in one pocket a silver kewpie doll from a local female admirer. Brown's wallet contained a tiny silk American flag given to him by his fiancée before he left England.

A small crowd gathered as the navigator loaded his instruments and charts and the small electric torch given to him by journalist Edward Klauber, after his own had failed. He put Twinkletoes, the smaller of the two black cat mascots, in his pocket and then tied the red-ribboned Lucky Jim to the strut behind the cockpit; the first felines to fly the ocean. To Brown's amazement a real black cat sauntered by the Vimy: 'Such a cheer-ful omen made me more than ever anxious to start!'

Reporters wanted to hear the aviators' last words before they flew. Brown explained that, unlike Mackenzie-Grieve, who had veered north to avoid bad local conditions, Alcock and he would head straight west on the Loxodrome Course. This was the nearest possible straight line between St John's and Galway, and only slightly longer than the Mercator Great Circle Course. Brown was so confident of hitting the Galway coast that Alcock laughed: 'Yes, we shall hang our hats on the aerials of the Clifden wireless station as we go by!'

Alcock estimated that they would fly the 1,900 miles at around 90mph. Their plan was to stop in Ireland and, after a night's rest and an overhaul of the aeroplane, to leave next day for Brooklands. As far as the *Daily Mail* prize was concerned, Alcock felt it was better to stop first in Ireland, so that everyone could see as soon as possible that they had crossed the ocean. He impressed reporters with his determination, born of experience, to nurse the Vimy's engines and to climb gradually after take-off: 'Perhaps at the very end when the Irish coast is in sight, I may try a whirlwind finish but not 'til then!'

It was now 10.30. The wind continued to gust across Lester's Field from west to east. Would it abate in time for a midday take-off? To everyone's relief it seemed to drop a little, but then it intensified. Alcock's original plan had been to take off in an easterly direction. Even if the wind was blowing from the west, the downhill slope would provide a much better run than if they taxied towards the west. The strength of the wind forced a change of plan. He had little choice but to take off uphill into it. The Vickers riggers and mechanics untethered the aircraft and, with the help of enthusiastic spectators, manhandled it all the way down the slope. Many observers felt that the heavily laden biplane would never climb the incline.

But just before the Vimy crew secured the machine again, a gust blew one of the ropes against the undercarriage. Tightened by the rolling wheel, it crushed a petrol supply line to the starboard engine. It looked as if the flight would have to be aborted and that another nightmare emptying of the tanks was inevitable, but the Vickers mechanics were as enterprising as their fliers. While one held back the fuel with his hand, another cut and fitted a new section of pipe. The operation took an hour. The team derived some consolation from the thought that the adverse conditions would also delay the Handley Page. They were sure that it was being readied for take-off, only 26 miles away from them by crow's flight, but at least it would be their only competitor. Freddie Raynham's engine was not yet installed.

Unknown to them, however, the Handley Page had developed radiator trouble. The tubes of the four radiators were too narrow, and the cooling water boiled over after the engines had run for only a couple of hours. Adm. Kerr was unwilling to start with such a problem, but the team worked from early that Saturday morning on modifications that they thought would work. Although aware of the risk, they persuaded Kerr that it was now their only chance of taking the honour of the first non-stop Atlantic flight. For them the wind was good news. The longer it lasted, the better their chances of completing the repairs and beating the Vimy. While Alcock and Brown fretted at Lester's Field, Brackley and his crew worked flat out to ensure that they would be first away.

While some onlookers had to brace themselves against the gusts, Alcock sat calmly on a wooden box near the Vimy. Once, when the wind seemed at its worst, he tore off a handful of grass blades, tossed them in the air and watched them scatter in all directions. 'No flight today,' he remarked, to the disappointment of those around him. But he added: 'That's what we used to do before the war. We would toss a handful of torn tissue paper into the air and, if there was the slightest puff of wind, we didn't go up. It is different now; I'm going.'

By 11.30 up to 150 hardy spectators had assembled at the exposed Lester's Field. For many it was not their first time to be on standby for a take-off. They congregated with the stoic expectancy of generations that had awaited the return of their fisherfolk. Their hats tightly secured, male elders lounged on the grass in the unaccustomed sun. But their enthusiasm was tempered by apprehension. Remembering the mishaps of Hawker and Raynham, not all of them were sanguine about the Vimy's prospects. A local reporter captured the mood:

There was a tense expectancy of danger; the very thought of flying any distance was fantastic to people who, only a few weeks earlier, had seen their first aeroplane. Many of the older folk believed that there was something devilish about the strange contraption in which Alcock and Brown were trying to fly across the Atlantic.

The crowd included a group of young girls on a weekend picnic. Among them were sisters Jean and Mollie Clinton and their friends, Sarah Andrews, Ethel Johnston and Stella White, who would long dine out on their memory of posing near Alcock and Brown in front of the Vimy. The aeroplane boasted no frills. Its clear lines were impressive, but its engine covers were unpolished. The fuselage fabric was more a dirty grey than white, the slightly yellowed wings finger-marked and stained. Mollie Clinton's daughter, Jean Kavanagh, remembered:

My mother told me how they were enjoying their basket of sandwiches and lemon crystals, when a man asked them to sit down in front of the 'plane so that he could take a picture before it took off. We still have that photograph.

The girls watched the aviators stretch out under the aeroplane and unwrap their sandwiches as if they too were on a picnic, instead of contemplating a feat never before achieved by man. A little boy arrived with a home-made wooden model of the Vimy, its propeller whirring in the wind. Alcock called him over and admired the aeroplane before handing it back. The *New York Times* noted:

Despite these delays, Alcock and Brown who retired at 7 o'clock last night and got their first good night's sleep in a week, kept in excellent spirits.

Both were happy and eager to be away. Alcock sat about on the grass, chatting, joking, laughing, and proving himself as calm, unruffled, and genial as he was when his big job was weeks away. His boyishness had won the hearts of all who knew him here, and this morning he was a bigger boy than ever as he told of his plans for flying back across the Atlantic again, if he succeeds this time, in a monster Vickers airliner which will take a year to build. This narrative, he interrupted long enough to squat on the ground and eat a luncheon of crackers, cheese and cold tongue, which Brown shared and which both washed down with hot coffee from vacuum bottles. Then there was much hand shaking and many sincere and genuine good wishes.

No sooner had the fliers re-corked their flask than Lt Clements arrived from the Admiralty Wireless Station with some encouraging news. His chart of the approximate strength and direction of the Atlantic air currents indicated that the high westerly wind would drop before the fliers were a 100 miles out to sea, and that the wind velocities for the rest of the journey would not exceed 20 knots, with clear weather over the greater part of the ocean. Clear weather; how welcome that would be after all they had experienced in Newfoundland! As if on cue, the wind seemed to slacken just before 1 o'clock. Pilot and navigator agreed to wait no longer. They knew now that they would leave as early as, if not before, the Handley Page. But their eagerness led to last-minute drama.

Percy Muller agreed with some observers that conditions were still too severe for a fully laden take-off. It would be catastrophic if the Vimy succumbed to the gusts that had caused the Raynham and Morgan debacle, particularly in front of the growing throng, which now included Mayor Gosling of St John's, Newfoundland Prime Minister Sir M.P. Cashin, and other government ministers. Although rumours were circulating that the Handley Page was preparing to leave, Muller was sure that Adm. Kerr would not risk a take-off in such weather. The tension grew within the Vickers team.

The *New York Times* reported the final pre-flight stand-off:

> There was a 40-knot half-gale blowing from the west. The wind was bucketing, veering and chopping about. Since its direction made necessary a take-off uphill, with only a comparatively short run available, P.M. Muller, head of Vickers Aviation Department, absolutely forbade the flight.

But Alcock, fearing that the four-engined Handley Page giant at Harbor Grace would get into the air and beat him in the race for the *Daily Mail's* $50,000 prize, begged and pleaded, insisting that he could get off without crashing. And, even if he did come to grief, he would be going so slowly that the chances of Brown and himself escaping from an accident were excellent. Finally, Muller agreed that it was better to try and fail than to remain idly on the ground and risk defeat. 'Go ahead, Jack. I assume full responsibility.'

The atmosphere in the Vickers team immediately lightened. The debilitating doubts had been articulated and overcome. A decision had been taken. Everyone was suddenly more positive. The flight was on. There was no turning back. It was ten minutes past one.

Fred Memory gave Brown a sprig of lucky white heather. With the eagerness to be off that attends all journeys into the unknown, the fliers said 'So long' to their mechanics. They promised them dinner in a London hotel, at which the menu, by agreement, would be duck and green peas. They donned their flying helmets and struggled to secure their dun-coloured Burberry flying suits and Gieves life-saving waistcoats. Each wore an electrically heated waistcoat, gloves and insoles. Because of his injured leg Brown had some difficulty in managing his suit. Bob Dicker was helping him when Alcock summoned him to start the engines.

With Alcock already aboard, Brown shook hands with Lt Clements and Percy Muller and clambered painfully up to the cockpit. Terra firma was now behind him; ahead was a great unknown. Muller reached up with the navigator's stick. High in their lofty cockpit and bulging in their flying suits and fur-lined helmets, both navigator and pilot now suddenly looked remote. Their eyes had altered focus and, under their goggles, they were already distant and semi-mythical figures, Alcock preoccupied with engine revs and temperatures, Brown checking his charts and navigation instruments.

The fliers secured their safety belts. It was almost 1.20 when Alcock's cry rang out, 'Contact!' Bob Dicker instructed a mechanic to swing the starting handle, while he prepared to disconnect the exterior magneto cut-out. The port engine had to be coaxed for a minute before it roared into life with a burst of exhaust smoke. Ten minutes later a second mechanic started the starboard unit. Alcock gave the motors maximum revs. The two four-bladed propellers became whirring blurs, spectators drew back in awe. Even the wind seemed to retreat in the face of such power. For six minutes there was no sound but the bellowing of the engines. The Vimy throbbed with life, as eager for action as its crew.

The fliers' senses went on full alert. The smell of warming oil, petrol and freshly applied dope percolated through the cockpit. As he checked the instruments and gauges, Alcock felt at home, doing what he loved best in life. He surveyed the undulating plain between the ridges and registered every bump and hollow in sharp relief. With so much fuel, he would have to deal gently with them, yet he would need maximum speed to lift off. It was some challenge. He throttled back the motors and the revs settled down. Dicker recalled: 'What beautiful music those two Rolls-Royce Eagle engines were playing! But I was a little apprehensive, knowing that it was now or never.'

Dicker was the same age as Alcock and one of his closest friends. The wiring specialist had interrupted his honeymoon to travel with the Vimy to Newfoundland. After the ever-supportive Freddy Raynham, he was the last to exchange words with the pilot. He wished him 'Good luck'. Over the noise of the engines, Alcock shouted back: 'See you in London.'

Alcock raised a hand. Percy Muller gave the signal to remove the chocks. Bob Dicker completed his disconnection and leaped off the starboard wing. The men who had been hanging on to the wings and tailplane let go. The engines roared once more as Alcock increased their supply of petrol, the noise reverberating back from the low hills. The Vimy started to roll through the diminishing lane of waving spectators, but more reluctantly than ever before, with its heavy load of petrol, oil and water. Nevertheless, grass blades flew and the young picnickers held their skirts in the draught.

High in the port side of the cramped cockpit, well forward in the Vimy's nose, Brown stared straight ahead. Beside him, Alcock sat rigidly at the controls, both hands gripping the wheel, his feet firmly on the rudder bar. None knew better than they the risks they were taking, apart from Lt Williams, Capt. Bennett and Freddie Raynham, who all watched anxiously. As Raynham knew from his own experience, take-off was possibly the most critical time of the whole endeavour. Hoping they would not be needed, doctors Campbell and Mitchell observed from the sidelines.

The thudding of the wheels reiterated that Lester's Field was no downy English meadow. Pushed back into their seat by the acceleration, Alcock and Brown held their breaths as they were jarred by the constant bumps. The vertical flexing of the wingtips alarmed spectators.

Young Harry Symonds and the picnickers hoped that the aeroplane would not hit his house or that of the nearby Lesters. Silhouetted against the skyline, two grazing horses and a band of hardy spectators seemed rooted to a nearby ridge. There was no doubting the Vimy's weight; it shuddered as it gathered speed across the uneven ground, the last land it would experience before it reached Europe. It was half a minute after 1.41 local time. One eyewitness said that the aeroplane's departure produced 'as beautiful a battle between the man on one side and the biplane and the wind on the other as possibly has even been witnessed'.

Alcock's subsequent account told more about himself than it did about the take-off drama:

> We made our long-hoped-for start. Some of the crosswind remained and the take-off was up a slight gradient, and there was insufficient room to start head to wind. We managed well, however, but a high range of hills on either side made climbing difficult and occasioned bumps which kept us down.

The uphill start looked much more dramatic to spectators and reporters. *The Times* correspondent recorded:

> Gradually increasing the pace, the Vimy slowly at first moved up the rather steep gradient of the aerodrome – 100 yards – 200 yards – 300 yards – and the machine still moved forwards, but showed not the least desire to leave the ground. Pessimists who had foretold that, with its exceptional load, it could not leave an uphill ground in the face of a 40 mile per hour gale began to croak disaster, when suddenly and just at the right moment Captain Alcock operated his controls.

The machine jumped off the ground, zoomed over a fence that was a few yards ahead, bounded over the end of the aerodrome and began to climb steadily. For a moment there was silence, for all but a few had failed to realise that the machine was off on its journey – the contour of the land gives a very poor idea of height – and then so loud a cheer was raised that it must have carried to the airmen even against the gale. Again there were cries of 'He's coming down', for the country gave the impression that the machine was scraping the treetops of a small wood directly in its path, when in reality it was many feet above, and climbing steadily.

Bob Dicker was one of those who held their breaths as the Vimy fought off the tugging wind and headed north-westward towards Topsail and Conception Bay:

I shall never forget the take-off. I can hardly put into words my feelings when I saw the Vimy heading for a small wall with the wheels firmly on the ground. I had visions of a large heap of wreckage after all our hard work and determination – not to mention the loss or injury to Alcock and Brown. Suddenly, the Vimy rose about five feet, fifty feet from the obstacle, then dropped and on hitting the ground bumped over the wall with about two feet of clearance.

Here, mother nature took a hand – the ground fell away into a steep valley. It was the one and only time I have seen a 'plane to fly downwards. With a very strong headwind, Jack was able to gain height but was going inland instead of out to sea – this was made necessary by the wind direction. The Vimy was lost to view for what seemed ages but was only a matter of minutes. I remember saying to Maxwell Muller as I ran to the old Buick, 'I'm going to find them', as I felt certain they were down in the woods that obstructed our view.

You can imagine the relief when Freddy Raynham, who was standing by my side, said 'Look Bob', and behold, there was the Vimy coming through a gap between the hills, going like an S.E.5 [fighter] or the like. They must have been doing 130 miles per hour with a machine capable of around 90 miles per hour – a marvellous sight. As they passed over at about 600 feet, they were waving vigorously and heading out towards Cabot Tower and they soon became lost from view.

136

Apart from Alcock, the man who most experienced the perils of the Vimy's departure was Arthur Whitten Brown. He recalled their take-off and early progress in the *Royal Air Force and Civil Aviation Record*:

The take-off up a slight gradient was very difficult. Gusts up to 5 knots were registered, and there was insufficient room to begin the run dead into the wind. What I feared in particular was that a sudden eddy might lift the 'plane on one side and cause the machine to heel over. Another danger was the rough surface of the aerodrome.

Owing to its heavy load, the machine did not leave the ground until it had lurched, at an ever increasing speed, over 300 yards. We were then almost at the end of the ground-tether allowed us. A line of hills on either side was responsible for much bumpiness in the atmosphere, and made climbing very difficult. At times, the strong wind dropped almost to zero, then rose again in an eddying blast. Once or twice our wheels nearly touched the ground again. Under these conditions we could climb but slowly, allowing for the danger of sudden upward gusts.

Several times I held my breath, from fear that our undercarriage would hit a roof or a tree-top. I am convinced that only Alcock's clever piloting saved us from such an early disaster. When after a period that seemed far longer than it actually was, we were well above the buildings and trees, I noticed that the perspiration of acute anxiety was streaming down his face.

We wasted no time and fuel in circling around the aerodrome while attaining a preliminary height, but headed straight into the wind until we were at about 800 feet. Then we turned towards the sea, and continued to rise leisurely, with engines throttled down. As we passed the aerodrome, I leaned over the side of the machine and waved farewells to the small crowd.

Between St John's and Conception Bay the air was very bumpy, and not until we reached the coast and were away from the uneven contours of Newfoundland did it become calmer. The eddying wind, which was blowing behind us from almost due west, with a strength of 35 knots, made it harder than ever to keep the machine on a straight course. The twin engined Vickers Vimy is not especially sensitive to atmospheric instability, but under the then conditions it lurched, swayed, and did its best to deviate, much as if it had been a little single-seater.

News quickly spread of the Vimy's take-off. As it roared over St John's, people in the streets below waved and cheered. This was their aeroplane, and they wished it a tremulous 'God speed' on its journey into the unknown. And from the harbour rose a rousing farewell from ships' sirens. The fliers saw the spurts of white steam, but could not hear the sirens above their own engine noise. Crewmen waved from the multi-masted barques with their lattice rigging, reminding Brown of the many times he had discussed navigation with their officers, weatherbeaten men who were at home with the currents and vagaries of the mighty ocean he was now about to cross.

The Vimy flew over the Narrows and Signal Hill, whose steepness the navigator had often walked. How minute it looked now, curling its cork-screw path back down towards Water Street. How the houses adapted to the contours, and those gravity-defying fishing shacks, clinging like red and green barnacles to the cliffs. How altitude, like ageing, revolutionised the perspective. He felt momentarily sad to be departing the place where he had made so many good friends. But not that airfield, it was not a place for taxiing a fully laden aeroplane. Smoke from a garden fire scampered seawards. The wind was behind them, a happy omen.

Fifteen minutes after take-off they crossed the coast at 1.57. As the wind whined a ghostly melody among the struts and bracing wires and drummed against the fuselage fabric, Brown concentrated on necessary work:

My mind merely recorded the fact that we were leaving Newfoundland behind us. Otherwise, it was too tense with concentration on the task ahead to find room for any emotion or thoughts on seeing the last of the square-patterned roof-mosaic of St John's, or the tangled intimacy of Newfoundland's fields, woods and hills. Behind and below was America, far ahead and below was Europe, between the two was nearly two thousand miles of ocean. But at the time, I made no such stirring, if obvious, reflection; for my navigation instruments and charts, as applied to sun, horizon, sea-surface, and time of day, demanded my close and undivided attention.

Above: John Alcock and Arthur Whitten Brown.

Left: John Alcock, 1914. (Tony Alcock)

Name of Ship _Mauretania_ Date of Departure _May 3rd 1919_ Where bound _Halifax_

Port of Departure _Southampton_ Steamship Line **CUNARD.**

P.M. 21.

NAMES AND DESCRIPTIONS OF **BRITISH** PASSENGERS EMBARKED AT THE PORT OF _Southampton_

(1) Contract Ticket Number.	(2) NAMES OF PASSENGERS.	(3) CLASS. (Whether 1st, 2nd, or 3rd.) A. C. I.	(4) Port at which Passengers have contracted to land.	(5) Profession, Occupation, or Calling of Passengers.	(6) AGES OF PASSENGERS Adults Not accom. by husb. Children Infants	(7) Country of last Permanent Residence.	(8) Country of Intended Future Permanent Residence.
43404	Pirie Geo.	1st	Halifax	Physician	39		Canada
43683	Cartwright Kate			Housewife	46	1	
43688	" George			Child	10		
43685	Wood Herry			Merchant	37		
43719	Cockshutt Henry			Manufacturer	50	1	
43725	Alcock John			Aviator	26		
43726	Brown Arthur			Engineer	32		
43727	Lyon Robert			aircraft	42		
43728	Montgomery Gordon			Geo.	24		
43729	Dicker Robert			Fitter	26		
43730	Black Harry			Joiner	51		
43731	Pitman Ernest			Contractor	41		
43732	Hunn Fred			Joiner	33		
43733	Davis Sidney			Engineer	41		
5485	Portlock Percy			Buyer	33		
43710	Burnside Josephine			Housewife	53		
	Johnston Eleanor			Spinster	48		
		16 1			33 1 / 15 / 2		

Alcock, Brown, Bob Dicker and the Vimy construction team signed aboard the Halifax-bound _Mauretania_, 3 May 1919. (Shane Joyce)

Opposite:

Top: St John's in ruins after the 1892 fire. (S.H. Parsons)

Centre: Lester's Field before the arrival of transatlantic fliers.

Bottom: Symonds Field farm, St John's, part of Alcock and Brown's take-off area. (Robert Symonds)

Above: Pioneer Harriet Quimby, the first woman to fly the English Channel in 1912.

Left: Blue Bird Restaurant, Brooklands, a cauldron of debate for a young John Alcock and fellow aviators.

First to bridge the Atlantic in stages over eleven days, the U.S. Navy's NC-4 piloted by Commander Albert C. Read takes off from Trepassey Bay, Newfoundland.

First Vimy test flight at Quidi Vidi, 9 June 1919.

Right: Harry Hawker's Sopwith Atlantic, from which its crew were rescued after a mid–ocean forced landing.

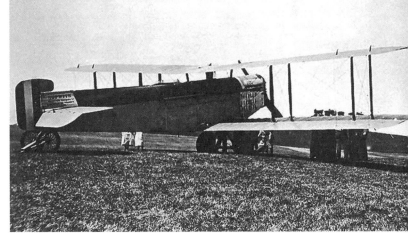

Below: Freddy Raynham prepares his Martinsyde Raymor.

Above: Crowds await Alcock and Brown's take-off from Lester's Field.

Left: Alcock hands Brown the first transatlantic mailbag before take-off.

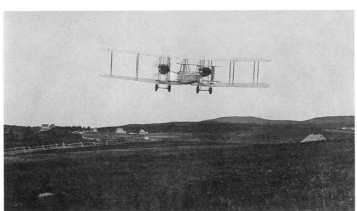

Above: Lt Clements affixes the Royal Aero Club seal to the Vimy. (Robert Holloway)

Left: The Vimy takes off, next stop Europe.

A Heavily-laden Vimy fights to gain height. (Robert Holloway)

The Vimy lands in Derrygimla bog, Connemara.

The stranded Vimy.

Many locals came to view the 'plane that had conquered the mighty Atlantic.

Clifden Marconi Station's wireless room, which relayed news of the fliers' arrival around the world.

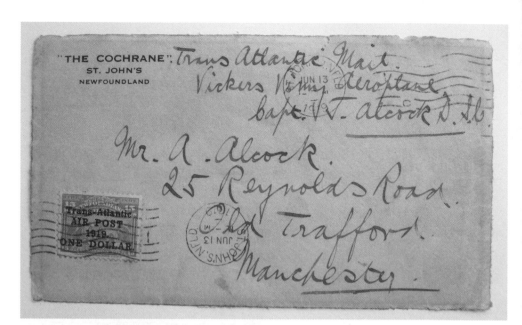

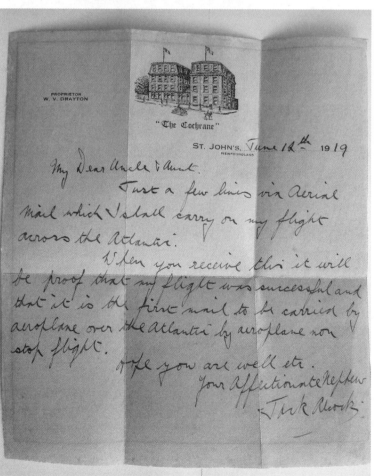

The first air mail letter carried across the Atlantic by John Alcock. (Virginia and Alan Payne)

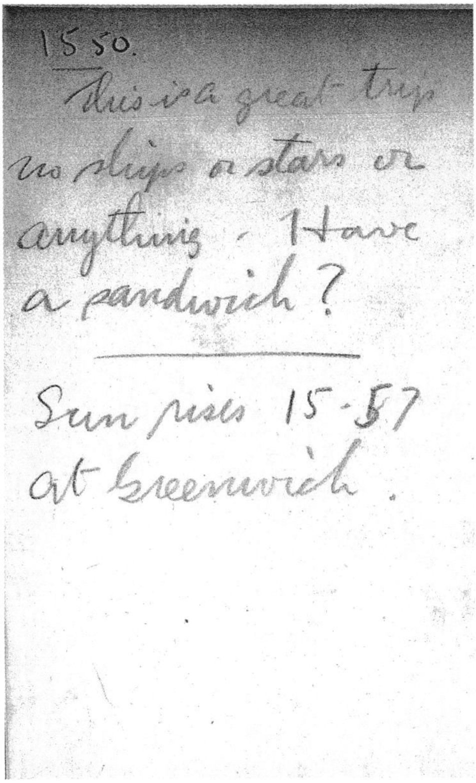

15.50.

This is a great trip
no ships or stars or
anything. Have
a sandwich?

Sun rises 15.57
at Greenwich.

The broken exhaust made conversation impossible. Log book directions written by Brown for Alcock during their flight.

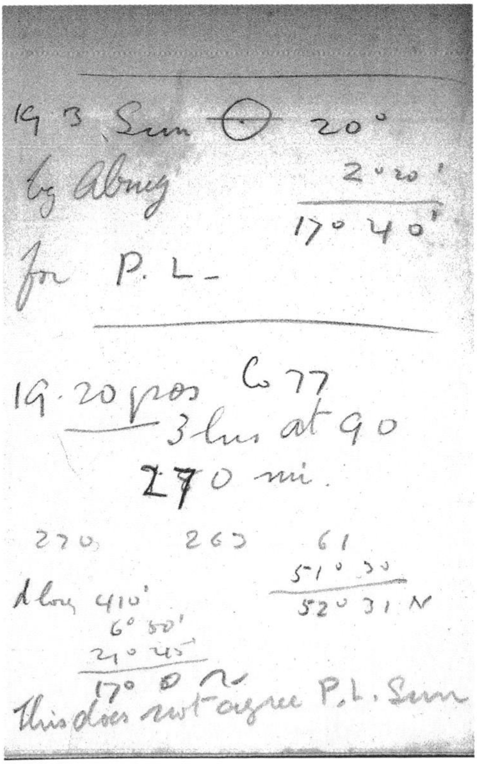

19 3 Sun ⊙ 20°
by Abney   2°20'
              17°40'
for P.L_

19.20 pos ⌐77
      3 hrs at 90
      270 mi.

270   263   61
                5-1°30
Δ log 410'   52°31 N
      6°50'
      2°45'
      17° 0
this does not agree P.L. Sun

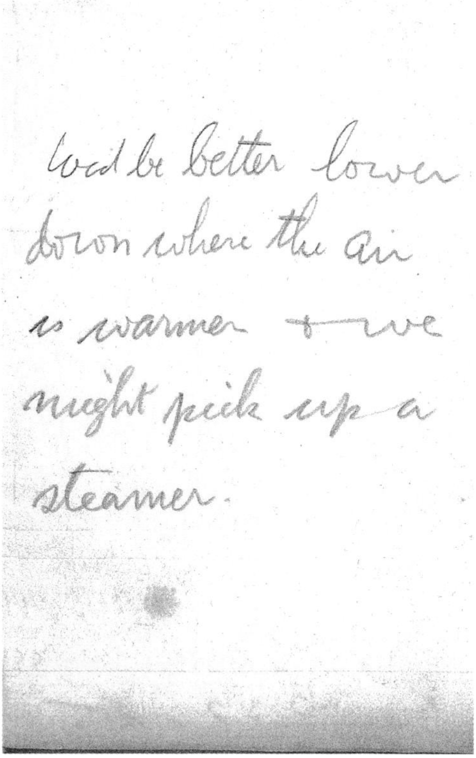

wd be better lower
down where the air
is warmer + we
might pick up a
steamer.

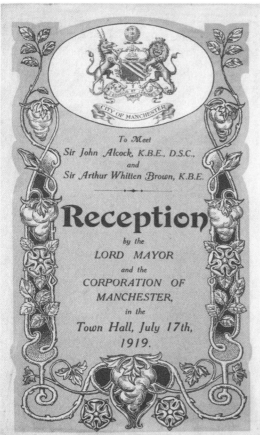

Above: Alcock and Brown are greeted at the Vickers works at Brooklands.

Left: Cover of the civic reception programme for Alcock and Brown, Town Hall, Manchester, 17 July 1919. (RuthAS via WikimediaCommons)

Alcock and Brown with Brown's fiancée, Kathleen Kennedy, Vimy designer Rex Pierson (left) and works manager, Bob Knight. (Tony Alcock)

Alcock and Brown after the flight with some of their Vickers Vimy team. Brown was rarely without a stick following his First World War crash. (Tony Alcock)

A monument on Ballinaboy Hill points to the Vimy's 1919 landing site. (Smb1001 via WikimediaCommons)

Above left: The sculpture of Alcock and Brown that was unveiled at London Heathrow Airport in 1954. (Adrian Pingstone)

Above right: Modern view of St John's Harbour, across which Alcock and Brown flew after starting their flight near the centre hill ridge.

Above: St John's airport plaque to Alcock and Brown.

Left: Major Scott, Lieutenant Arthur Whitten Brown, Captain Alcock, Haus des Glockenspiels in der Böttcherstraße, Bremen. (Bernhard Hoetger CC.2.0)

Arthur Whitten Brown relaxing in the 1940s.

The author examining Brown's navigation chart at London's RAF library.

The late Harry Symonds (seated), who witnessed Alcock and Brown's take-off from Lester's Field. (Robert Symonds)

Harry Sullivan, Clifden's last witness to Alcock and Brown's 15 June 1919 arrival, chats with Margie Lynch.

Steve Fossett and Mark Rebholz prepare to re-enact Alcock and Brown's flight, 2005. (Gary J. Hebbard)

The author (right) with Flier John Dodd in the Vimy in which Steve Fossett re-enacted the Atlantic flight in 2005.

10

THE VIMY LOSES RADIO AND EXHAUST

◆◇◆

As we droned our isolated way eastward and upward, nothing could be seen outside the cockpit, except the inner struts, the engines and the red-glowing vapour ejected through the exhaust pipes.

Arthur Whitten Brown

◆◇◆

As soon as the aeroplane was out of sight, Lt Clements dispatched his official cable to the Royal Aero Club in London: 'Captain Alcock and Lieutenant Brown left St John's, Newfoundland, in a Vickers Vimy machine on a flight to England today, June 14th, at 4.13 GMT.' This was a minute later than the time Brown recorded in his log, in which the hours would likewise be expressed in terms of Greenwich Mean Time (which, with summer time adjustment, was two hours thirty-one minutes ahead of Newfoundland time).

The Admiralty Station at Mount Pearl informed all ships equipped with wireless on the Atlantic to watch out for the aeroplane, whose call signal was DKG. Fred Memory forwarded an equally urgent report to the *Daily Mail*: 'The Vimy on its Way. Brown Flying to His Bride.' But, after all Lord Northcliffe's endeavours, the choice of a Saturday take-off could not be worse for the *Mail*, which had no Sunday edition. The paper's reporters were already *in situ* in Ireland, where they had primed coastguards to alert them of any aeroplane sightings. But there was only a skeleton staff on duty at Carmelite House in Fleet Street. Depending on the Vimy's arrival, the *Mail* would surely be scooped by rival media.

Reaching the coast, Brown unwound the wireless cable by his side. As it rolled free in the air beneath him he wondered how effective the radio would be. The American flying boats had experienced many problems with their equipment. With little inclination now to study the icebergs, he tapped out what he thought would be the first of many messages to Mount Pearl: 'All well and started.'

Brown remembered his father's excitement as he told him about the laying of the first transatlantic cable in 1858. How greatly communications had developed since that courier who sped from Marathon to Athens in 490 BC, or the Chappe brothers' semaphores of 1790s France. And how quickly even the cable had been overtaken by the new 'wire-less' system. This was proving itself on ships and was surely the means of future communications, but it was still far from being practical for aircraft, particularly over longer distances and ocean crossings. And, as Alcock had hinted more than once, the uncertain wireless was still as heavy as it was bulky!

The navigator took his pencil and, ignoring the engine noise and the occasional tug of the slipstream, concentrated on his first log book entry:

GMT 4.28. Lat 47.30. Long 52.30. GS [ground speed] 120mph. AS [air speed] 70. Wind 30. Height 1,100 feet. RPM 1750. Engine Temperatures – Port 85, Starboard 85. Remarks: Wind strong and gusting. Heavy bumps, taking off and climbing. Port engine started 3.55, starboard 4.05. Took off 4.12. Left land on course 4.28. Low clouds. Sent message to BZM.
[BZM was the Mount Pearl Admiralty Station's call sign.]

Message sent, the navigator looked over the side of the cockpit. Gone was the spectacular blue he had noticed on their first Newfoundland trial. The ocean looked darker, more sullen, and contrasted sharply with the brilliant whiteness of the icebergs. Its foam-enfolded trawlers were diminishing toy boats. What a harsh life those fishermen endured, combing the freezing waters day after day, at risk of storms and the ubiquitous bergs. Death from hypothermia awaited anyone who slipped overboard from a heaving deck.

Even at colder altitude and with the engine din and the buffeting, Alcock and Brown's Vimy seemed a cosier and safer haven. Their boots and coats protected them from the incessant draughts common to all early cockpits. The wind whistled through the struts and wires, but the modest height of the fairing and windscreen shielded both men from its force. Their helmets protected the tops of their heads, which were in the slipstream. The fur gloves and electrically heated suits further cosseted them. The adjacent throbbing engines suggested additional warmth.

As he settled himself for their long flight, Alcock reflected on how lucky they were that all their rivals had dropped out. They now only had the Handley Page to contend with. If she had not left before them, they were certainly in with a chance of beating his former pupil, Brackley, and his crew. And, as he later related to Bob Dicker, how much more flexible the Vickers team had proved compared with what one observer had called 'Kerr's committee'. But that was the way flying seemed to be going now. It was becoming more technical, more expensive and involved many more people. Suits would probably soon replace oily overalls. There would be no scope for individuality, everyone would be part of a team. The days of Santos-Dumont, Farman, the Wright brothers and the spectacular Cody constructing and flying their own aeroplanes were now past. They were real fliers. He remembered building that scout biplane at Mudros. How lucky he was to have this Atlantic opportunity.

Engine noise made conversation impossible. Pilot and navigator attempted to communicate through the throat microphones and earpieces in their fur caps, but Alcock discarded his earpieces as they were uncomfortable. With the exhausts so close the two men could only communicate by gestures and scribbled notes. Jammed tight beside Alcock, Brown found that his flying coat limited every movement, particularly when he swivelled around for his preliminary checks of the rpm and petrol-overflow gauges. He would have a struggle with his chart and instruments. The restricted space of the St John's cinema seats suddenly seemed expansive. For how many hours would he be confined to this much sparser bench in the sky?

The first hour of flight was uneventful, but Alcock had to work at the controls to counter the frequent gusts. Occasional downdraughts made both men feel as if their seat was about to drop out from under them. The Vimy was no longer the feather-light machine of the test flights. How sluggishly she now responded with all that fuel. How on earth would the bigger Handley Page cope, despite her superior engine power? Alcock wondered if their rival had yet taken off. That following wind would surely negate the speed differential and favour the Vimy.

Clumps of Capuchin-like cloud, white with dark shadows on the water below, started to infiltrate the comparatively clear sky. It seemed odd that cloud shadows should make a land-like impression on the water but, on land, looked like pools of water. They encroached slowly at first and, through the ceiling, Brown could observe speeding patches of blue sky. Sunshine escaped to glint off the Vimy's wingtips and lighten the water below. In case the clouds thickened, the navigator wisely decided to make an observation: 'The Baker navigating machine with the chart lay on my knees. I knelt on the seat, and made haste to take observations on the sea, the horizon and the sun, through intervals in the covering of clouds.'

As Brown had earlier explained to reporters, wind drift and the aeroplane's superior speed ensured that aerial navigation was infinitely more complicated than its maritime counterpart. Directional wireless navigation was undoubtedly the system of the future but not yet practicable for ocean voyages. Hence his decision to rely on traditional Dead Reckoning (DR), which ensured that his side of the cockpit resembled a mathematician's den. He had adapted the normal navigational tools to his own special aerial requirements:

My sextant was of the ordinary marine type, although it had a more heavily engraved scale than is usual, so as to make its reading easier amid the vibrations of the aeroplane. My main chart was on the Mercator projection, and I had a special transparent chart which could be moved above it, and upon which were drawn the Summer circles for all times of the day. I took with me a similar chart for use at night, giving the Summer circles for six chosen stars. To measure the drift, I had a 6-inch Drift-Bearing plate. Besides its ordinary use, this enabled me to measure the ground speed, with the help of a stop-watch.

In addition, I carried an Appleyard course and distance calculator, and also Traverse tables for the calculation of 'dead reckoning'. As the horizon is often obscured by clouds or mist, making impossible the measurement of its angle with the heavenly bodies, I had a special type of spirit level, on which the horizon was replaced by a bubble. The bubble of course was less reliable than a true horizon, being affected by variations of speed, but it was at least a safeguard.

Brown's early observations proved wise. The fleeting sunshine and its encouraging brightness soon disappeared. Finally there was only the odd island of water down a funnel of obstinate cloud. The Vimy headed into an immense bank of fog. They hoped it would just as quickly exit the other side, but, to the contrary, the cloud thickened until the sky was completely obscured. The sea became a dull grey. Soon, it too disappeared entirely from view. Where was Lt Clements's clear weather? Suspended between an imperceptible sky and an equally invisible ocean, the Vimy crew were floating in a damp and eerie no-man's-land. Only the constantly eddying slipstream told them that they were moving forward. Brown reached for his log again just before 3 p.m. (Newfoundland time) and recorded that air speed was 70, height 1,500ft, latitude 47.52°, longtitude 50°. He noted plaintively: 'Impossible to get observation of sun – between fog and high clouds.'

Fifty degrees west. The navigator recalled the *Titanic's* last recorded position on 15 April 1912: latitude 41.44°, longitude 50.25°W. What a brave wireless operator Phillips had been, sending out messages until the ship took him to the bottom of the ocean. Whatever problems Alcock and he might experience with the clouds, at least they were free of icebergs and the other hazards of the water below. The deaths of 1,500 people in those freezing seas was hard to comprehend. And the *Titanic* was not the only local disaster. The steamship *Atlantic,* also built by Harland & Wolff, had sunk off Halifax in April 1873 with the loss of over 500 souls. East of foggy Father Point in Quebec, only five years ago, the *Empress of Ireland* had collided with a Norwegian coal ship and over 1,000 had perished. And people spoke about flying being dangerous. Perhaps the air would one day provide a safer travel environment? In machines that would not, hopefully, oscillate and roll as their Vimy did.

Brown soon had a rude reminder that the era of safe flying was not yet at hand. His problem with visibility was compounded by an unforeseen mechanical mishap. His instinct not to rely entirely upon wireless was rudely endorsed as he attempted to transmit a message. There was no power; the generator on the lower port wing was not working. The wind buffeted the navigator's head as he leaned over the side of the cockpit and looked down. No wonder the generator had failed, its little wind-driven impeller was nowhere to be seen. It had sheared off and fallen into the sea, fortunately without damaging the wing or rigging.

Although Brown could still receive messages, he would no longer be able to transmit. It seemed ironic that one of his earlier worries had been that the generator would supply too much power and burn out the wireless. The demise of the machine after only seventy minutes also meant that their electrical suits would soon grow cold, not a cheerful prospect in the clammy cloud and with the long evening and night ahead of them. They had been right to discard the Vimy's running lights, which would have absorbed even more power.

The navigator scribbled a note and held it up for Alcock to read: 'Wireless generator smashed – the propeller has gone.' Brown never found out why the generator impeller failed. It was one of the few mistakes made by the crew who had so swiftly and capably assembled the Vimy. Years later, W.J. Richards recalled:

The machine failed because of the failure of a screw. The propeller was fastened to the generator spindle. At the boss, the centre of the prop, there was one screw which had to be tightened on to the spindle. When it was reassembled for the final time, someone just mounted the prop on the spindle but forgot to tighten the grub screw. That was why the generator failed, though knowing what Alcock thought about the wireless, I'd say it didn't bother him in the least!

Richards was correct. It would take more than such a mishap to disturb the pilot's equilibrium. Alcock only gave an ironic smile as he held on to the control wheel, his eyes never wavering from compass and invisible horizon. Disappointed that the wireless on which he had worked so hard would now be of little use, Brown wound in the redundant aerial. He remembered a flier returning from patrol in France who had forgotten to do this. As he passed over a group of officers preparing evening tea, the lead weight on the cable's end had caught their trestle table, plucked it into the air and scattered delph in all directions. But it had not been the pilot's fault. The 120ft cable had wrapped itself around the fuselage when he had dived to escape German fighters. Nonetheless, new orders were posted: 'Before engaging enemy aircraft or returning to the aerodrome, particular care must be taken to rewind aerials to avoid danger to, or dis-organisation of, ground staff.'

As Brown well knew, Alcock had long doubted the potential of the newfangled wireless. While the navigator implicitly trusted his pilot, Alcock in turn had every confidence in Brown's navigation, with or without wireless direction or weather forecasts. He showed no emotion as he acknowledged Brown's additional note, which explained: 'I can't get any obs in this fog. Will estimate that same wind holds and work on DR.'

With sky and sea no longer visible, the pair were now flying blind. They were flying on faith alone and Brown's navigation, in a dank and forbid-ding world traversed by none before but Hawker and Mackenzie-Grieve. The wind gusted and the nose of the Vimy continually swayed from the right direction. Alcock had to make rapid allowances for the deviations. Both men accustomed themselves to the damp and gloom. They had known well in advance that fog and cloud would be part of the menu, and how much better to be on their way, even in fog, than facing another delay or the perils of take-off. Brown would acknowledge later that the loss of wireless transmission even added a certain sense of finality to the adventure. The insistent hum of the engines also made the solitude seem more normal:

> The long flight would have been dreadful, had we made it in silence; for, shut off as we were from sea and sky, it was a very lonely affair. The spreading fog enveloped the Vimy so closely that our sheltered cockpit suggested an isolated but by no means cheerless room.

The engines' reassuring hum was, however, about to change its tone. The fliers were to face a further character test. Shortly after 3.30 the starboard motor startled them with a loud clattering noise. Both men instantly recalled the drama of Hawker and Mackenzie-Grieve. Was an engine problem also going to force them down, so early into their flight? The navigator thought of their life-saving suits, which had been delivered to the Bank of Montreal and mistakenly stored as typewriters.

Brown looked across to the right over Alcock's shoulder, and immediately saw the problem. A section of exhaust pipe had split away from the engine. It turned red hot, then white, and started to melt before his eyes. Diverted flame from the exhaust played directly on to one of the bracing wires and turned it red. If Alcock throttled back the engine it would probably reduce the fiery tongue, but it would also cost them valuable altitude.

Brown watched anxiously, but, before the wire melted, the pipe broke away. The navigator feared it would damage the fuselage as it fell. Luckily the slipstream took it well clear and it whirled down towards the invisible sea. The wire soon regained its metallic colour, but a slight flame remained and would pursue them all the way to Ireland. The incident was a sudden reminder of their vulnerability. Would the loss of the exhaust pipe section reduce the engine power?

The navigator sharpened his hearing as he had done at this altitude during the war. But there was no frightening vibration, nothing to denote the engine failure that had nearly killed William Allcock and himself in France. The motor continued to function perfectly, but the noise was almost unbearable. The racket of the cylinders venting straight into the air beside them deafened the two men. As with the weather, they did not allow this additional handicap to intimidate them. Brown recalled:

> The chattering swelled into a loud, jerky thrum, much more prominent than the normal noise of a Rolls-Royce aero engine. This settled down to a steady and continuous roar. Until we had landed nothing could be done to the broken exhaust pipe, and we had to accept it as a minor disaster, unpleasant but irremediable. Very soon my ears had become so accustomed to the added clamour that it passed unnoticed.

Fretting over the impossibility of making observations, Brown checked the interior and exterior gauges and pencilled another entry in his log book at 3.49 Newfoundland time: '6.20 GMT. AS 65. Height 2,000. Lat 48.16. Long 47. GS 120mph. Clouds above and below. Readings impossible.' He followed this with a note to Alcock: '6hrs more daylight and we must then be sure of clear sky.'

Alcock urged the Vimy into a gentle ascent. Moisture condensed on Brown's goggles and on the wires, dials and switches as the aeroplane climbed. If Harriet Quimby could cope with these conditions, so could they. What a courageous woman, one of the earliest to fly in America, as well as the first woman to cross the English Channel. The Michigan lady had no sooner left England than she had also run into a bank of fog, which she finally only cleared by rising to 6,000ft. She was one of the few who knew exactly what they were now experiencing. And how accurately she had described it: 'The fog quickly surrounded me, like a cold, wet, grey blanket. The mist felt like tiny needles on my skin.'

Despite the conditions, Alcock disdained the use of goggles. Brown used his only when leaning over the side of the cockpit to take observations. Shortly after 4 o'clock they broke clear of the clouds at 2,000ft, but there was no hoped-for sun. Only another impenetrable bank about 3,000ft above them. Brown congratulated himself on having taken that early observation, as the Vimy continued in a sea of nothingness. They were sandwiched between the clouds, guided only by the navigator's dead reckoning.

At 5 o'clock Brown reached back to the cupboard for their own sand-wiches. He passed one to Alcock with some chocolate and uncorked the Thermos flask. The pilot made use of only one hand for eating and drink-ing, keeping the other constantly on the wheel. Throughout the journey the pair were to have no regular meals. Although they frequently took something to drink, they never experienced hunger and ate only when they felt like it.

Brown became anxious for further observations. After they had eaten, he reassured Alcock that the starboard engine temperature was back to normal and he pencilled a reminder: 'If you get above clouds we will get a good fix tonight and hope for clear weather tomorrow. Not at any risky expense to engines though. We have four hours yet to climb.' The pilot nodded and the Vimy climbed steadily; 3.000ft, 4,000ft. But the increased altitude brought no respite from the gloom. How far higher must they go to see the sky? The navigator made another log book entry at 5.50: 'AS 65. Height 4,300. Lat 48.54. Long 42.32. Total time 3' 52'. Too cloudy for drift observation.'

Brown listened to the wireless, as the receiver was still working. Across the ether he suddenly heard a message. Maybe the Handley Page? It was not for the Vimy, but it was an encouragement nonetheless. A sign that there was life out there, somewhere far below or behind them. How dif-ferent flying over water was. With no sea or landmarks to observe, it was hard to gauge their speed. But with that generous tailwind they were already over 400 miles into their journey. America was now well behind them; there was no going back. They were heading towards their home continent. Although it was only weeks, it seemed a lifetime since they had left Europe.

The navigator was further cheered to think that waiting for him in England was his bride-to-be, Kathleen Kennedy. He wondered if she had heard of their departure. He had had no choice but to postpone their marriage. Soon that disappointment would be merely an entertain-ing anecdote. Flying to meet his fiancée; not many people had enjoyed that privilege! He remembered essayist Joseph Addison's forecast of the romantic advantages of aviation:

Flying would give such occasions for intrigues as people cannot meet with who have nothing but legs to carry them. You should have a couple of lovers make a midnight assignation upon the top of the Monument, and see the cupola of St Paul's covered with both sexes like the outside of a pigeon-house. Nothing would be more frequent than to see a beau flying in at a garret window, or a gallant giving chase to his mistress, like a hawk after a lark.

Shortly after 6 o'clock the Vimy unexpectedly nosed through a gap in the upper layer of clouds. After four long hours of unsighted flying, the evening magically brightened. How like France the sky suddenly seemed, as it evoked memories of wartime homecomings through curtains of bright rain. At last there was the opportunity for an observation. Brown quickly reached for his instruments, but the welcome following sunshine almost blinded him as it flooded their craft, casting its shadow on to the clouds ahead. As the ghost aeroplane expanded and contracted on the shifting and distorting vapour, Brown put his instruments to work. He did not know it, but ten minutes was all he had.

I got my observations while kneeling on the seat and looking between the port wings. I was obliged to bring the spirit level into play, as the horizon was invisible, and the sextant could not be used. The calculations showed that if we were still on the right course the machine would be further east than was indicated by 'dead reckoning'. From this I deduced that the strength of the wind must have increased rather than fallen off, as had been prophesied in the report of the meteorological expert at St John's. The supposition was borne out by the buffetings which, from time to time, swayed the Vimy.

Brown celebrated their speed with an underlined '143 knots!!!' note that he showed to Alcock. But no sooner had the navigator completed his task than dense cloud once again blotted out the sun. Glimpses of patches of sea tantalised Brown, but not for long enough to permit fresh observations. For these he would have to wait almost another four hours. They were now at just over 4,000ft. Immobile as ever, Alcock stared straight ahead, alert for any deviation by the aeroplane. Still concerned about their position, Brown nudged him with another note to say that he thought they must be further east and south than he had calculated. Alcock climbed steadily, but at 5,000ft the cloud remained resolutely dense. It was noticeably cooler at this altitude. Remembering the non-charging battery, Brown reminded Alcock to use only two of the three 'hands, feet, and body' variables of his heated flying suit.

Dusk encroached prematurely and intensified the enveloping gloom. What a forbidding nothingness it was. Cloud to the left, cloud to the right, cloud below, cloud above. The light between the layers of cloying vapour waned. The exhaust flame assumed a cheekier presence. Concerned about his calculations, the navigator pencilled another request at 7 o'clock: 'Can you get above these clouds at, say, 60 deg? We must get stars as soon as possible.'

Alcock nodded, and continued to climb. Twilight gradually over-came them. Within half an hour they were in complete darkness. Brown recalled balloonist Thomas Monck Mason's account of a similar night flight: 'We could scarcely avoid the impression that we were cleaving our way though an interminable mass of black marble.' The luminous glow of the instruments came to life, before Brown switched on the tiny bulb that illuminated the compass. He used the electric torch to read the outside gauges and the chart spread on his knees.

It was 8 o'clock as they sped into the night far from the sight of fellow men, and apparently equally remote from any possibility of fixing their position. Brown noted in his log book: 'Lat 50.23. Long 32.00. Dense clouds below and above. No observations and DR apparently out. Could not observe sunset. Will await checks by stars.'

The clouds grew more opaque as they flew through the void without respite from the raucous starboard exhaust. The darkness was a new expe-rience for Brown. He hoped that he could cope with its disconcerting challenge. While Alcock's gaze was resolutely horizontal, the navigator constantly peered aloft for a sight of those elusive stars.

Few aviators knew either the loneliness or demands of night flying. Subsequent Atlantic flier Charles Lindbergh described its challenges in his book *The Spirit of St Louis*:

By day, or on a cloudless night, a pilot may drink the wine of the gods, but it has an earthly taste; he's a god of the earth, like one of the Grecian deities who lives on worldly mountains and descended for intercourse with men. But at night, over a stratus layer, all sense of the planet may disappear. You know that down below, beneath that heavenly blanket is the earth, factual and hard. But it's an intellectual knowledge; it's a knowledge tucked away in the mind; not a feeling that penetrates the body. And if at times you renounce experience and mind's heavy logic, it seems that the world has rushed along on its orbit, leaving you alone flying above a forgotten cloud bank, somewhere in the solitude of interstellar space.

11

NOTHING BUT CLOUD

I do not think that either of us had any thought of what we were flying over, being merely intent on getting the machine across. There was no sense of remoteness, we were just too keen on our work.

John Alcock

Back in Newfoundland, news of Alcock and Brown's departure reached Harbour Grace two hours after their Vimy had crossed Signal Hill. The adjustments to the Handley Page radiators were not completed until one hour later, at 5 o'clock. Adm. Kerr and his crew were forced to acknowledge that, even if they risked leaving now, they would not be able to overhaul their nimble rival. Reluctantly, they agreed to postpone their Atlantic attempt until the arrival of four larger radiators, which were due from England. It was a bitter blow after all their early preparation and hard work. Now, like the rest of the world, they could only bide their time and see how Alcock and Brown fared.

Stirred by the Vimy's take-off, spectators debated excitedly at Lester's Field. How had Alcock lifted off that aeroplane with such a load? Could he and Brown really cross the ocean to Europe – and in one day? What courageous men they were, flying into the unknown. The spectators had witnessed something special, but they were fearful for the outcome. They gradually drifted away. Bob Dicker and his companions tidied the field and collected their belongings. For the first time in weeks the old Buick stood silent and neglected. Soon it was as if the Big Top had left town. Lester's Field was left to the gusting wind and the freed horses. They regained their territory and stampeded happily across its open undulating space.

After eating a well-deserved dinner, Percy Muller, Dicker, and the Vickers team decamped to the Admiralty Station. They waited anxiously for news, hoping to catch regular progress reports from Alcock and Brown. Unaware that the wireless generator had failed, they paced up and down the station floor. It was a fruitless experience. They heard that the Handley Page had not taken off, but how could they tell the non-communicating Vimy crew? Despite the frustrating silence they were confident that their men were safely on course. Most of the team had been on their feet for almost forty hours. They finally trudged back to their hotel. They had done their best, it was now all up to the fliers.

The radio silence also worried Alcock and Brown's many local supporters. The St John's and Cape Race wireless stations maintained a ceaseless vigil without result. The steamers *Faraday* and *Mackay Bennett*, which were repairing cables between 80 and 250 miles offshore in the Vimy's projected path, likewise reported no sighting. The SS *Digby* docked just before midnight and was besieged by a huge crowd. Its final 100 miles had been right under the Vimy's planned early route. Among its passengers was Lt Charles Biddlecombe, Freddy Raynham's new navigator, and Maj. Fiske of the Boulton and Paul Company. The ship also brought new radiators for the beleaguered Handley Page. But the crowd was disappointed to hear that the *Digby*'s crew had not spotted the Vimy. The captain explained that they had been in fog for much of the time. He and his crew had kept a sharp lookout, but they had neither seen nor heard the aeroplane. They had also transmitted numerous messages to which the fliers did not respond. It was the captain's opinion that the Vimy's wireless was malfunctioning.

While some thought that Lt Brown was simply too busy to send messages, concern inevitably grew for the safety of the fliers. Aware of the Vimy's earlier transmitter problems, others surmised that the newfangled radio had indeed failed. The Sopwith crew had had the same problem. But many feared that the aircraft had come down in the sea. They recalled the ditching of Hawker and Mackenzie-Grieve, whose lives had only been saved by the last-chance sighting of a ship. Such good fortune was unlikely to recur. Whatever their opinions, like the Vickers staff, the late-night crowd could now only wait and hope.

Brown's wait for those elusive stars was equally trying. Now attuned to Greenwich Mean Time, he noted in his log book at 11.20 (8.49 Newfoundland time) that they were still climbing to get above the clouds for a star fix. The engines never missed a beat as Alcock coaxed the aeroplane to over 5,000ft, but the clouds both above and below them remained dense, with only an occasional lightening of the upper layer. Brown noted: 'Nothing could be seen outside the cockpit, except the inner struts, the engines, the red-glowing vapour ejected through the exhaust pipes, and portions of the wing surface, which glistened faintly in the moon-glimmer.'

They continued to climb. Midnight approached, and passed. Fitful moonlight added a ghostly luminosity to the Vimy's wings and fuselage as they reached 6,000ft. This was their highest altitude so far, and appreciably colder. How fortunate the navigator's favourite nature poet, Wordsworth, had been on those cloudless Lake District crags, when he had mused on navigation:

Chaldean shepherds, ranging trackless fields
Beneath the concave of unclouded skies
Spread like a sea, in boundless solitude,
Looked on the pole star, as on a guide
And guardian of their course, that never closed
His steadfast eye.

Dispiritingly, instead of a Pole Star sighting, the Vimy pair found yet a third layer of cloud several thousand feet higher. They continued to climb. Suddenly, to Brown's delight, he observed that the new layer was much less dense than the previous clouds. Focusing his eager eyes, he managed to see some stars. He grabbed his instruments and renewed his vigil. At 12.17 (9.46 Newfoundland time) he finally spotted a gap, and there were

Vega and the Pole Star glowing brilliantly to the north-east! Using the stars and a cloud horizon, he quickly used the sextant to fix their position. They were at latitude 50° and 7', longitude 31° west, only slightly to the south of their planned course. He passed a note to Alcock: 'Air Speed 106. 850 miles. Half Way!!! South of course. Alter to 110 degrees.' He followed the note with a celebratory hot coffee from the faithful Thermos. Who needed batteries?

Alcock marvelled at how smoothly the engines continued to run. With that broken exhaust to starboard over his head, the din was still terrific, but high as he urged the Vimy, its motors never missed a beat. The Rolls-Royce Eagle was definitely the right choice, but how about those other vitals, the Claudel-Hobson carburettor and the Watford magneto? How well these also were standing up to the trials of the damp and variable weather. If he had not experienced these conditions he would not have believed that there was such cloud over the Atlantic. Hawker and Mackenzie-Grieve had also encountered fog and cloud, but it had not been on this scale. With the growing reliability of engines and aeroplanes, it seemed that the weather was now the only remaining obstacle to oceanic flight. He hoped that next time he flew this way there would be some means of more accurate forecasting. But how lucky they were to have that following wind! All the time it was blowing them closer to Ireland. It would be an entirely different story had the wind been in the opposite direction. Then they would have had the additional worry of running out of fuel, and over the Atlantic was not a place for that to happen.

Brown was relieved that his navigation had been accurate so far. His only miscalculation had been due to the incorrect forecast, which had underestimated the strength of the following wind. Alcock had suggested that the flight would take them up to twenty hours. Should the wind maintain its present speed, they would reach Ireland three or four hours earlier. It was an encouraging thought. Pleased with their progress, the navigator took stock. Having succeeded in making a sighting, he agreed with Alcock that there was no further need to climb, but what a struggle it had been to find those stars. The persistent cloud suggested he would have difficulty with future sightings.

Equally impressed with Brown's navigation, the pilot nursed his constant engines by descending gently. He was not a man to take unnecessary chances. Ever since his youthful silk-and-bamboo balloons and model aeroplanes he had learned to understand and care for his machines. Like Brown, he wondered what the Vickers team were doing now. Without their skill and commitment, Brown and he would not have come so far. It was frustrating not to be able to communicate with them. But if flying had taught him anything, it had taught him the virtue of patience and self-reliance. Their crew in St John's would have to contain themselves.

On they roared into the night that was now early morning. The engine tumult no longer discomfited them. Alcock reflected that the Vimy had reached the point at which Hawker and Mackenzie-Grieve had come to grief, latitude 50.20° north, longitude 29.30° west. What an achievement to bring the Sopwith down among the unpredictable waves and so close to that ship. Hawker had a great reputation, and that descent showed why. The Aussie and he would have a lot to talk about when they next met at Brooklands. Brooklands! Was it really only six weeks ago that Brown and he had left? Steaming to an unknown country on that ocean way down there. And now they had covered half the week-long journey in less than half a day. It might be the fastest liner afloat, but the *Mauretania* was no match for their Vimy. The aeroplane age was at hand!

Brooklands was his favourite part of the world. How his life had opened up when he first arrived there as a young mechanic. Seven years ago already? How lucky he had been to get that break with old Ducrocq with the funny accent. The man had taught him everything about tuning an aero engine. And then the other Frenchman, Coatalen, and his Sunbeam motor. He would have liked to have tried those racing cars. He would never forget the wind in his hair and the sensation of speed as, chest to the tank, he roared over the bumps and banking of the Brooklands track on Bob Dicker's motorbike. 'With those sharp eyes and your understanding of machinery, you'd make a great driver,' Dicker had coaxed. But neither the racing cars nor bikes offered anything like the thrill of flying and the joy of soaring above England's green fields. The wide open air also offered a greater recovery margin than a narrow track. As he had told Bob Dicker, you could not loop the loop in a racing car. He remembered fearless Bob's retort: 'You can, Jack – and I could show you the marks.'

When the war came he had enjoyed training young pilots. But it had been no substitute for the camaraderie of the workshop and the earlier schools, and the beer-fuelled arguments with the likes of Hawker and Raynham, all of them reeking of oil after a hard day's flying. All through his imprisonment he had dreamt of getting back to Brooklands. How fortunate he had been to be able to return there immediately he was demobbed. But it had changed. Many of his friends had not survived the war; much of the fun had gone. The aeroplane factories now seemed more professional, and competition had bred secrecy, but his disappointment had ebbed smartly when Vickers offered him the transatlantic Vimy. He had been lucky once again. And now, according to Brown, they had covered almost half the distance to Europe. What an aeroplane! Which meant that they had almost another 1,000 miles to fly. He must concentrate on his work. He felt at home now in the Vimy, but, like a wayward horse, she required a tight rein. Occasional gusts on the ailerons threatened to snatch the control wheel from his grasp.

He envied Brown, who was not a slave to the controls as he was. The navigator could move about and juggle his instruments and clap his gloves any time he felt chilled. He could only risk an occasional flexing of his arms and legs. Alcock admired people who worked and constructed things. He did not set as much store by books as Brown did. But though he might recite poetry, Brown was certainly a professional. He knew the stars in real life as well as in verse. And he was as enthusiastic as he was courageous. Alcock had heard him discussing navigation at Mount Pearl, just as animatedly as Hawker and he had debated engine revs and stalling angles. Brown knew his stuff.

The navigator noted in his log book at 2.20 a.m. (11.49 Newfoundland time) that they were now at 'Latitude 50.49, Longitude 26.15. Horizon too indefinite to get any good readings.' Ten minutes later the Vimy had descended to 3,600ft. As they were flying so far north and against the Earth's revolution, it would not be long before the sun rose again. Kathleen was waking up to the new dawn somewhere there ahead of them, and, lucky her, probably to a clear sky. He wondered if she had got his letter. 'I'll try to time our arrival so that we can drive straight to the Registry [sic] office.'

The fitful moon occasionally bathed the Vimy and played on the constantly changing clouds. How many lonely mariners the moon had superintended over aeons, but few like Alcock and himself! After reading Jules Verne's *From the Earth to the Moon* as a child, Brown had wondered if the intrepid Impey Barbicane and his friends were still up there. Tonight, Alcock and he were the nearest on planet Earth to the moon. Would real men ever land there? Would this flight be a stepping stone? Brown remembered H.G. Wells and *The First Men in the Moon*. If Alcock and he only had Dr Cavor's cavorite, which repelled gravity, they could quickly get above these clouds and savour the heaven's complete panoply – and get those much-needed sightings.

He was growing fanciful, but no wonder:

An aura of unreality seemed to surround us as we flew onward, towards the dawn and Ireland. The fantastic surroundings impinged on my alert consciousness as something extravagantly abnormal. The distorted ball of a moon, the eerie half-light, the monstrous cloud shapes, the fog below and around us, the misty indefiniteness of space, the changeless drone, drone, drone, of the engines.

Brown was not the only transatlantic flier to experience strange sights in the upper reaches. Shortly afterwards, J.C. Shotter flew this way in the R.34 airship. He would long remember his uncanny experience in the cloud and fog: 'I opened the cabin window and received a big shock. I saw another engine room opposite and a man's figure looking out!' Shortly after this cloudy mirage, Shotter discovered a stowaway cat in the airship. He knew it was a real one when it made a beeline for the airship's carrier pigeon. Shotter and his companions enjoyed luxuries unknown to Alcock and Brown. They could walk around their small cabin and dine to 'Back Home in Tennessee' on their gramophone. Shotter marvelled at how lucky Hawker and Mackenzie-Grieve had been. During his R.34 Atlantic trip he had not spotted one ship between Ireland and Newfoundland.

The fliers' sense of isolation and the lack of radio communication were a contrast to the armada that had accompanied the US Navy flying boats. Alcock and Brown had witnessed its scale when they saw one of their depot-ships at Halifax. Like Lord Northcliffe, *The Times* would later berate the UK government for its lack of support for the British transatlantic entrants:

> The official tradition in this country of leaving pioneer work to private endeavour – with a substantial reserve of disapproval in case of failure – dates back at least to that gaunt patroness of official meanness, Queen Elizabeth. It is our way, but we question whether the country can afford to keep it so far as civilian flying goes. The Americans, with NC-4, have shown us that there is another way and a very efficient way.

By now Alcock and Brown had been flying for ten hours. It was over twenty since they had left their comfortable beds in the Cochrane, yet neither of them felt the least sleepy. The navigator conjectured:

> During the war, pilots and observers of night-bombing craft, their job completed, often suffered intensely on the homeward journey from the effort of will necessary to fight the drowsiness induced by the relaxed tension and the monotonous, never-varying hum of the engine – and this after only four to six hours of continuous flying.
>
> Probably however, such tiredness was mostly reaction and mental slackening after the object of their journeys had been achieved. Our own object would not be achieved until we saw Ireland beneath us, and it could not be achieved unless we kept our every faculty concentrated on it all the time. There was, therefore, no mental reaction during our long period of wakeful flying over the ocean.

Alcock later told a journalist:

> I had done a considerable amount of night flying in the past, and the sense of loneliness that might be supposed to accompany it had long since worn

off. Indeed, I do not think that either of us had any thought of what we were flying over, being merely intent on getting the machine across. There was no sense of remoteness, we were just too keen on our work.

It was time for an early morning snack. Brown reached behind to their food cupboard and extricated sandwiches, chocolate and the trusty Thermos flask of coffee. They were to drink four coffees each during the flight, while Alcock would eat three of their meat sandwiches and Brown five. Although it was cold outside the cockpit, inside the men still felt warm. The coffee heated them further, as well as keeping them awake and alert. Once again Alcock freed only one hand from the controls and Brown passed him a sandwich, a section at a time. The pilot massaged a stiff arm before he knocked back his coffee, and then requested another. While Brown at least had the distractions of his regular engine and navigation checks, Alcock's world remained confined to the joystick, rudder controls and the dashboard compass. Although he did not show it, controlling the heavy Vimy was a demanding and full-time job.

Melvyn Hiscock, who later piloted a replica Vimy, wrote:

The flying characteristics of aircraft of that period mean they are not one hundred per cent stable, you have to be flying them all the time. The controls are heavy, the ailerons are draggy. The downgoing aileron will drag and cause the wing to drop at the same time as it is trying to aerodynamically rise! You have to control the aeroplane mostly on rudder and use the ailerons to balance the turn rather than instigate it. It requires constant attention to maintain a heading and there are no trim tabs to take out the control forces. To fly in bumpy weather it would be a real handful as, at top weight, it is not responsive on the controls and any gusting headwind would cause severe drag and almost stop the aeroplane.

Changing direction was equally problematical:

You also cannot bank the aeroplane too steeply, as there is not enough performance to get you out of trouble. At thirty degrees of bank your stall

176

speed rises by thirty per cent. For a forty-five degree bank the stall speed is even higher and you need a lot of power to get you out, or a lot of height. To fly an aeroplane that primitive over the Atlantic is nothing short of inspiring. To do this in bad visibility, rotten weather and without having anyone pave the way before you takes real guts. Alcock was some pilot.

It was approaching 3.00 a.m., and Alcock and Brown thought they had experienced the worst of the fog and clouds. They were looking forward to greeting the dawn. How nice it would be to feel warm sunshine on their faces. The navigator had worked out a table of hours, angles, and azimuths of the sun at its rising, to serve as a check on their position. At five minutes before three he pencilled an optimistic request that he held in front of Alcock: 'Immediately you see Sun rising, point machine straight for it and we'll get its compass bearings.' But, rather than the heartening sun, the aviators were heading straight for the biggest crisis of their transatlantic attempt. Alcock's flying skills were about to be tested to the limit.

The cloud around them gradually lightened, as Brown turned around and picked out the exterior gauges with his torch. But it was a false promise; there was no sign of the sun. Then, at ten minutes past three, the weather conditions suddenly deteriorated. Brown's hopes of a sun sighting were rudely dispelled when the sky darkened dramatically. He was going to have to fight for his next observations. It was now clear to him that accurate weather forecasting was as necessary to long-distance flight as reliable engines or crew. What did mainly ground-based forecasters know of fogs, turbulence and the variations of weather at these heights?

Meteorological knowledge had developed slowly since the time of Aristotle's *Meteorologica* in 340 BC, the first major study of the atmosphere and the phenomena of rain, wind and lightning. Galileo invented the thermometer in 1592. The barometer, which measured atmospheric pressure, appeared 50 years later. By the mid-1800s meteorologists realised that clouds, winds, and rain were produced by large weather systems that grew and changed as they moved across the face of the Earth. But this knowledge was hardly useful until the electric telegraph of 1837 ensured that data could travel faster than the weather itself.

In 1849 the Smithsonian Institution established an observation network across the USA. Five years later the United Kingdom Meteorological Office became the first such national service in the world. In 1909 transatlantic shipping introduced wireless telegraphy to transmit weather messages ashore. The first aviation weather forecast was issued on 1 December 1918 by the US Weather Bureau, based on data collected from instruments carried aloft by balloons and kites. The Bureau undertook to provide information on wind directions and speeds, optimum altitude for most favourable wind, altitude of the cloud layers and a forecast of probable changes in the succeeding twenty-four hours. The British Air Ministry issued its first aviation meteorological report two months later. For 1 February 1919 it forecast: 'Low clouds, poor visibility and snow showers are likely to continue today over the British Isles. Cross-country flying will be dangerous on these accounts.'

The transatlantic flights accelerated co-operation between the meteorological services of Britain, Portugal and the USA, but weather forecasting in 1919 was still as primitive as the wireless, and more relevant to shipping than to flying. There was little available information for aviators in the upper atmosphere or far out to sea. As he faced the sinister gloom, Brown recalled Lt Clements's final confident prediction: 'Diminishing westerly wind for the first 600 miles. Then, mild west to south-west wind. No area of depression reported at any place along your route.'

As if to confirm that their Atlantic attempt was a voyage into the unknown, Alcock and Brown were immersed in a dense bank of whirling vapour that suddenly reached up from the lower layer of cloud. Had this been England or France they could put down and take a breather, but not over the hidden ocean. They had no choice but to fly into the maelstrom. It was so thick that they could no longer see the wingtips or the extremities of the fuselage. The Vimy shuddered, as if recoiling from some unseen terror beyond the dark curtain. The flexing of the wings added to their sense of vulnerability. The turbulence tossed the aeroplane around as if it were a toy.

Brown remembered being thrown about during the war by the passage of shells en route to enemy lines. But this was as if a giant hand had caught hold of the aeroplane and was jerking it in all directions, while pummelling them continuously under their seat. At the centre of this whirlwind both fliers lost all sense of balance. It was just after 3.20 and they were beyond the chance of rescue by fellow men. Only by their instruments, or a sight of either the sea or sky, could they now restore their sense of the horizontal.

It was an experience faced by many pilots, including war veteran Cecil Lewis:

> A pilot flies by his horizon. He keeps his machine on an even keel, or indeed in any position, by reference to it. Take away the horizon and he doesn't know where he is. In a cloud, there is no horizon, nothing above, below, in front, behind, but a thick white mist. It's apt to make you panic after a while. Many a man has fallen out of the clouds in a spin through losing his head and, without knowing it, standing his machine on its ear.

The Vimy's air speed increased. Alcock pulled the control stick back and the aeroplane nosed upwards, but the needle remained poised at ninety. The air-speed indicator was jammed.

The pilot later recalled: 'The air-speed indicator failed to register, and bad bumps prevented me from holding to our course. From side to side rocked the machine, and it was hard to know in what position we really were.'

The Vimy stalled. It hung motionless for an instant before falling into a deep downward spin from 3,500ft. The fliers' stomachs lightened, as if on the crest of a roller-coaster. For Brown it was the terror of Hulluch all over again. His pilot had saved him then. Would John Alcock's skill and strength rescue him this time? Would anyone ever discover what had happened should they disappear into the watery depths? Only an observation of the sea would enable his pilot to regain equilibrium. Down they spiralled.

12

SURVIVING A STALL

The sleet embedded itself in the hinges of the ailerons
and jammed them, so that for about an hour the machine
had scarcely any lateral control.

Arthur Whitten Brown

The Vimy's stall was the most demoralising of Alcock and Brown's Atlantic tribulations. The aeroplane was completely out of control. The navigator later remembered:

> The compass needle continued to revolve rapidly, showing that the machine was swinging as it dropped. But, still, hemmed in as we were by the thick vapour, we could not tell how or in which direction we were spinning. Before Alcock could reduce the throttle, the roar of the engines had almost doubled in volume. Instead of the usual 650 to 1,700 revolutions, they were running at about 2,200 per minute.

Alcock throttled back the engines, but the diving biplane continued its plunge. Apart from the changing levels on the aneroid barometer, only the fact that the fliers' bodies were pressed tightly against the seat indicated that they were falling. How and at what angle, they had no idea. They plummeted downwards. What if the aneroid's accuracy had been affected by differences between local barometric conditions and those at St John's, where the instrument had been set? The Vimy descended: 2,000ft, 1,500ft, 1,000ft, 500ft. If the cloud mass stretched down to the surface of the sea they would be in the water before they could react. Brown loosened his safety belt and pocketed his flight log. Kathleen Kennedy, would he ever see her again? Both he and Alcock knew that if they hit the water at this speed they would not survive to see any chance passing ship.

The navigator recorded their near-miraculous delivery:

> Then, while these thoughts were chasing each other across my mind, we left the cloud as suddenly as we had entered it. We were now less than a hundred feet from the ocean. The sea surface did not appear below the machine but, owing to the wide angle at which we were tilted against the horizontal, seemed to stand up level, sideways to us.
>
> Alcock looked at the ocean and the horizon, and almost instantaneously regained his mental equilibrium in relation to external balance. The Vimy responded rapidly to his action in centralising the control column and rudder bar. He opened up the throttles, and the Rolls-Royce Eagles came back to life in an instant. The danger was past. Once again disaster had been averted by the pilot's level-headedness and skill. The compass needle, which had continued to swing, now stabilised itself and quavered towards the west, showing that the end of the spin left us facing America!

It was 3.30 a.m. Brown estimated that when the Vimy levelled out, they were no more than 50ft above the water. He felt that he could have almost reached down and touched the crests of the greedy swells. Even the phlegmatic pilot acknowledged that it had been a trying experience:

> When we at last emerged from the fog we were close down over the water at an extremely dangerous angle. The white-capped waves were rolling along too close to be comfortable, but a quick glimpse of the horizon enabled me to regain control of the machine. The salty taste we noted later on our tongues was foam.

Alcock started climbing again; 100, 200, 300ft. For the second time the Vimy was heading west, as it had been at the start of their flight. Safely clear of the water, Alcock turned the aeroplane around in a wide semi-circle and resumed course again towards Ireland. As he regained direction and height, he reflected that it could have been worse. At least half their fuel load had been burnt off before the incident. He would not have pulled out of the dive so quickly had the tanks been full. He liked the sea, but not at such close quarters. Much better St Anne's on Sea, where he had stayed as a child, than those menacing Atlantic waves. But at least there had been no bullets pinging off the engines, as in his last aquatic adventure in Suvla Bay, when Turkish soldiers had used his crashed aeroplane for target practice. How fortunate he had also been there. To be able to swim to the safety of the rocks where, even if he had been captured and manhandled, he had not been shot.

And, as he had told Bob Dicker, how lucky he had been compared with so many of his Eastchurch students who had perished in the war. Like young Lt Rex Warneford, who won the Victoria Cross in 1915 for being the first to shoot down a Zeppelin, only to die in a flying accident ten days later. It was curious that Warneford was buried in Percy Pilcher's Brompton Cemetery, so close to racing driver Percy Lambert, whom Dicker and he had seen regularly seen at Brooklands. Everyone was delighted when little Percy became the first man to cover 100 miles in an hour at the track in February 1913, but he was killed eight months later in another record attempt. Alcock felt that he had lost too many friends. But at least they had died doing what they liked most; better to go that way than lingering in a bed.

Since leaving St John's, Alcock had treated his engines gently, never running them at more than half to three-quarters throttle. With plenty of fuel in hand he had no compunction in urging the Vimy upwards, back into those forbidding clouds, which were at least safer than the water they had so narrowly avoided. What limited choices ocean flying presented. High as the aeroplane climbed, they could not escape the saturation thay had haunted them since they left Newfoundland. Moisture dripped off the cockpit instruments and switches. Animated equally by relief and frustration, Brown scribbled an ironic note at 3.50 a.m.; 'This is a great trip. No ships or stars or anything. Have a sandwich?'

The food and drink refreshed them after their narrow escape. Soon, they were over 6,000ft high and above the lower range of clouds. But ascend as they would, they could not escape the next cloudbank. The higher they went, the thicker it got. Nothing could be seen beyond the Vimy's wingtips. Where was the sky? Where was the sun? Brown had visualised a Turneresque dawn, but he would be disappointed. He needed to make an observation soon. He urged Alcock to continue climbing and pencilled a log book entry at 4.20 a.m.: 'AS 55, Height 6,500. Engine temps Port/Starboard 80. Oil 72. RPM 1650. Lat 51.30. Lg 21.45. Above clouds but still between two layers.'

Suspended for so long in the uniform and intangible cloud, the Vimy crew frequently felt as if they had entered an alien world hitherto unknown to man. It was as if they were frozen motionless or ghosting along in some unearthly eternity. The regular tattoo of the engines and the metronomic beat of the propellers reinforced the seductive fantasy that they could float there perpetually. The broken exhaust proved a blessing in disguise. Its constant tail-glow betrayed their forward motion, its reverberations restored a sense of reality to their numbed senses.

Brown continued his regular checks of the gauges, but his concerns were now more navigational than mechanical. He again requested altitude and the Vimy ascended higher still into the dark and forbidding mist. Not only dark but cold, much colder than either man had experienced before. At this rate they would be frozen before they would see the sky. How far up did the cloud go? There must be an end to it somewhere. Even Alcock grew frustrated: 'I climbed to 7,000 feet above sea-level. Occasionally we saw the moon, but Brown could get no reading. I hoped to get above the fog and clouds, but it seemed impossible. Climb as we might, the clouds seemed to climb still faster.'

It was almost 5 a.m. and they had been flying for over twelve hours. Brown estimated that they had covered three-quarters of their journey, and that they were within 450 miles of Ireland. Surely nothing would stop them now. But the elements held one last unpleasant surprise. A barrier of glowering denser cloud suddenly materialised ahead of them. It was like solid water. Without warning they were enveloped by heavy rain, most certainly not the welcoming and gentle mist of Yeats's mystical land of which the navigator had dreamt.

The aeroplane shuddered beneath the onslaught, and Alcock wrestled once again for control. The force of the rain was many times that of a normal vertical downpour. It hammered the windscreen and fuselage and the fliers' heads. The tumult rivalled the navigator's wartime experiences with Archie, but Archie had been spasmodic. This drenching torrent was as constant as it was inescapable. The maelstrom was a major trial on top of the affliction of that seemingly eternal cloud. Sisyphus had had it easy, Brown thought.

Incredibly, the conditions became even worse. The din increased as the rain turned to hail, and then to sleet and snow. Were they heading north for Iceland or east to Ireland? It was so vicious that Alcock insisted afterwards: 'It chewed bits out of our faces. Having a love of freedom at the neck, I left my suit open there, and so shipped sleet and rain in fairly generous quantities.'

It would take more than such a storm to defeat the Vimy's pilot. He fought the controls and continued his dogged search for the elusive clear sky. It had to be up there above them, somewhere. They reached 8,800ft, their highest altitude so far; and the coldest. Although the sleet persisted, the storm finally started to subside at 5.20. They were now thirteen hours out of Newfoundland. John Alcock's mother never doubted his ability to conquer the elements. After the Vimy's departure she informed a *Sunday Chronicle* reporter:

> I have heard nothing since my son left home to cross to Newfoundland. But now that he has started, I am delighted. I am absolutely confident of his success, for throughout his flying career he has been so lucky. I have no fear of his failing.

Yet the fliers faced one further test. Brown turned to make his regular inspection of the petrol-overflow gauge on the centre-section strut immediately behind him, about three feet above his head. He was shocked to find that the gauge's face had become obscured by the driving snow. 'To guard against carburettor trouble, it was essential that the pilot should be able to read the gauge at any moment. It was up to me, therefore, to clear away the snow from the glass.'

Brown stood up in the cockpit and swivelled around. It was difficult in the restricted space. His bad leg ached miserably, and the heavy coat limited his manoeuvrability. He knelt on his seat, as he had for his first observation, held on to the strut with his left hand and reached up past the now-sodden Lucky Jim. The sudden exposure to the ice-cold exterior shocked him. The slipstream almost whipped his arm away. It glued the soaking coat collar to his neck and forced his chest into the back of the seat so that he could hardly breathe. As Alcock struggled to keep the aeroplane on an even keel, Brown held tight and worked away at the snow with his free gloved hand.

In his *Royal Air Force and Civil Aviation Record* account the navigator wrote that he had knelt on the fuselage, rather than on his seat and *against* the fuselage. This misstatement may have encouraged the subsequent fiction that he had walked out on the wings. The navigator downplayed the danger of the operation:

> I had no difficulty, however, in reaching upward and rubbing the snow from the face of the gauge. Until the storm ended, a repetition of this performance, at fairly frequent intervals, continued to be necessary. There was however scarcely any danger in kneeling on the fuselage, as long as Alcock kept the machine level.

Brown inched his feet back down to the floor. He shivered from the cold and the shock of his sodden exposure. Cramped it may have been, but the shelter of the cockpit was a relief. It represented a homely refuge, as Alcock and he cleaved their discordant way through the obdurate cocktail of cloud and sleet. The navigator had had more than his share of aerial exposure. From one extreme to another; the last time he had battled the slipstream was to escape those engine flames in France.

Besides, how much better it was to be shivering than to have suffered the fate of his former pilots, Allcock and Medlicott. Their skills had saved his life but they themselves had perished. Without their own war experience, it was doubtful if Alcock and he would have survived this flight so far. Daily confrontation with danger and death had undoubtedly honed their reflexes and their instincts of self-preservation. How fortunate he had been with his pilots, he thought, as Alcock continued to fight the oscillating Vimy to maintain its course.

The cloud was still so thick that it periodically blotted out the aeroplane's wingtips. As the navigator thawed out and resumed his regular engine checks, Alcock continued his stubborn quest for clear air and the sun. Brown recorded in his log book that they reached 9,400ft at 6.20 a.m. Alcock climbed higher, but still no sun. At 7 a.m. the Vimy peaked at 11,000ft, the highest altitude of their flight. Almost immediately Brown caught a glimmer of sun through a cloud gap.

The chilling temperatures had not cooled his reactions. Although there was no horizon, he raced to obtain a reading with the help of his Abney spirit level. What would he not give to have a table like those American fliers, on which to rest his navigation equipment? The observation confirmed that they were right on course and nearing Ireland. He recalled later: 'I could afford no spare time for speculation on what a safe arrival would mean to us. As yet, neither of us was aware of the least sign of tiredness, mental or physical.'

Arthur Whitten Brown was an exceptionally modest man. While Alcock had the responsibility of piloting the Vimy, it was Brown's navigation in extreme conditions that guided the aeroplane across the ocean wastes. One error, one miscalculation, one lapse of concentration or judgement could have resulted in a catastrophic deviation from their course and an unmarked and unmourned watery grave, like that of many a subsequent ocean aviator. Typically, Brown later insisted: 'To Hawker and Grieve we owed particular thanks, in that we profited to a certain extent by what we learned from the cabled reports of their experience.'

Kenneth Mackenzie-Grieve described the conditions under which the navigation was conducted:

One's quarters are pretty cramped. The small space in which one can move does not make the taking of sights easy, for to use the sextant involves a good deal of neck twisting and looking round the corner. A buffeting eddying slipstream does not conduce to holding the instrument steady, and one has to brace oneself as stiffly as ever one can.

So far as warmth was concerned I had nothing to complain of, for our suits kept us quite comfortable. Until I had to make an observation with the sextant. Then, conditions were not quite so good, as the working of this instrument and the subsequent calculations meant taking one's gloves off. At an altitude of 10,000 feet or more, the temperature was about zero Fahrenheit. Whilst messing about with my instruments I was lucky not to get badly frost-bitten, as a matter of fact I did get a touch which numbed my fingers for a week or two. What was even more distressing was the fact that my handkerchief got frozen as stiff as a board!

Tantalised by further fleeting glimpses of the sun through the incessant sleet, Brown recorded their new bearing at 7.30 a.m.: latitude 52.30 north, longitude 17 west. Although Alcock and he were nearing their goal, their Sisyphian trials were not yet ended. The freezing altitude temperatures brought a new danger: the Vimy was gradually being covered in ice. Brown noted:

The sleet embedded itself in the hinges of the ailerons and jammed them, so that for about an hour the machine had scarcely any lateral control. Fortunately, the Vickers Vimy possesses plenty inherent lateral stability; and as the rudder controls were never clogged by sleet, we were able to hold to the right direction. We therefore remained at 11,000 feet until, at 7.30 a.m., I had definitely fixed the position line. This accomplished, I scribbled the following message and handed it across to the pilot: 'We had better go lower down, where the air is warmer, and where we might pick up a steamer.' We started to nose downward.

No sooner had Alcock started their descent, however, than the exhaustless starboard engine began to misfire. Brown turned around. Had that flame finally escalated? The sound was clearly audible above the racket of the motors, as if it was backfiring through one of the carburettors. Had the petrol been contaminated despite their best filtering precautions, and so close to their goal? The pilot immediately throttled back. It was likely that water caused by melting ice had caused the aberration. He did not panic, but maintained a steady glide until they had descended to 1,000ft. They were still surrounded by cloud, but it was lightening and was warmer than that which had dogged most of their journey. As Alcock eased their descent the disconcerting noise gradually ceased.

The rise in temperature also dissipated the ice. Alcock exercised the ailerons and the lighter Vimy responded immediately to his touch, a good job, as the aeroplane was now assailed by a strong breeze that had veered to southwesterly. The Vimy's centre of gravity had also altered with the gradual emptying of the rear tanks. Alcock felt as if he was handling a different machine. As it became increasingly nose heavy he had to maintain a backward pressure on the column. It was tiring work; he had not stirred from the controls since they left St John's. Before their departure a mechanic had improvised an elastic device that he had attached to the column to ease the strain, but in the rush before take-off he had cut it too short to be of any use.

Despite their demanding fifteen hours, both pilot and navigator were as alert as they had been at the start. Their tribulations had made them doubly vigilant. Unsure of how far down the cloud descended, Alcock took the precaution of loosening his safety belt. Suddenly, at 500ft, the fliers found themselves in clear air, practically the clearest of their entire journey. They could see the heaving water below them. Dull though it appeared in the early morning light, it was a welcme sight, and immediately restored their sense of security. The pilot opened up both engines in a full-throated celebration. Brown remembered Alcock's pre-departure words: 'Perhaps at the very end when the Irish coast is in sight, I may try a whirlwind finish!'

But they had not yet reached their destination. Brown promptly put his instruments to work:

I reached for the drift-bearing plate, and after observation on the ocean, I found that we were moving on a course 75 deg true, at 110 knots ground speed, with a wind of 30 knots from the direction of 215 degrees true. I had been reckoning on a course of 77 degrees true, with calculations based on our midnight position; so that evidently we were slightly to the north of the prescribed track. Still, we were not so far north as to miss Ireland.

In my correction of the compass bearing, I could only guess at the time when the wind had veered from its earlier direction. I made the assumption that the northerly drift had existed ever since my sighting on the Pole Star and Vega during the night. I reckoned that our position at eight o'clock would consequently be about 54 degrees N latitiude, 10 degrees 30 min W longitude. Taking these figures, and with the help of the navigation machine which rested on my knees, I calculated that our course to Galway was about 125 degrees true, allowing for variation and wind. I therefore set a compass course of 170 degrees.

Brown indicated the necessary change with a diagram and another note to the pilot: 'Don't be afraid of S but we have had too much N already.' Alcock nodded and gently ruddered the Vimy on to its adjusted course. As they skimmed the water at 300ft both men now knew that they were nearing terra firma and, finally, relief from the all-enveloping dampness. The navigator thought of the early Viking explorer who released a hungry raven when he felt he was near land. If, instead of circling aimlessly, the bird took off in a certain direction, the boat followed, knowing that it was heading for shore and replenishment.

Securing himself against the swaying of the aeroplane, Brown reached to the food locker for the last time. Neither of them felt hungry, but the 8 o'clock breakfast would both kill time and take their minds from the rising excitement of impending landfall. It was ironic that impatience should manifest itself now, when they were so close to the end of their long flight. Brown placed a sandwich in Alcock's left hand. He followed it with some chocolate.

It was the pilot who first sighted land. Brown recorded the moment:

I had screwed on the lid of the flask, and was placing the remains of the food in the tiny cupboard behind my seat, when Alcock grabbed my shoulder, twisted me round, beamed excitedly, and pointed ahead and below. His lips were moving, but whatever he said was inaudible above the roar of the engines.

I followed the direction indicated by his outstretched forefinger; and, barely visible through the mist, it showed me two tiny specks of – land! This happened at 8.15 a.m. on June 15. With a light heart, I put away charts and tables of calculation, and disregarded the compass needle. My work as a navigator of the flight was at an end.

The land that the keen-eyed pilot had spotted was the two islands of Eeshal and Turbot, situated off the coast 5 miles from Clifden. Mist obscured the mainland but, a few minutes later, Alcock and Brown saw the white breakers beating against the shoreline. The cloud, still only 200ft above them, masked the top of a distant mountain range, but at least they were finally free of its relentless clutches. They would have to land before they reached those peaks. Despite the distraction of journey's end, Brown made his hourly log book entry at 8.20 a.m.: 'AS65. Height 400 feet. Engine Temps 75/76. RPM 1750.'

They crossed the coast at 8.25 a.m., at an altitude of 250ft. Behind the sea was a small town. Brown wondered if perhaps they still had not veered sufficiently southwards. He pencilled a final note: 'Probably N Ireland. Can you carry on & go farther S. Follow the railway.' But a few minutes later he saw the tall masts of a radio station and knew that they had arrived over Clifden. He was finally in the land of Yeats, the land of his fiancée's forebears. It would not be long before she and he would be together for good. He remembered a verse from fellow war veteran Paul Bewsher's 'The Dawn Patrol':

My flight is done. I cross the line of foam
That breaks around a town of grey and red,
Whose streets and squares lie dead
Beneath the silent dawn …

For a disconcerting moment, however, Brown thought that he was back in Newfoundland. The rocky terrain, the watery pools and the radio masts uncannily mirrored their distant departure point of St John's. It was not good landing ground. He felt the ghost of Marconi at his shoulder as he reflected that they had reunited the inventor's two stations on opposite sides of the ocean. Thanks to his navigation they were only 20 miles north of their original planned course, after an almost totally blind flight of 1,900 miles with only four fleeting observations; the longest distance ever flown by man. Thales of Miletos would have been proud of him.

Alcock and Brown circled Clifden in the gusts and slight mist. There was no movement below them, none of the town's population of 1,000 could be seen on its wide curving streets. It was indeed as if they were returning from a dawn patrol, or had hit a ghost town. Brown fired two red flares from the Very pistol. But, even with a second circle, the noisy Vimy with its broken exhaust brought only a few people out. The fliers did not realise that most townspeople were attending either Sunday service or morning Mass in the two churches whose gaunt spires were within touching distance of their undercarriage. A scant 200ft was all that prevented a collision of faith and technology. The first persons to see them were a honeymooning Australian soldier and two 8-year-old boys, Harry Sullivan and Albert Millar. The latter recalled: 'I was ready to go to Sunday School when I heard a commotion in the sky and rushed on to the street. I looked up and saw this thing flying very low between the houses. The pilot was waving down.'

Another who waved, but in annoyance, was the Rev O'Shea, who was on his way to a prayer service for the Marconi staff at their Derrygimla station. The Vimy swooped over his motorcycle and almost caused him to lose control on the narrow track. The noisy machine also drew reproachful braying from the donkeys that carted turf to the station.

Although Brown's work was done, his pilot's responsibilities were not yet at an end. For Alcock, it was a relief to be flying over solid land at last, but he remembered from his war experience how many a landing had been spoiled by the excitement of homecoming. He must keep a clear head. His economical flying meant that they still carried almost a third of their fuel. He would prefer to land with less. But those mist-shrouded mountains banished his already ebbing aspirations of continuing to their home base at Brooklands. Alcock now faced every pilot's most difficult hazard after take-off: the landing. His senses speeded up as he prepared to bring the Vimy down in a place he had never seen before.

13

A BOGGY LANDING

---◆◇◆---

The only thing that upset me was to see the machine at the end get damaged. From above, the bog looked like a lovely field.

John Alcock

---◆◇◆---

Antoine de Saint-Exupéry described the joy of homecoming at journey's end in *Night Flight:*

> The job has its grandeurs, yes. There is the exultation of arriving safely after a storm, the joy of gliding down out of the darkness of night or tempest toward a sun-drenched Alicante or Santiago; there is the swelling sense of returning to repossess one's place in life, in the miraculous garden of earth, where are trees and women and, down by the harbour, friendly little bars. When he has throttled his engine and is banking into the airport, leaving the sombre cloud masses behind, what pilot does not break into song?

Misty Connemara was far from Alicante, but the sensation was as heartening for Alcock and Brown as they prepared to touch down. The pilot sharpened his eyes in search of a likely landing spot. His sixteen hours of concentration were almost at an end. As they circled the Marconi station, Brown looked down and recalled Alcock's breezy pre-departure remark: 'We shall hang our hats on the aerials of the Clifden wireless station as we go by!'

The surrounding rocky ridges and boggy pools did not look promising to Alcock. But, to his delight, he spotted a pristine field in the level vastness behind the station masts. Flat land, clinging grass, every flier's dream. How welcoming compared with the undulations of St John's and the war-cratered fields of continental Europe. A tailor-made and treeless landing site. He did not need a second invitation. He circled to ensure that there were no boulders or hidden stumps, which could terminate their mission in a tangle of splinters and blazing fuel. He turned the aeroplane westward for the last time. Hands and feet alert for any sudden gust, he descended into the slight wind. The noise of the Vimy alerted some of the Marconi staff. Brown mistook their waving as a welcome and cheerfully returned the compliment, but their waving had been a warning. As Alcock shut off the engines near the condenser house and descended expectantly, the groundlings waved even more.

Brown described the approach to the field, as the earth rose up to meet them:

> With engines shut off, we glided towards it, heading into the wind. Alcock flattened out at exactly the right moment. The machine sank gently, the wheels touched earth, and began to run smoothly over the surface.
>
> Already I was indulging in the comforting reflection that the anxious flight had ended in a perfect landing. Then, so softly as not to be noticed at first, the front of the Vickers Vimy tilted inexplicably, while the tail rose. Suddenly, the craft stopped with an unpleasant squelch, tipped forwards, shook itself, and remained poised on a slant, with its fore-end buried in the ground, as if trying to stand on its head.
>
> I reached out a hand and arm just in time to save a nasty bump when the shock threw me forward. As it was, I was only stopped a jarring collision with the help of my nose. Alcock had braced himself against the rudder control bar. The pressure he exerted against it to save himself from falling bent the straight bar, which was of hollow steel, almost into the shape of a horse-shoe.

This was each flier's third violent landing in four years. Brown was lucky not to lose teeth, as he had at Valenciennes. After a run of 50yd the Vimy had come to rest at an angle of almost forty-five degrees. Its nose and half its propellers were buried in the bog, while the tailplane with the now redundant rations was poised 16ft high in the air. Instead of fog and insubstantial cloud, pilot and navigator found their gaze locked on to heather and hardy green scrub. Alcock later told Bob Dicker:

> I made a perfect approach but, on touching down, I soon discovered that there was something wrong. I immediately thought of the damaged axle that had been repaired a few hours earlier in Newfoundland. But then I realised we were in a bog and that the machine was sinking slowly. Bob, I could have cried.

Ironically, the winds that had accelerated the fliers' progress also caused their unexpected entrapment. Moisture carried from eastern America by the prevailing westerlies, rather than indigenous conditions or basins, maintained the waterlogged conditions that were responsible for the phenomenon of Derrygimla's blanket bog, one of the largest in Europe. Sphagnum moss was among the bog's happiest and well-nourished flora. Being able to absorb many times its weight in water, its sponge-like properties contributed generously to the sticky wetness that now held the Vimy in its unyielding embrace.

Unaware of the adaptation of bog plants to their nutrient-poor surroundings, Brown reached for his Very pistol and fired two white distress flares. At ground level he was amazed at the infinity of the greeny russet expanse in which they had landed. In the distance, to his right, he spotted a party of army officers and men from the station zigzagging across the low wet bog. How strange to see fellow humans again, but what an incongruous sight! Some were in uniform, others in pyjamas and overcoats. Several tripped as they ran. The navigator performed one last task before he prepared to leave the aeroplane. He noted the time. It was 8.40 a.m. Alcock and he had been in the air for sixteen hours and twenty-eight minutes. Thanks to that following wind they had completed the 1,880-mile coast-to-coast flight in fifteen hours and fifty-seven minutes, at an average speed of 118.5mph.

The fliers had landed in one of Ireland's most beautiful places, between the background serrated hump of Roundstone's Errisbeg Mountain and the distant sea off Ballyconneely village. Immortalised by artist Paul Henry, this part of Connemara was described by naturalist Robert Lloyd Praeger:

> On a day of bright sky, when the hills are of that intoxicating misty blue that belongs especially to the west, the bogland is a lovely far-reaching expanse of purple and red brown; and the lakelets take on the quite indescribable colour that comes from clear sky reflected in bog-water, while the sea inlets glow with an intense but rather green blue. On such a day the wanderer will thank his lucky star that it brought him to Connemara.

Although he was in no mood to appreciate the scenery, Brown's scratched nose pleasantly recorded the reviving scent of wild flowers. A reflection of the cloud they had finally vacated, fluffy white bog cotton waved a demure welcome. Disturbed by their unruly arrival, curlews, skylarks and snipe twittered around the unexpected interlopers, but neither Alcock nor Brown could hear them. After their long exposure to the engines and broken exhaust, they were both almost completely deaf.

While the navigator savoured the wild scents, the pilot suddenly sniffed petrol. With one-third of their fuel still on board, they were not safe yet. Their abrupt stop had ruptured a petrol supply pipe, and fuel was seeping into the tilting cockpit. Had the impact dazed them and their aeroplane caught fire, both men would have been consumed before any possible rescue attempt. Fortunately Alcock had already anticipated the danger and switched off the magneto current. With the chance of a random spark reduced, the two men clambered from the cockpit; Brown first, the captain last.

One advantage of the Vimy's buried nose was that the fliers no longer needed a ladder to descend from 9ft. They simply stepped on to the wind-grained carpet of moss and stubby heather. Soft it might be, but how solid it felt after their long suspension in space. It seemed an eternity since they had last touched ground in America, now almost 2,000 miles away. How fresh the morning air felt after their long confinement amid oil and petrol fumes, and how strange and disconcerting the lack of motion. And the all-enveloping quiet, after the constant engine noise. As if the world was holding its breath.

Brown safely extricated his log book and notebook. Only his chart and the Baker navigating machine were slightly damaged. The fleetest of the men arrived and struggled to catch their breaths. 'Anybody hurt?' was the not unexpected first question that Alcock and Brown eventually understood.

'No!' was the loud response.

'Where are you from?'

'America.' Alcock yelled back. 'Yesterday, we were in America.'

This response provoked some good-humoured laughter. In addition to their hearing problems, the violent landing had obviously affected the fliers' mental condition.

'We're Alcock and Brown!' the pilot shouted again.

This meant nothing to their would-be rescuers, who thought they were the crew of a search aircraft on the lookout for Atlantic aviators. Surely the station men would have relayed Lt Clements's cable yesterday about the Vimy's departure? Alcock in desperation showed the white sealed air-mail bag from St John's. Slowly, realisation grew. Alcock and the equally unshaven and bloodshot Brown must be two of those Atlantic fliers who had been mentioned in the papers! As more staff arrived, cheers rang out across the empty bog. Sodden cigarettes from the Vimy changed hands. Hearty handshakes were followed by equally painful welcoming hugs. It was as much as the tired fliers could bear.

Brown recalled:

I felt a keen sense of relief at being on dry land again, but this was coupled with a certain amount of dragging reaction from the tense mental concentration during the flight, so that my mind sagged. I was very sleepy but not physically tired. My hands were very unsteady. My mind was quite clear on matters pertaining to the flight, but hazy on extraneous subjects. After having listened so long to the loud-voiced hum of the Rolls-Royce engines, made louder than ever by the broken exhaust pipe, we were very deaf. Our ears would not stop ringing.

Although the mist had dissipated, the trek of almost a mile to the Marconi building was a trial.

Burdened as we were with flying kit and heavy boots, the walk over the bog was a dragging discomfort. In addition, I suddenly discovered an intense sleepiness, and could easily have let myself lose consciousness while standing upright. We lurched as we walked, owing to the stiffness that resulted from having sat in the tiny cockpit for seventeen hours. Alcock, who during the whole period had kept his feet on the rudder-bar and one hand on the control lever, would not confess to anything worse than a desire to stand up for the rest of his life – or at least until he could sit down painlessly.

Flaunting the latest technology in one of the most deprived corners of Europe, the sprawling Marconi station provided a surrealistic spectacle in the middle of the boundless bog. Set against a background of mountains whose colours constantly changed with the light, it consisted of over thirty buildings and even boasted a tennis court. The steel masts from which the transmitter aerials hung reached over 200ft into the sky. The multi-wire aerials covered an area of one-quarter of a square mile. Plumes of smoke rose from the competing chimney towers of the generating plant. Six constantly hissing steam engines provided the station's power. The smell of burning turf perfumed the immediate locality. Giant ricks of the convenient fuel flanked the 75ft-wide condenser house, which ranged for 350ft along a nondescript lake. The station was equally spectacular at night, its illuminations casting an unearthly glow over the bog whose peripheral homesteads were lit by candles.

Their enthusiastic escorts brought Alcock and Brown to the cluster of neat bungalows housing the 150 permanent staff. It was in one of these that the *Titanic's* wireless operator, Jack Phillips, had earlier lived. In the time-honoured tradition of Connemara accommodations, the station crew quickly treated the fliers to a full Irish breakfast. The involuntary bog walk had whetted their appetites. Washed down with generous mugs of tea, the sizzling bacon and egg quickly disappeared. The crisp linen tablecloth was luxury, the fresh crusty bread a welcome change from soggy aerial sandwiches. Less so the questions with which their hospitable hosts bombarded them. The fliers would endure more of these before the day and the following weeks were over. But there was one big question they themselves wanted to ask.

When Alcock and Brown finally recovered their hearing they enquired about the Handley Page. No one had heard of the aeroplane, of either its departure or arrival. And if the Marconi operators had not heard about it, then it had not even taken off. But might it have flown direct to England? Later they found out that radiator problems had grounded their rival. Not only had they crossed the Atlantic, they were also the first to do it non-stop. They had won the *Daily Mail* prize! Brown's fortune-teller had been right on all counts. And they had handsomely beaten Lt Cdr Read's previous NC-4 distance record of 1,380 miles. Brown turned to Alcock: 'What do you think of that for fancy navigating?'

'Very good,' was the reply. They shook hands.

Later, Wg Cdr J.L. Mitchell commented:

> Brown's navigation in adverse conditions was a triumph of experience, coolness and finesse, which set the pace in navigational techniques that were to remain in vogue for the next twenty years, until the advent of hyperbolic radio fixing systems and aircraft radar.

The flight might be completed, but there was still work to be done. Cables to be dispatched to the *Daily Mail*, the Royal Aero Club and to Vickers. The fliers could not have picked a more convenient landing site than the Marconi station. One of its operators, Frank H. Teague, would later win the *Wireless World* award for being first to get news of their arrival to London. Alcock and Brown remembered the crew still waiting anxiously in St John's, and it was to engineer Sidney C. Davis and these workers who had become friends that they dispatched the first message: 'Your hard work and splendid efforts have been amply rewarded. We did not let you down. Alcock and Brown.'

Worn out by their take-off efforts, Muller, Dicker, and the Vimy crew were fast asleep in the Cochrane when they were awakened that Sunday morning. The tidings from Mount Pearl quickly banished their fatigue.

Those long days in the cold and wind had not been in vain. Although the news was first received with caution, their joy was soon shared by everyone in St John's. Their aeroplane had conquered the mighty Atlantic, another first for their historic city! Dicker insisted: 'But I think we were still far too tired to celebrate. I did have an ice cream. We had expected them to do it anyway, so perhaps that was why we did not go wild.' Not everyone believed that the Vickers team confined themselves to straight ice cream that day.

Word of the Vimy's triumph reached Adm. Kerr's team as they were fitting the Handley Page's new radiators. The engines performed faultlessly during a three-hour test. Kerr decided to fly to England four days later and attempt to better Alcock and Brown's time. But, instead of the winds that had favoured the Vimy pair, a mid-Atlantic depression was forecast which forced a final postponement.

In Derrygimla, with Frank Teague taking his dictation, Alcock next cabled the Royal Aero Club:

> Landed Clifden 8.40 a.m. (Greenwich Mean Time) June 15, Vickers Vimy Atlantic machine, leaving Newfoundland 4.28 p.m. (Greenwich Mean Time) June 14. Total Time, 16 hours 12 minutes. Signed Captain Alcock (Pilot). Lieutenant Brown (Navigator).

The club promptly responded:

> Keep machine intact until observer arrives.

Alcock and Brown's speedy arrival had taken both the club and the Air Ministry by surprise. They had understood that inclement weather would delay the Vimy's take-off for another week. Plans were hurriedly made to welcome the fliers to London.

Alcock then contacted the *Daily Mail*. At 12.55 p.m. Brown sent a special personal cable to Kathleen Kennedy: 'Landed Clifden Ireland safely this morning. Will be with you soon. Love, Teddy.' The grateful aviators also cabled Rolls-Royce managing director Claude Johnson:

'Congratulations on performance of the two Eagle Rolls-Royce engines, which propelled the Vickers Vimy safely across the Atlantic.'

After breakfast, having finally regained their ground feet, the fliers washed and shaved. Brown carefully skirted his bruised nose. Alcock was equally cautious with his face, which was sore and swollen after its long exposure to the elements. While the navigator lay down to rest, Alcock returned across the bog to see their Vimy, now guarded by two soldiers. Much of its nose and four propeller blades were under the bog surface. The top wing was at shoulder height, and the leading edge of the lower plane, on which the generator impeller had been mounted, was bent and broken. But its solid structure had saved the Vimy from further damage and, thanks to the rear tanks having emptied first, the aeroplane did not break its back. The pilot reiterated: 'The only thing that upset me was to see the machine at the end get damaged. From above, the bog looked like a lovely field.'

W.J. Richards of Vickers later suggested that, had the Vimy retained the protective front wheel with which it was originally fitted, it might not have tipped over. Those more familiar with Irish bogs thought to the contrary. The aeroplane might have dug in sooner and possibly even somersaulted.

The Vimy shed more parts after the crash-landing than during it. Many locals helped themselves to souvenirs. Artist-to-be Alannah Heather was one of the first who went to see it. She knew the quickest way; Guglielmo Marconi had stayed with her grandmother at Errislannan Manor:

We heard the aeroplane, then saw it above Clifden castle across the bay, possibly hoping to land on the steep sloping field. Then it made for the Marconi station. It was not long before the soldiers from the Marconi station came to their aid and took them back to their huts. We could see all this as we beat up the horse, hurrying over Ballinaboy Hill. In that dark land of heather and the inky-blue of Errisbeg, the white plane stood out distinctly.

We were joined by a few others as we trudged across the bog, but most people were at Mass and in their Sunday clothes, and gumboots were needed. Without newspapers or radio we did not realise the special importance of this plane. It appeared to be made of canvas tied together with string. As the wings were broken we began pulling the plane apart, taking pieces of canvas and wood. Squares of this tough canvas crowned little haycocks for many years to come. Then we went home for our cameras, bringing all our souvenirs, some of which I still have. We took photographs from different angles with the family posed in front of the plane.

Alannah's brother had served with the Loyal North Lancashire Regiment, so perhaps it was appropriate that she should have had a keepsake from the Lancastrians' aeroplane, but a guard was quickly posted to ensure that there was no further pilferage. Having seen the machine in Clifden, 8-year-old Albert Millar lost no time in organising his family to go out and view it:

After Sunday school I came home and the whole family drove out in my father's pony trap to the bog. As we walked up the railway line which linked the Marconi station with the road, we met two farmers coming down. My father asked did they see the plane. 'We did, Sir, it's a hell of a yoke.' I ran ahead of my parents and saw the plane lying in the bog. I ran back and said: 'I've seen the hell of a yoke lying in the bog but it has no wheels.'

Despite his tiredness, Brown had been unable to sleep. Alcock returned at lunchtime and the two men did a tour of the wireless station before preparing to leave. But first they had to meet such local dignitaries as parish priest Canon McAlpine, Eddie King, chairman of the local district council, and the first journalists on the scene, Tom Kenny of the *Connacht Tribune*. They were packing their flying gear and instruments when the *Daily Mail*'s J.L. Hodson arrived with a photographer. It was to be the first of many interviews.

I congratulated them on behalf of the Daily Mail. Capt Alcock's face just lit up into a smile and Lieutenant Brown bent further over his sextant and said 'We didn't do it badly, did we?'

They might have come 10 miles, but they told me they had come 1,800. It was difficult to conceive that these two quite young men –

Capt Alcock in a blue lounge suit, with a ruddy face and light tousled hair, and Lieutenant Brown in the Royal Air Force blue uniform – were in Newfoundland yesterday. Captain Alcock said with a laugh 'I am not at all tired', but Lieutenant Brown confessed 'I am a bit fagged out.'

His eyes are a wee bit bloodshot, but otherwise they both look as if they had not traversed 100 miles.

Both pilot and navigator agreed that it had been a rough flight. Brown insisted: 'I got more fun out of my first solo.' Alcock, who admitted to being still deaf, said:

'This was a job of work. It was a difficult task, but we are too near to it to realise what we have done. We have had a terrible journey. The wonder is we are here at all. We scarcely saw the sun or the moon or the stars. For hours we saw none of them. The fog was very dense, and at times we had to descend to within 300 feet of the sea.'

Marconi staff listened spellbound as Alcock described the drama of the flight for Mail readers:

At the start, we had to drive up a valley and we got some very bad bumps. That was the only time I had the engines full out. We climbed quickly up to a height of 1,000 feet. At Signal Hill, Lieutenant Brown set our course for the ocean at a 124-degree Compass course. We kept the course until well on in the night. I had the engines throttled down and let her do her own time.

After the first hour we had got in these clouds – one lot 2,000 feet up and the other 6,000 feet up – it was impossible to see the sea to get our drift. The clouds above were obscuring the sun, and when night came we could neither see the stars nor the moon. We flew on our original course until we saw a clear patch about 2 a.m. Then we saw a few stars.

Brown gave me a new course of 110 compass points. We went on steadily until the weather got very thick again. That would be about 3 or 4 a.m., and we could see nothing because the bank of fog was extremely thick. We began to have a very rough time. The air speed indicator jammed and stopped at 90, and I did not know exactly what I was doing. It jammed through sleet freezing on it, and it smelt smoky.

We did some comic stunts then, and I believe we looped the loop, and by accident we did a steep spiral. It was alarming! We had no sense of horizon.

We came down quickly from about 4,000 feet until the water was very near. That gave me my horizon again, and I was then all right. That period only lasted a few seconds, but it seemed ages. It came to an end when we were within fifty feet of the water, with the machine practically on its back.

We climbed after that and got on fairly well until we got to 6,000 feet, and fog was there again. I climbed twice on top of it, only to find banks of cloud. We went higher and saw the moon and half-stars. We carried on until dawn. We never saw the sun rise. There was another bank of fog on top of the lower one. Lieutenant Brown was only able to take four readings of his position.

Asked about the future of transatlantic flight, Alcock opined: 'The flight has shown that the Atlantic flight is practicable, but I think it should be done not with an aeroplane or seaplane, but with a flying boat.' Praising the Vimy and its engines, the pilot said: 'The engines are Rolls-Royces and they ran perfectly all through. We did not lose a spoonful of water on the journey and no petrol. When I landed, I had only two-thirds of the supply exhausted.'

The pilot's relaxed demeanour was captured by the *Manchester Guardian* correspondent:

When I saw Capt Alcock at the residential bungalow of the Marconi station, some hours after he landed, he looked as spruce – attired in navy lounge suit and cheerfully smoking a cigarette – as any city man enjoying an hour's leisure. He received congratulations with a cheery smile. 'Yes' he said frankly, 'I'm glad we did it.'

A *Despatch* reporter contrasted the two fliers:

Alcock, 26 – bluff, big-faced, ruddy. Strong with a good deal of Northern directness in his manners and a trace of Lancashire accent in his speech. Lt Brown says that Captain Alcock has no nerves, and I can believe him.

Lt Brown is different – of medium height, rather slightly built and with fine blue eyes, a cultured intellectual face, and wavy brown hair that is turning grey and that falls in disorder away from his forehead. He might be a poet or a lawyer or inventor. He has been wounded in the foot, and has trouble with it sometimes. This morning, he was limping a little, and is still very tired, but Captain Alcock, except that he is stiff with long sitting, is as fit as a fiddle.

Brown shed some of his fatigue when he received a reply cable from his fiancée: 'Magnificent. Never doubted your success. Wire when leaving for Brooklands. Will meet you there. Micki.'

Sunday was a quiet day in the west of Ireland, and only meagre details of the Vimy's arrival trickled slowly to the outside world. But once the news had broken in England, crowds started to assemble outside the fliers' homes and that of the Kennedys, which was decorated with flags. Ignorant of the damage to the Vimy, some Londoners hoped that the aeroplane would continue and make a celebratory flypast over the city. Congratulatory flowers were followed by the media.

The photogenic Kathleen Kennedy was much in demand:

The suspense of waiting for the news was terrible. I will sleep sounder tonight. A message from the *Daily Mail* on Saturday evening told us that the flight had begun. I did not expect to hear anything further before noon Sunday at the earliest, and when I learned of the safe arrival of the plane during the forenoon I was almost beside myself with joy.

Kathleen told another newspaper: 'I am going to fly in the Vimy myself when it comes back. I am going to try for a pilot's licence and I shall get him to teach me.'

News of the fliers' departure from Newfoundland only reached the Air Ministry in London on Saturday evening. Unaware of the landing, Flt Lt Bill Urqhart Dykes was sent from Castlebar at lunchtime to patrol the entrance to Galway Bay. He braved the coastal mists until he reached the Marconi masts, where he saw the grounded Vimy. After circling, he returned to base and telegraphed the Ministry. His decision not to land was a wise one. However, shortly afterwards, Capt. Bowen from Oranmore ensured that the Vimy would not be without company. As Alcock pointed out to a journalist, even such a light machine did not stand a chance on that surface. Bowen rashly attempted a landing just 50yd away, and his Bristol biplane buried its nose in homage to the off-white conqueror of the Atlantic.

Alcock and Brown left the Marconi station at 2 o'clock. They paused for a last look back at their stranded aeroplane. The Vimy looked in the distance like a stranded whale, its tail waving a reproachful farewell. Preparations were already being made for it to be dismantled and brought to Oranmore Aerodrome. Although Alcock and Brown knew they would all be reunited again at Brooklands, they were sorry to leave their aeroplane behind. They had watched it from its first assembly and nursed it through its test flights, and it had not let them down. Far from the company of man and top-heavy with cumbrous fuel, the uncomplaining Vimy had brought them through those clouds and storms all the way from America. Its fuselage and fabric had withstood the assaults of wind and savage rain, its struts and wires had resisted the deadly forces of their stall. It had suffered their every trial and now shared with them the honour of being the first to bridge the mighty ocean non-stop. In one peaceful mission it had achieved more than it would have done on countless raids. The fliers knew that the aeroplane would now be a part of their lives forever.

14

INTERNATIONAL ACCLAIM

The achievement is more than remarkable, it is sensational. It is one of
the greatest exploits of aviation. Not only has the Atlantic been crossed
but an immense horizon has been opened to long-distance flight.

Matin, Paris

Alcock and Brown travelled the mile to the glistening main road in a car
whose wheels had been adapted for Marconi's light railway. Assemblies of
locals and flying hens greeted them as they turned right under Ballinaboy
Hill and at crossroads along the 3-mile route to Clifden. A large throng
awaited on the outskirts of the town and escorted them to the Railway
Hotel for a reception arranged by the district council. Built in 1895, the
railway was a window to the outside world for the blighted and otherwise
isolated area. It enabled the transportation of local produce, as well as the
region's main export, tearful emigrants.

Formalities were kept to a minimum as Chairman Eddie King insisted
they must not delay the tired aviators from a well-deserved rest in Galway.
Alcock repaid this considerate gesture by not revealing that he and Brown
would have landed at Oranmore had they known there was a base there.
Vickers had not provided them with a map of Irish airfields. After congratulating the fliers and apologising for the deceptive nature of Irish bogs, King
assured them that they had landed in the most appropriate place: 'During
the years of the famine, many thousands of poor souls quit the shores of

Connemara for a better life in America. Surely, it is only right and proper that the first fliers from America should be landing here in Connemara.'

The Vimy pair set off for Galway shortly after 4.00 in the car hired by J.L. Hodson, who interviewed them further as they drove. On the way they were waved down by Maj. Mayo of the Royal Aero Club, en route to Derrygimla to check the aeroplane's official seal. They passed the Ballinahinch home of animal welfare pioneer 'Humanity' Dick Martin, a man after Brown's own heart. The navigator remembered Newfoundland as they negotiated the twisting, undulating road between the crags and grey stone walls. But this seemed a more gentle and friendly landscape, with rushing brown streams and a playful railway line that ran, first on one side of the green-bordered road, and then the other. Orange-hued woodbine perfumed their car, bright meadow-sweet and mombrecia as delicate as any Yeats lyric waved from lush verges. An ivy-covered castle graced a little island out on one of the lakes, the poet's restful land at last:

And I shall have some peace there, for peace comes dropping slow,
Dropping from the veils of morning to where the cricket sings;
There midnight's all a glimmer, and noon a purple glow,
And evening full of the linnet's wings.

For the sleep-challenged navigator, the 50-mile drive to Galway was a surreal experience:

It was a strange but welcome change to see solid objects flashing past us, instead of miles upon monotonous miles of drifting, cloudy vapour. Several times during that drive, I lost the thread of connection with tangible sur-roundings, and lived again in near retrospect the fantastic happenings of the day, night and morning that had just passed. Subconsciously, I still missed the rhythmic, relentless drone of the Rolls-Royce engines. My eyes had not yet become accustomed to the absence of clouds around and below, and my mind felt somehow lost, now that it was no longer preoccupied with heavenly bodies, horizon, time, direction, charts, drift, tables of calculations, sextant, spirit level, compass, aneroid, altimeter, wireless receiver, and the unexpected.

For a while, the immediate past seemed more prominent than the immediate present. Lassitude of mind, coupled with the reaction from the long strain of tense and unbroken concentration on one supreme objective, made me lose my grip of normal continuity, so that I answered questions mechanically, and wanted to avoid the effort of talk. The outstanding events and impressions of the flight – for example, the long spin from 6,000 to 50 feet, and the sudden sight of the white-capped ocean at the end of it – passed and repassed across my consciousness. I do not know whether Alcock underwent the same mental processes, but he remained very silent. Above all, I felt the need of re-establishing normal balance by means of sleep.

Sunday or not, the navigator was surprised at how quickly tidings of their arrival had travelled:

The wayside gatherings seemed especially unreal – almost as if they had been scenes on the film. By some extraordinary method of news transmission the report of our arrival had spread all over the district, and in many districts between Clifden and Galway curious crowds had gathered. A reception had been prepared in Galway, but our hosts, realising how tired we must be, considerately made it a short and informal affair. Afterwards we slept – for the first time in over forty hours.

The fliers were about to discover that they would need their rest in the Great Southern Hotel. But for its damage, the Vimy could have taken off again for England. Thanks to the following wind and Alcock's husbandry, it had more than enough fuel left for the journey. Had the pair known of the public and media frenzy they were about to face, they would happily have waited for a repair crew to arrive from Brooklands. Even with their wartime prison experiences they had rarely been as isolated in all their lives as on the long flight. It had seemed at times as if they were the only persons on the planet, and that the world had entirely forgottenn about them. But their transatlantic success changed all that.

NEWFOUNDLAND TO IRELAND. UNDER 16 HOURS. ALL-BRITISH TRIUMPH.

So read the headline that greeted Alcock and Brown on Monday, 16 June 1919. They awoke to find that the world was knocking on their door. Trying as some of the Marconi station interviews had been, these only marked the start of a new ordeal. Their achievement had made the fliers public property. They were celebrities. Everyone felt entitled to an answer, an interview, an autograph.

The pair began the day with the first recorded manifestation of modern jet lag, or, more correctly, propeller lag. Brown recorded:

> Alcock and I awoke to find ourselves in a wonderland of seeming unreality – the product of violent change from utter desolation during the long flight to unexpected contact with crowds of people interested in us. To begin with, getting up in the morning after a satisfactory sleep of nine hours was strange. In our eastward flight of 2,000 miles we had overtaken time, in less than the period between one sunset and another, to the extent of three and a half hours. Our physical systems having accustomed themselves to habits regulated by the clocks of Newfoundland, we were reluctant to rise at 7 a.m., for subconsciousness suggested it was but 3.30 a.m.
>
> This difficulty of adjustment to the sudden change in time lasted for several days. Probably it will be experienced by all passengers travelling on the rapid trans-ocean air services of the future. Those who complete a westward journey becoming early risers without effort, those who land after an eastward flight becoming unconsciously lazy in the morning, until the jolting effect of the dislocation wears off, and habit has accustomed itself to the new conditions.

Brown was allowed little time to dwell on his unique condition:

> After breakfast – eaten in an atmosphere of the deepest content – there began a succession of congratulatory ovations. For these we were totally unprepared; and with our relaxed minds, we could not easily adapt ourselves

to the conditions attendant upon being magnets for a few days' curiosity from the world.

News of the Vimy's arrival in Ireland dominated all the local, British, and international media. Alcock and who? Hitherto unknown to the general public, Alcock and Brown's names and photographs were emblazoned on news stands from Dublin to London, Paris, and New York. Their success against overwhelming odds had touched all strata of society. The fliers had become instant heroes, harbingers of change and a brighter future for the millions who were weary of the plagues of war and flu, and the endless post-Armistice recriminations.

The conquest of the Atlantic was the sole topic of conversation at British breakfast tables. At first there had been incredulity at the speed with which the journey had been accomplished. It seemed as if the fliers had only left Newfoundland and, one newspaper edition later, they had arrived in Europe. 'Yesterday we were in America' became a much-repeated catch cry. In London there was particular pride. The Vimy had been constructed just down the road at Weybridge. There was even greater joy in Manchester, where both men had studied and lived. Soon, welcome ceremonies were being planned.

The cabled news of Alcock and Brown's success had reached the *Daily Mail's* Carmelite House at 10.50 on Sunday morning. But with no Sunday *Mail*, the tidings of both the Vimy's departure and arrival was first published by rival media. The *Express's* Newfoundland correspondent, Edwin Cleary, dispatched news of the departure in time for his paper's Sunday morning edition. Its 'GREAT BRITISH AIR TRIUMPH' headline ensured record sales for the night-extra edition of the *Sunday Evening Telegram*.

All of Monday's international newspaper front pages were devoted exclusively to the Vimy's arrival. From the earlier derisory 'Weather Delays Fliers' paragraphs, Alcock and Brown now pushed Germany and the Versailles Conference off the main pages. The media surpassed themselves in superlatives. The *Daily Mail* insisted:

Greater glory attaches to the flight for the reason that it was accomplished under bad weather conditions. Fog and drizzling rain obscured vision to such an extent that at times the machine was discovered to be flying upside down and once only 10 feet from the water. The world will acclaim the cool courage and flying skill of Alcock and the wonderful navigation of Brown which alone could bring the machine to its landing on the west coast of Ireland after such a perilous passage of the trackless waste.

The Times carried a full report on the flight and added its congratulations:

Captain Alcock and Lt Brown had no landsman's crossing. They started in perilous fashion and with a real risk of ruining their hopes before they could get into the air; and even when they had escaped the type of disaster that overtook Raynham and his Martinsyde machine, their flight was beset by fog and ice-sleet. They have attempted, and have performed, a feat which is a great step forward in human accomplishment.

Continental media showered further compliments. In Paris, *Matin* insisted: 'The achievement is more than remarkable, it is sensational. It is one of the greatest exploits of aviation. Not only has the Atlantic been crossed but an immense horizon has been opened to long-distance flight.' *Le Journal* agreed: 'Performances like that of Alcock and Brown are lofty and powerful beacon fires on the road of progress.'

In the USA *The World* wrote: 'The flight of Captain Alcock and Lieut Brown as a splendid feat of scientific skill, pure sportsmanship, physical endurance and indifference to danger, has never been surpassed in the records of aviation.'

After describing the fliers' performance as worthy to rank among the greatest of human achievements, the *New York Times* soared:

Like Alexander, the record-making aviator will soon weep because he has no more worlds to conquer. After such a flight what is a small voyage like death, across a peaceful river, to a fate determined? For human daring our hats are off to these Englishmen who fought the sun, the stars and Sir Isaac

Newton's best theory and beat them all. Neither nightmare nor Samuel Taylor Coleridge ever did better.

The *Irish Times* celebrated: 'The NC-4 frustrated the obstinacy of the Atlantic with three sups; the Vickers Vimy has drained it at one gulp.' The paper optimistically concluded: 'We are certain, as we were not certain yesterday, that we stand on the threshold of rich and wonderful developments in the arts of peace and the fellowship of mankind.'

Alcock and Brown were delighted with Orville Wright's reaction: 'What? Only sixteen hours! Are you sure?' But they were embarrassed to read British media reports of what each had said about the other. One newspaper reported:

Lt Brown said to me 'Right from the beginning when we first met, we worked together splendidly. To my mind Alcock has the ideal temperament for flying. Nothing seems to upset him, and he does not appear to have any nerves. He is always bubbling over with good humour. The way he nursed the engines on the flight was great.'

Alcock said; 'I consider that the navigation on the trip under the trying circumstances and bad visibility was really wonderful.'

The pilot was further mortified to read of his parents' interviews. Messages of the fliers' arrival had been telephoned by the *Daily Mail* to the relatives of both men. But, worried about her son, Mrs Alcock had earlier cycled into Fallowfield to telephone Vickers, who were the first to give her the good news. Well-wishers then stood in a line outside the Alcocks' Manchester home to shake their hands. A newspaper quoted the pilot's parents:

At Didsbury, my son told me 'Father, I am going to fly.' He had confidence. I've never known him to fail at anything he had undertaken. If he says he will do a thing, he does it, however difficult it is.'

Mrs Alcock said that her son began to study books about mechanics at the age of thirteen. He would sit up at night, poring over textbooks. She once caught him hard at work at 3 a.m.! Mrs Alcock expressed the fervent hope that there would not be too much fuss. 'He never liked fuss.'

To the embarrassment of the *Mail*, it was an *Express* reporter who first told the Kennedy family of Alcock and Brown's safe arrival. The very private navigator was disconcerted to read the 'AIRMAN'S PROUD BRIDE' headline. The *Express* continued:

> Miss Kennedy, to whom Lieutenant Brown is shortly to be married, told a Daily Express representative last night that she was delighted with the success of the flight.
>
> 'It is splendid,' she said. 'I am tremendously proud. My family and I were deeply concerned when the flight started, but now all is well and Captain Alcock and Lieutenant Brown have reached their goal.'
>
> Major and Mrs Kennedy were equally elated. They have been the recipients of countless congratulations. 'We share our daughter's pride,' said Major Kennedy, 'and Lieutenant Brown is assured of an ovation when he arrives.' Hundreds of spectators yesterday assembled outside Miss Kennedy's home at Ealing and cheered for Lieutenant Brown and his bride.

While trying to come to terms with their new-found fame, the fliers were inundated with congratulatory cables. The messages included one from the King, whose father had previously toured the area where the fliers landed:

> The King was delighted to receive your welcome announcement that Capt Alcock and Lieut Brown have safely landed in Ireland after their Transatlantic flight. His Majesty wishes you to communicate at once with these officers and to convey to them the King's warmest congratulations on the success of their splendid achievement.

US President Wilson sent his congratulations, as did one of the country's foremost pioneers, Glenn Curtiss. Future New York mayor Fiorello la Guardia recommended that Alcock and Brown be awarded Congressional Medals of Honor. British Prime Minister Lloyd George wrote to Alcock:

'Heartiest congratulations to you and Lieutenant Brown on your audacious and splendid flight. It is a splendid achievement. I am especially
delighted that two British officers who fought in the war should have
been the first to Europe from America in a non-stop flight.'

Alcock and Brown were particularly pleased with the Royal Aero
Club's congratulatory cable and with Harry Hawker's reaction:

> I am sending my heartfelt congratulations to Captain Alcock and
> Lieutenant Brown. A very, very fine performance indeed. My only regret is
> that I was not able to be at Clifden to congratulate the conquerors of the
> Atlantic personally. There is, of course, always an element of luck in such
> enterprises but the Vickers achievement is really an amazing one. I am more
> gratified than I can say that British air supremacy has been maintained by
> British aviators and a British machine has made the first successful crossing.

An equally appreciated message arrived from Lord Northcliffe, who was
awaiting a thyroid gland operation. He reminded Alcock and Brown of
the implications of their success:

> A very hearty welcome to the pioneers of direct Atlantic flight. Your jour-
> ney with your brave companion, Whitten Brown, is a typical example of
> British courage and organising efficiency.
>
> Just as in 1913 when I offered the prize, I thought that it would soon be
> won, so do I surely believe that your wonderful journey is a warning to cable
> monopolists and others to realise that within the next few years we shall be
> less dependent upon them unless they improve their wires and speed up.
> Your voyage was made more quickly than the average Press message of 1919.
>
> Moreover, I look forward with certainty to the time when London
> morning papers will be selling in New York in the evening, allowing for
> the difference between American time and vice versa in regard to New
> York evening journals reaching London the next day. Then we shall no
> longer suffer from the danger of garbled quotations due to telegraphic
> compression. Then too, the American and British peoples will understand
> each other better as they are brought into closer daily touch.

Like every other Irish and British town, Galway buzzed with the news of the transatlantic achievement and the additional pride that their city hosted the two most famous men on the planet. It was too good an opportunity to lose. Calligraphers worked into the early hours of Monday on special addresses from the urban and county councils. The city's normally quiet post office played a major role in relaying the story of the Vimy's arrival to the outside world. Journalists praised its staff's efficiency during the previous evening's news frenzy: 'Their interest never flagged; their courtesy remained undisturbed. They did more than they could have been expected to do, playing a worthy part in giving to the world the airmen's story. Some of them worked fourteen and a half hours at a stretch.'

The Lieutenant for County Galway, Lord Killanin, was unsurprised that Alcock and Brown had chosen his bailiwick as their destination:

Not at all. In my part of the country, we knew that they would land in Galway. As I have always maintained in the House of Lords, Galway is the natural port for the traffic from America to Great Britain because it is the shortest route, as Captain Alcock and Lieutenant Brown have proved beyond our wildest expectations.

Galway's council officials assembled at the hotel at 1 o'clock. Thomas Macdonagh delivered the first address:

On behalf of the citizens of the County of Galway, which has the honour of being the landing place of the first non-stop Transatlantic flight, the Galway County Council heartily welcomes the intrepid airmen who successfully carried out this magnificent feat. On account of the shortness of the notice we regret that this meeting is not more representative of the county, but we feel assured that we voice the feeling of the whole county and of all Ireland in congratulating you on the success of your courageous and sporting exploit. In the record of which we are glad to know that the name of our country, linked with your own, will go down in history. Wishing you both long life to enjoy the unique honour you have so well earned.

After Capt. Redington read the urban council's contribution, Alcock rose to make his first public speech: 'I hope you will excuse me. I am not used to this sort of thing. I wish to express to you our feelings of deep gratitude, and if you will kindly excuse me.'

The pilot was cheered loudly, as was Brown after his equally brief thanks. Then each man was presented by local jeweller William Dillon with a gold Claddagh ring. One of the world's most distinctive bands, with two hands holding a crowned heart, the Claddagh ring was allegedly designed by Richard Joyce, whose life was as adventurous as that of the fliers. Captured by Algerian corsairs and sold as a slave to a Moorish goldsmith, he returned to Galway in 1689 and set up in the same trade. Claddagh rings were worn by both Queen Victoria and King Edward VII, who holidayed in Galway in 1903. As Alcock and Brown tried on their rings there was a call for 'three cheers' and all the officials joined in singing 'For They Are Jolly Good Fellows'. Alcock responded: 'I shall always keep my ring and wear it as a lucky charm.'

If the fliers had thought this was the end of the celebrations, they were mistaken. Outside the hotel door they were acclaimed by a vast crowd. The wind and rain failed to dampen the spirit of the Galwegians, who noisily escorted their guests to the 2.25 Dublin train. Brown later wrote: 'The warm-hearted crowd that we found waiting at Galway station both amazed and daunted us. We were grateful for their loud appreciation, but scarcely able to respond to it adequately. Flowers were offered and we met the vanguard of the autograph hunters.'

A British journalist explained:

The modest unassuming demeanour of the airmen has won all hearts in Galway. They have been besieged by autograph hunters, and Army officers, navy officers, local dignitaries, and priests have struggled in concert for the honour of shaking their hands. 'You have Galway more talked about than Paris!' said one gentleman, wringing Brown's hand. The press of people on the platform was terrific, and the airmen had difficulty in making their way along to their reserved compartment. More autographers here; more handshakes, and then at length, to the accompaniment of deafening cheers and to the explosion of fog signals, the train steamed out from Galway.

Between the newspapers, congratulatory messages and the receptions, both Alcock and Brown felt that they had already had a long day. The Claddagh rings gleamed on their left hands as they settled into their seats for the journey to Dublin and the Holyhead boat for home. Alcock shared his seat with Twinkletoes and a bunch of flowers given to him by a girl. It was a relief to bathe their tired eyes with the gentle countryside rolling past their window. But it was to be a brief respite. Not even the presence of their escorts, Lord Killanin and Maj. Mayo, could save them from the ovations at almost every station along the 130-mile journey. Even where there were no stops, crowds waved flags as the Midland and Great Western train slowed to an accommodating rate. At Oranmore, officers from the air station invaded the train to greet their fellow fliers and take photographs. The train was over a quarter of an hour late by the time it left Athenry, where children presented Alcock and Brown with further flowers.

A more official welcome greeted them at Mullingar. The War of the Roses was forgotten as the band of the 3rd East Yorkshires played 'Hail the Conquering Hero Comes' for the two Lancastrians. Alcock and Brown were invited to inspect the assembled troops and, as they were leaving, a schoolboy presented the pilot with a wooden model aeroplane he had made himself.

Brown was moved and equally bemused by the unexpected adulation:

We must have signed our names hundreds of times during the journey to Dublin – on books, cards, old envelopes, and scraps of paper of every shape. This we did wonderingly, not yet understanding why so many people should ask for our signatures, when three days earlier few people had heard our names. The men, women and children that thronged every station on the way seemed to place a far higher value on our success than we did ourselves. Until now, we had been too self-centred to realise that other people might be particularly interested in the flight from America to England. We had finished the job we wanted to do, and could not comprehend why it should lead to fuss.

Now, however, I know that the crowds saw more clearly than I did, and that their cheers were not for us personally, but for what they regarded as a manifestation of the spirit of Adventure, the True Romance – call it what you will. For the moment this elusive ideal was suggested to them by the first non-stop journey by air across the Atlantic, which we had been fortunate enough to make.

Few manifested the spirit of adventure more than the students of Trinity College, who were celebrating their Trinity Monday that day. As Alcock and Brown faced another cheering throng and waving flags at Dublin's Broadstone Station at 6 o'clock, a group of students 'kidnapped' Alcock and drove him to their college. Officials of the Royal Irish Automobile Club (RIAC) brought Brown to their Dawson Street headquarters for the reception they had organised on behalf of the Royal Aero Club. They thought Alcock had preceded them, and it was some time before they heard that he was in Trinity, from whose Commons the Provost eventually liberated him. The students escorted the pilot's car to the RIAC. Brown admitted to being still tired. Asked how he felt, Alcock laughed: 'If I am due for a reaction from the strain and excitement of the flight, it is a long time coming!'

The fliers were given a special guard as they left for the lodge of the Chief Secretary, Mr Macpherson. It was their last night in Ireland, a country whose people they had conquered, unlike their government, which was unable to cope with the increasing clamour for independence. Having had to deal with so much acclaim from Galway to Dublin, the fliers were right to wonder what the following day's return to London might bring.

15

HOMECOMING AND HONOURS

Their exploit is so great that we must get further away in the perspective. When we look back a thousand years, how it will shine in the head-roll of history.

Col Arthur Lynch, MP

Early on the morning of Tuesday, 17 June, Alcock and Brown embarked on their triumphant return home in the SS *Ulster* from Kingstown (now Dun Laoghaire). Not recognising Brown, a ship employee asked for his ticket. Leaning over the ship's starboard side, the two fliers gazed peacefully at the harbour and the hills before they were finally spotted by their fellow passengers. For once the pilot was not short of words when asked what he thought of Ireland:

> I want to thank the Irish people for the royal reception they have given to Lieutenant Brown and myself on our way from Galway to Dublin. It was really wonderful. This reception is really harder than the actual flight and entails a bigger strain. I was nearly torn to pieces yesterday!

Hundreds acclaimed the fliers when they came down the gangway in Holyhead at noon. Ships' sirens competed with a welcoming band. The pair were delighted to be greeted by some of those responsible for their success, particularly Capt. Vickers and designer Reginald Pierson, and

Lord Northcliffe's friend, Claude Johnson, general manager of Rolls-Royce. Scenes along the *Irish Mail's* 270-mile journey to London replicated those of the previous day. As they steamed across Robert Stephenson's Menai Straits bridge, Brown was right to be concerned. How nice it would be to turn the clock back six weeks to their unacknowledged departure from Southampton, but now bands played, flags waved and crowds cheered. How removed this joyous clamour was from the lonely reality of their long flight and their fraught departure but seventy-two hours earlier from Lester's Field.

Britain witnessed the greatest national outpouring of joy since Armistice Day. Brown had to rescue Alcock from a mob of autograph hunters at Chester. The Mayors of Chester, Crewe and Rugby greeted them as if they were returning war heroes.

A barrier of milk churns erected by station porters at Rugby was no match for the surging throng, who shouted 'Good old Lancashire'. *The Times* recorded the Crewe welcome:

> Women and men struggled together to touch the Captain or the Lieutenant
> – both for preference – and imperative demands from the rear ended in a
> kind of slow procession past the saloon door. Suddenly, an Australian soldier
> called to a porter 'Up with him', and Lieutenant Brown was lifted shoulder-high so that all the people could see and cheer him. Another soldier
> with assistance hoisted up Captain Alcock. Then the whistle blew and the
> throng had to let them go.

Kathleen Kennedy was among the crowd waiting at Rugby. Alcock was reminded of the distant London–Manchester air race when he saw aeroplanes circling overhead. He was told that they were waiting to escort himself and Brown to London. *The Times* noted:

> At Rugby, Brown's shyness must have finally got the better of him. For
> instead of leaving the train to greet Miss Kathleen Kennedy, his fiancée –
> who with her father, Major D.H. Kennedy, had travelled to meet him – he
> remained in the saloon and Miss Kennedy, pretty, slim, tall and daintily

dressed, stepped into the carriage. Capt. Alcock immediately jumped out to face the enthusiastic crowd and to write more autographs, and then before the train left, brought Lieutenant Brown and Miss Kennedy arm in arm to the door to get their share of the cheers.

Hawker and Grieve had been overwhelmed by their reception at Euston on their return. That welcome was about to be eclipsed, despite the rival attraction of Ascot Races and the sweltering beaches. Long before the train's scheduled 6 p.m. arrival, thousands swamped the station forecourt and platform. Sir Andrew Caird represented Lord Northcliffe. Accompanied by his mace-bearer and aldermen, the Mayor of St Pancras was one of the first to greet the fliers. As he was swept away by the throng, Gen. Groves presented the Vimy pair with letters of congratulations from Gen. Trenchard of the RAF and Gen. Seely from the Air Department.

Alcock and Brown were thrilled to be reunited with Harry Hawker, who, a month earlier, they had thought they would never see again. But they were shocked by the mass of people and the waves of cheering that engulfed them in the heat outside the station. As the fliers entered their flag-adorned open Rolls-Royce, helmeted policemen jumped on the running boards to protect them from over-eager admirers. Hawker and his wife rode in a second car behind them.

Hundreds of thousands more lined the route via Portland Street, Oxford Circus and Regent Street, which mounted police were required to clear several times. Young and old waved Union flags and called out the fliers' names. Acclaim and confetti rained down from balconies. Bewildered but moved by the happy throng, Alcock and Brown smiled and saluted in return. They were touched that their achievement had inspired so many people, but relieved finally to reach the Royal Aero Club. As vice-chairman Gen. Holden welcomed them home again, Alcock handed over his white bag of mail from Newfoundland. 'I am the first transatlantic postman,' he joked.

Once the cheers had subsided, Gen. Holden said: 'The first non-stop flight across the Atlantic will ever live as one of the most remarkable feats. Columbus must now fade into the shade.' The general remarked on the modesty of the Vimy pair: 'They appreciate that we appreciate what they have done, but they do not appreciate themselves what they have done.'

The fliers were forced to make brief speeches. Standing on a chair, Alcock paid generous tribute to his partner's navigation, while Brown insisted:

> In a flight like this, the essentials to success are, first, the design of the machine, for which our thanks are due to Messrs Vickers and to the workmen who built it. Second, the engines, the Rolls-Royce engines. Third, the instruments with which the machine is equipped, and for these we have to thank the Air Ministry, who helped us to obtain the most modern equipment which has been designed. And last, but not least, the pilot Captain Alcock. For with all these things, the machine could not have made a successful flight without such a pilot as Captain Alcock.

It did not take that pilot long to get up to his old tricks. Before he left the club, Alcock completed his entry for the following Saturday's Aerial Derby at Hendon Aerodrome. Then he went for a Turkish bath before going to the British Heavyweight Championship boxing match at Olympia. Brown faced yet one further reception at 9.00 p.m. in Ealing Town Hall. The mayor, council members and the Kennedys' neighbours thanked him for the honour he had brought to his fiancée's borough. In response to popular demand, the councillors also promised a substantial present for his forthcoming wedding.

The crowning celebration would be the presentation of the *Daily Mail* cheque on Friday, 20 June. But Alcock and Brown's first loyalty was to Vickers and, despite their weariness, they returned to Brooklands the day after their arrival in London. Flags and bunting decorated the factory gates, 'WELCOME' was painted in large letters across the roof of one of the sheds. Work was suspended for the day as the entire staff turned out to greet them. The cheering did not subside for ten minutes. A manager insisted:

> We always thought a lot of Alcock here at the works. He was very popular and the enthusiastic way he worked in preparing his machine inspired us

all. We do not know Brown so well but Alcock does know him and had every confidence in him.

To the stirring accompaniment of the band of the nearby New Zealand Soldiers' Hospital, the fliers were chaired across the sunny grounds by the riggers who had built the aeroplane. Eighty-year-old Albert Vickers thanked the Vimy crew for having maintained the company's tradition for efficiency, originality and good workmanship. In addition to remembering Maxwell Muller and Archie Knight, Alcock also praised Bob Dicker, Gordon Montgomery and foreman Ernie Pitman. He paid a special tribute to the staff of riggers, carpenters and mechanics who had worked so hard in such difficult conditions at St John's: Messrs Chick, Couch, Davis, Humm, Potter, Wand and Westmacott. Saddened by the death of Albert Vickers the following month, Brown recorded: 'It was to be the welcome we appreciated most.'

The conquerors of the Atlantic savoured their first day's rest in weeks, before the *Daily Mail*'s grand celebratory luncheon at the Savoy Hotel. This would be their last official reception before their achievement was celebrated in their home city of Manchester. Not only were the fliers to receive the *Mail*'s £10,000 prize, they were also to be awarded £1,000 by Mr Lawrence Phillips for being the first Britons to fly the Atlantic, and another 2,000 guineas by the State Express Cigarette Company. Alcock discarded his suit and donned a uniform like Brown. A specially printed menu displayed their photographs and a sketch of their aeroplane. In contrast to their Vimy sandwiches, the fare featured such delights as *Oeufs pochés Alcock*, *Suprême de sole à la Brown*, *Salade Clifden* and *Gateau Grand Succès*.

The quality of the speechmaking matched the grandeur of the occasion. Winston Churchill, Secretary of State for War and the Air, was at his Ciceronian best:

This is an achievement which marks the advance of science and of engineering and the increasing triumph of man over nature. But it is also an event which shows that, while we have become more powerfully equipped in all that sort of apparatus, we have also preserved as a race the audacity, the courage, the physical qualities of the old heroic bygone times.

Churchill painted a graphic picture of the perils the fliers had faced:

Think of the broad Atlantic, that terrible waste of desolate waters, tossing in tumult in repeated and almost ceaseless storms, and shrouded with an unbroken canopy of mist. Across this waste, and through this obscurity, two human beings, hurtling through the air, piercing the clouds and darkness, finding their unerring path in spite of every difficulty to their exact objective across those hundreds of miles, arriving almost on scheduled time, and at every moment in this voyage liable to destruction from a drop of water in the carburettor, or a spot of oil on their plugs, or a tiny grain of dirt in their feed pipe, or from any of the thousand and one indirect causes which in the present state of aeronautics might drag an aeroplane to its fate.

When one considers all these factors I really do not know which we should admire the most in our guests – their audacity, their determination, their skill, their science, their Vickers Vimy aeroplane, their Rolls-Royce engines, or their good fortune. They are the victors. They are the real victors, and they are the only victors. It is no disparagement to the brilliantly executed exploits of the US Navy, if we say in surveying the Atlantic flight made by Alcock and Brown, 'This is it!'

Lord Northcliffe was represented by *Daily Mail* editor Thomas Marlowe, a graduate of Queen's College in Galway, from which the aviators had just arrived. Alcock expressed his regret at the absence of Lord Northcliffe: 'I hope he will soon recover and be strong and well enough to further the cause of aviation as he has done in the past.' Brown surprised the audience and himself with an eloquent account of the flight, his navigational difficulties and how he made drift bearings by observations on icebergs from 1,000ft. After paying tribute to the Vickers designer and workers, and to Rolls-Royce, he concluded to laughter: 'No doubt, you are all anxious to know what is to be done with the money. When Captain Alcock and

I landed from St John's, the first thing we saw in a newspaper was a paragraph headed Buy War Loans. We made our mind up in two minutes!'

Like Alcock, the navigator was himself in turn taken aback when Churchill announced to lusty cheers: 'I am very happy to be able to tell you that I have received His Majesty's gracious consent to an immediate award of the Knight Commandership of the Order of the British Empire to both Captain Alcock and Lieutenant Brown.'

The fliers were invested the following day, Saturday, at Windsor Castle. Alcock cancelled his Aerial Derby entry and wore uniform for the royal occasion. The Mayor of Windsor greeted them at the station, from which Eton College boys escorted their carriage to the castle. Alcock presented a Newfoundland airmail stamp to the King, who told them that it was his idea that they should be knighted. The King said that he would convey their good wishes to the people of St John's, whom he would be visiting the following month. To cries of 'The First Knights of the Air', the young Etonians cheered the fliers back to the Paddington train. Alcock rushed to Hendon to catch the end of the flying, while Brown made a well-planned secret visit to his parents' home. He had the train stopped at Withington and then boarded a local train to Chorlton, where he spent the weekend indoors before returning to London the following Monday.

Alcock and Brown's final reception was in Manchester. Both men turned out in uniform, the last time Alcock would be so attired. The event was noteworthy for the number of eligible young ladies who turned out to welcome the fliers home. Sadly, their hopes of capturing a transatlantic airman were in vain. Brown was due to marry shortly afterwards, while Alcock thought only of returning to fly at Brooklands and of opening a motor business.

Hitherto, Brown and Kathleen Kennedy had been making plans to live in the USA, where he had been confident of finding engineering work. He had told an American journalist that the Atlantic would be his last flight and that he intended to resume his interrupted career. But the Vimy success and the prize money changed all that. The navigator no longer needed the CV with which he had previously limped around London and Manchester in vain search of employment. He could now remain in England, where there was the prospect of a full-time position with Vickers.

Back in St John's, news of Alcock and Brown's success was still being celebrated. Homes and stores rejoiced with flags and bunting. Many recalled how Alcock had practically fought his aeroplane into the air. The story of his take-off and battle against the elements was told and retold, and would be recalled around many a future fireside. Those who sent airmail letters were doubly elated. Never before had letters travelled so swiftly from one continent to the other. A reporter noted:

> Even the worst pessimist of yesterday is perfectly willing today to theorise over the possibilities of flying to the moon or to Mars or anywhere else, and those who pinned their faith on Captain Alcock and Lieutenant Brown today have the satisfaction of unlimited 'I told you so's'. Amazing and almost unbelievable as the feat seemed, even more astonishing was it to those who received cable messages from the pilot and navigator dated at Clifden. Yesterday in Newfoundland, today sending messages from another hemisphere! It seemed almost incredible as one stared at those two names – Alcock and Brown – on a cable blank.

With consummate bad timing, Maj. Alfred Fiske had arrived in St John's on 14 June, the day of the Vimy's departure, to prepare for the Boulton and Paul transatlantic effort. One look at Lester's Field was enough to convince him of its limitations, and he went immediately to Harbour Grace. But with Alcock and Brown already in Ireland the company then called off its attempt 'due to adverse public reaction'. This did not inhibit it from naming its new eight-seater biplane Atlantic. Lieutenant Williams and the Alliance team, who had already planned a hangar at Ropewalk, announced their retirement the following week.

Although beaten to the *Daily Mail* prize, Freddie Raynham prepared his Martinsyde for one further Atlantic bid. With his new navigator, Lt Charles Biddlecombe, he made a successful test flight on 14 July. Three days later, after fixing a radiator fault, he confidently taxied the Raymor down the Quidi Vidi strip. The aeroplane made a better take-off than on its first fully laden attempt, but after only 50yd it once again tumbled back to the ground. The weight of the fuel seemed too much for such a small machine, and the airmen said they felt the aircraft sag as it lifted into the air. Neither man was injured but, with fractured petrol tanks, Raynham considered themselves lucky to have once again avoided a conflagration. He decided on no further attempts, and a Cochrane Hotel wag suggested that he might find difficulty in raising a third navigator. Raynham returned to England and subsequently became chief test pilot for H.G. Hawker Engineering, which had been founded by his old friends, Harry Hawker and Tommy Sopwith.

The Handley Page saga suffered an equally inauspicious conclusion. With the Atlantic now conquered, the company's US representative suggested that the V/1500 should make a demonstration flight to New York. Adm Kerr argued against this, but commerce prevailed. They headed south, but luck was not on their side. The radiators once again overheated and forced them down at Parrsboro, Nova Scotia. Another emergency landing near Cleveland wrecked the repaired aeroplane, though fortunately without injury to its crew. Apart from the overheating, the responsibility of British naval backing was perhaps the main reason for Kerr's indecision and his failure to race the more flexible Alcock and Brown. A cautious and conscientious career man, the admiral took his responsibilities seriously and would only let Maj. Brackley and his crew leave in a perfect aeroplane.

Once the elation had died down there was more sober assessment of the Vimy achievement's implications for the future of aviation. The aeroplane's success helped to ensure the future of Vickers. Concerned by the British advance, the chief of US naval aviation asked for an extra $20 million, stating that, otherwise, his country would fall behind other nations in aircraft development. The *Manchester Guardian* agreed that the airship seemed the most ideal means of transatlantic flight for the foreseeable future, but insisted: 'To make the aeroplane safe enough for business use on such sea routes we should have to have all the cyclones of the Atlantic marked on the chart, and their progress marked in from hour to hour.'

The *Empire Mail* saw a future for both airships and aeroplanes:

This flight will no doubt be a great incentive to all countries to organise and equip aerial passenger and freight services for distances not exceeding about 1,000 miles. For greater distances, it seems likely that the lighter-than-air machines will play the more important part. What the future will bring in this direction, it is impossible to say. For all will depend on development and experiment, the present trend of which would indicate that the heavier-than-air machine will assume far larger dimensions and power, and will probably be in the nature of a sea-plane capable of descending on dry land. It is likely that the development in design will necessitate the machine being made entirely of metal, even the wings being of this construction.

Arthur Whitten Brown particularly appreciated the *Daily Mail* prizes:

I desire to pay a very well-deserved tribute to the man who from the beginning has backed with money his faith in the future of aviation. The pioneer work of aeronautics has been helped enormously by the generous prizes of Lord Northcliffe and the *Daily Mail* for the first flights across the Channel, from London to Manchester, around the circuit of Britain and, finally, across the Atlantic.

Ironically, however, Brown felt that money should now be diverted into research, rather than into such awards. He pointed out that Vickers had helped to make the British aircraft industry the greatest in the world, thanks to its specially established experimental department, which had quickly led to the production of superior aircraft:

There are plenty of men able and anxious to devote themselves competently to seeking for yet hidden solutions whereby flying will be made cheaper, safer, and more reliable. What is especially wanted for the moment is the financial endowment of research into the several problems that must be solved before the air age makes the world a better place to live in, and, by eliminating long and uncomfortable journeys, bring the nations into closer bonds of understanding and commerce.

Like Alcock, the navigator always played down his role in the conquest of the Atlantic. And he never forgot the debt he owed to earlier pioneers:

It is an awful thing to be told that one had made history or done something historic. Such an accusation implies the duty of living up to other people's expectations; and merely an ordinary person who has been lucky, like myself, cannot fulfil such expectations. Sir John Alcock and I were told so often by the printed and spoken word that our transatlantic flight was an important event in the history of aviation that, almost – but not quite – I came to believe. And this half-belief has made me very humble, when I considered the splendid company of the pioneers who, without due recognition, gave life, money, or precious years, often all three, to further the future of aeronautics – Lilienthal, Pilcher, Langley, Eiffel, Lanchester, Maxim, the Wrights, Blériot, Cody, Roe, Rolls, and the many daring men who piloted the weird, experimental craft that were among the first to fly.

John Alcock noted:

We were too tired to think much of the feat at the time. Our subsequent experiences having been of an even more strenuous if gratifying nature, it is only now, when in possession of some leisure, that any sort of retrospect is possible. Although the actual time occupied by our transatlantic flight was under sixteen hours, it may be fairly said that it took ten years to accomplish. It was perhaps owing to the knowledge of this fact that the public appreciation of the feat overwhelmed me in no small degree. To them it was a sudden and perhaps sensational achievement; but it was really but the successful outcome of much preparation.

The Vimy pilot explained:

There is always satisfaction in being first to do anything, whatever it may be, and while the lapse of time may intensify that feeling, the flight was nothing more than the execution of a long conceived plan. It was not the happy issue of a hastily planned venture, nor was it seizing the favourable factors. At the risk of appearing egotistical, I would lay stress on this fact, for before leaving Newfoundland we felt confident of our arrival on the other side; but the confidence was derived very largely from experience and the knowledge of a machine capable of the journey.

As in everything else, there is no royal road to long-distance flying. Physical fitness and technical knowledge are essential, for the strain is certainly heavy both on man and machine. Ten years of continuous flying undoubtedly stood me in good stead. Had I been less fit or less experienced, the excellent machine produced by Messrs Vickers and the Rolls-Royce engines must have been sacrificed.

Although he was impressed by the modesty of the Vimy aviators, Col Arthur Lynch MP, who had witnessed many pioneer flights, had the final word on their achievement: 'Their exploit is so great that we must get further away in the perspective. When we look back a thousand years, how it will shine in the head-roll of history.'

Once the celebrations were over, the conquerors of the Atlantic went their separate ways. Brown to get married at last, and his pilot to resume flying for Vickers and to plan the launch of his motor business. Alcock had dared the ocean because he was a flier, not for the money. His prize, however, would now help him to open a motor showroom. He had dreamt of having his own garage while a young apprentice in Manchester. Now he would be independent at last, at the young age of 26. Sadly for such a capable and deserving man, he was not destined to realise that cherished ambition.

16

ROUEN CLAIMS ALCOCK

I heard engine noise and looked up in the sky. I saw a large plane speeding from the north. It became very unsteady in the wind. Then, it gave a great sway and fell to the earth.

M. Pelletier

Over the following months both Alcock and Brown endured sittings for official portraits. War veteran Sir John Lavery painted the studies, which are now in the RAF Museum at Hendon. Ambrose McEvoy produced the more stylised picture of Alcock that hangs in London's National Portrait Gallery. Their Vimy was not neglected either. Mahogany models of the aeroplane sold briskly for 10/6d. The propellers revolved as the model was wheeled and, instead of emergency supplies, its tail acted as a receptacle for matches.

The fliers yielded to pressure and wrote accounts of their joint achievement. Alcock's brief factual description was published in the September 1919 issue of *Badminton Magazine.* He concluded by revealing that his hearing had been affected by his exposure to the Vimy's broken exhaust: 'I suffer still as a result of long proximity to the deafening exhaust. Travelling as we were at over two miles a minute with the exhaust rattling like a machine gun battery, this is hardly to be wondered at.'

Brown collaborated with journalist Alan Bott on a more elaborate but equally understated version, later published in the *Royal Air Force and*

Civil Aviation Record. While John Alcock saw flying as a challenge and an adventure to be savoured, Arthur Whitten Brown idealistically surveyed the long-term implications of their Atlantic success:

> I realise that our flight was but a solitary finger-post to the air traffic – safe, comfortable, and voluminous – that in coming years will pass above the Atlantic Ocean. But even had the winning of the competition brought us no other benefit, each of us would have remained well content to be pioneers of this aerial entente which is destined to play such an important part in the political and commercial co-operation of Great Britain and America.

The Vimy navigator envisioned a glowing future:

> The present generation is lucky in that, despite this instinctive longing since the beginning of human history for the means of flight, it is the first to see flying dreams and theories translated into fact. The coming generation may see the realisation of even wilder dreams. The development of practical aviation within the past fifteen years has been startling. The aeronautical wonders of the next fifteen years are likely to be yet more startling. To come within sight of world intercommunication as rapid as is indicated by the signposts of present-day aeronautics would make possible an era of greater prosperity and peace. If people, their written communications, and their goods can be taken from continent to continent as quickly, or nearly as quickly, as cablegrams, the twin evils of state parochialism and international misunderstanding will less often be dragged from the cupboard in which the world's racial skeletons are kept.

There was one final public appearance that Brown would not miss. Resplendent in his blue RAF uniform, he and Marguerite Kathleen Kennedy were married at the Chapel Royal, Savoy, off London's Strand, on Tuesday, 29 July 1919. Alcock was among the guests who attended the wedding and the breakfast in the nearby Savoy Hotel. He had hoped to arrive unnoticed, and was embarrassed to be cheered by spectators. After their honeymoon, Brown and his new bride set off on an extended trip to America on the *Mauretania*. Five months earlier he had studied navigation on the ship's bridge. Now he was cheered as he explained to an afternoon concert audience how he had navigated the Vimy across the skies high above their ship.

He was also fêted by the Aero Club of America when he lectured on 7 October about the Atlantic flight to a huge audience at Carnegie Hall. A journalist noted: 'Brown, despite the success and the honours which had intervened, was the same modest unassuming agreeable person who had been so well liked by both rivals and associates in the days when the race was yet to be flown.'

Photographs showed him unfamiliarly capless and in civvies, as he and Kathleen circled New York harbour on their first trip in a flying boat. Lady Whitten Brown, as Kathleen was now known, was the subject of a fulsome full-page *New York Evening Word* interview, in which she was described as having 'large blue-grey eyes, curly dark hair, pink cheeks, and a most engaging smile'. The couple also visited Pittsburgh, where Brown had trained, and Seattle, where Boeing's test pilot, Eddie Hibberd, flew them around.

John Alcock was happily back at Brooklands, testing aeroplanes for Vickers. Plans were well advanced for his new business in London's West End. Bob Dicker, now selling motorcycles on which he would later set up world speed records, recalled:

I met Jack five weeks after the flight. We sat on the edge of Brooklands track having a chat about the crossing when I learned that his greatest disappointment was still the landing in Clifden. I saw him on several other occasions and I agreed to go at his request to help him in his new business which he was going to start. A motor agency in, I believe, the Burlington Arcade. He had several good makers to back him.

While Brown was still in the USA, Alcock celebrated his 27th birthday on 5 November with some friends at Brooklands. One week later he saw the brothers Ross and Keith Smith lift off their Vimy from Hounslow on the first-ever flight to Australia. Aviation's continuing hazards were further underlined when four Australian fliers perished in the race to lead the eighteen entrants home. Capt. Roger Douglas and Lt Leslie Ross crashed at Surbiton, while Capt. Cedric Howell and Lt George Fraser disappeared near Corfu.

On 15 December, three days after Adm. Kerr finally arrived back in Britain, Alcock made his last public appearance in London. It was a heady time for Vickers, whose aeroplane, piloted by the Smith brothers, had completed the first-ever England–Australia flight on 12 December. Together with Douglas Vickers, Moore-Brabazon and Claude Johnson of Rolls-Royce, Alcock attended the presentation by Vickers of the trans-atlantic Vimy to London's Science Museum. Washed clean of Irish peat and with its nose repaired, the aeroplane was original in every detail apart from its propellers, which had been replaced by two spares. Douglas Vickers warned museum officials: 'The curio-hunter was there and made bounty of the machine – so that this is not the only place where relics of the Atlantic machine would be shown.' The Vimy's pilot interjected to laughter: 'I can vouch for that!'

After leaving South Kensington, Alcock headed back to Brooklands, from where he was to fly a single-engined Vickers Viking Mark 1 amphib-ian biplane to the first post-war aeronautical exhibition in Paris. The show was a special one. It marked the tenth anniversary of the earliest exhibi-tion dedicated to aviation, and was to be opened by President Poincaré and Marshals Foch and Petain. The plywood-hull Viking with its novel enclosed cabin had only recently been flown for the first time. Bob Dicker's own entrepreneurial flair prevented him from sharing the trip: 'He invited me at short notice to fly over with him for the weekend in Paris. But I was trying to sell the local chemist a motorcycle combination!'

Just as in Newfoundland six months earlier, the English weather was at its worst for the preceding days. Low cloud and wind-driven rain ensured a miserable morning for those who braved the wide-open spaces of Brooklands on the morning of 18 December. When Alcock arrived early from his home in Mayfield Road, Weybridge, his col-leagues suggested he postpone the trip, particularly as he was taking the six-seater aeroplane without a navigator. But the pilot felt that he had already waited too long, and he was anxious to have the machine in Paris for the following day's official opening. He shrugged off their concerns and headed once again into the clouds. Southern England was such familiar territory since those halcyon pre-war days flying Ducrocq's faithful Farman. Having coped with the Atlantic weather, the English Channel held no fears for him.

Despite the blustery conditions, Alcock safely negotiated the Channel and reached the Normandy coast. It is likely that he was following the Seine when heavy mist suddenly reduced visibility to 100yd, less than 100 miles from Paris. He descended, either to find the river again or a town he could identify. He would have recognised Rouen, but he was never to see its shuttered houses, nor its lines of docks and telltale cranes.

At 1 o'clock in the afternoon a farmer named Pelletier was working in his fields at Côte d'Evrard, 25 miles north of Rouen, when he heard the Viking approach:

> There was a strong wind coming in from the channel. I heard engine noise and looked up in the sky. I saw a large 'plane speeding from the north. It became very unsteady in the wind. Then, it gave a great sway and fell to the earth.

The farmer surmised that the pilot was flying too low in the mist. The aeroplane touched the top of a tree before hitting the ground. Alcock was pitched forward into the windscreen; his head was thrown back and the base of his skull was fractured. When he was found, his hands were still gripping the spade-handles on each side of the control column. The farmer and a friend carried him into the farmhouse. A priest, Father Collpiur, arrived and administered the last rites. Alcock was identified by an inscription on his watch and papers found in his civilian suit.

The crash site was in a remote area, and the farmer sent another friend to the road to flag down a passing car for assistance. There was little traffic, and it was some time before a British Army lorry arrived. Its driver went immediately to No. 6 British General Hospital at Rouen. A doctor was dispatched, but Alcock had died at 4 o'clock without regaining consciousness. The medic took the flier's body back to the hospital, where it was laid out under a Union flag in the wooden shed that served as a chapel. The children of the sergeant major laid some flowers with a message:

In loving memory of one of our dead heroes, Jean and Normand.

Alcock had been desperately unlucky. Had he been able to reach Rouen he would have found clear air all the way to Paris, where winter sunshine gilded his target berth opposite the Grand Palais. An investigation showed that he hit the ground at comparatively slow speed. *Flight* magazine concluded that Alcock had been attempting an emergency landing. After circling the farmhouse he had turned into the wind and was almost safely down when he spotted a wire fence running across the field. His wartime reflexes to save the aeroplane enabled him to rev the engine and clear the fence, but the machine then stalled and nosed into the downward sloping field. At low forward speed the force of the impact was small but, sadly, sufficient to kill the Viking's conscientious pilot. Alcock was not to be the only high-profile Viking fatality. A similar machine later killed J.M. Bennett and Ross Smith, first to fly to Australia, when it spun into the Byfleet banking at Brooklands.

The Aeroplane wrote in a tribute to Alcock:

Quiet, unassuming, earnest and confident, he had no enemies.

The journal reiterated that Alcock, the fearless pilot and acrobatic specialist, was no unthinking risk-taker:

He always knew what the machine and engine would stand and drove them just to the limits of safety, but never beyond. His was always plain straightforward flying which inspired confidence. Mr Coatalen will agree when one says that much of the reputation of his engines was built up on the results achieved by the skill and sound common sense with which Jack Alcock handled the early engines.

In San Francisco, Brown was shocked when he heard of Alcock's death. His shoulders heavy with sadness, he mumbled before fleeing reporters: 'A true sacrifice for humanity.' Their shared Atlantic experience made it seem as if he had known Alcock for a lifetime, rather than nine brief months. The news was received with similar disbelief throughout the world. A spokesman for the American Flying Club said: 'The science of aviation has lost one of its most daring and beloved leaders.' While mourning Alcock, Parisian media reflected proudly that it was Frenchman Maurice Ducrocq who had first taught him to fly. News of Alcock's death coincided with another tragedy: the discovery off Corfu of the body of Australian flier Capt. Cedric Howell.

The British government provided a military escort to accompany Alcock's coffin across the Channel from Le Havre. A special message was sent to Alcock's parents by the King who, six months earlier, had honoured their son.

Alcock's parents and representatives of Vickers met the cortège at Waterloo Station, where Alcock had often entrained for Brooklands. The flier's body was removed to his parents' parish church in Fallowfield on Christmas Day. Representatives of all the companies who had sent aeroplanes to Newfoundland attended the subsequent service in Manchester Cathedral. France was represented by its leading aviation hero, Lt René Fonck. Aeroplanes flew overhead as the coffin, escorted by RAF cadets, was carried on a gun carriage through crowded silent streets. The Mayor of Manchester and Corporation officials joined the cortège. A friend quoted Robert Louis Stevenson in tribute:

> Under the wide and starry sky,
> Dig the grave and let me lie.
> Glad did I live and gladly die,
> And I laid me down with a will.
> This be the verse you grave for me:
> Here he lies where he longed to be;
> Home is the sailor, home from the sea.
> And the hunter home from the hill.

The pilot who had conquered the Atlantic was buried in the city's Southern Cemetery, north of the Barlowmoor Road entrance. One wreath of the three coachloads read: 'He flew by the light of Heaven and may Heaven's light be his own light ever more.' Three volleys were fired and the Last Post sounded by his graveside. Appropriately for a man whose historic adventure had concluded in Ireland, a Celtic Cross was later erected over his grave, an aeroplane propeller carved on its base.

Alcock's friends and admirers took some consolation from the fact that he had died doing what he loved best. Charles Lindbergh described the attraction of their mutual passion:

> I began to feel that I lived on a higher plane than the sceptics of the ground; one that was richer because of its very association with the element of danger they dreaded, because it was freer of the earth to which they were bound. In flying, I tasted a wine of the gods of which they could know nothing. Who valued life more highly, the aviators who spent it on the art they loved, or these misers who doled it out like pennies through their antlike days? I decided that if I could fly for ten years before I was killed in a crash, it would be a worthwhile trade for an ordinary life time.

Still grieving for Alcock, Arthur Whitten Brown returned to England shortly afterwards with his new bride. He spent a brief spell with Cecil Lewis in China, to whose government Vickers had sold some Vimy Commercials. On his return, Brown and his wife moved to Swansea, where Metropolitan Vickers employed him as their general manager. After living in Overland Road, Oystermouth, the couple moved to 24 Belgrave Court, Uplands, before finally settling at number 3. The Vimy navigator was happy in his marriage, and particularly with the arrival of their son, Arthur junior, born in 1922. But he was further saddened by the death of Lord Northcliffe, to whom he paid tribute: 'All who flew on active service during the first three years of the war realise what they owe to Lord Northcliffe's crusades for more and better machines.'

The *Daily Mail* proprietor willed three months' salary to each of his 6,000 employees. Unlike most prophets, he lived long enough to be able to celebrate shortly before his death:

> The prizes given by my journals were devised to these two ends – to encourage the flying man and to interest the public. Both aims were, I am assured, achieved. Aerial progress in the design, construction, and handling of craft, followed upon the winning of these prizes; and I have the word of the flying men themselves that the encouragement came, so far as they were concerned, just when it was most required. The first direct trans-Atlantic flight of the late Sir John Alcock and Sir Arthur Whitten Brown was an example of unparalleled courage and endurance, of navigational skill in a new element, and of the reliability attained already with a mechanism which is still admittedly crude.

A measure of Alcock and Brown's achievement is that no aeroplane repeated their non-stop crossing for eight years. But they were not the only ones to fly the Atlantic in 1919. In addition to Lt Cdr Read and his NC-4 flying boat, a British airship made history in July with the first west–east crossing and the first return Atlantic trip. Commanded by Maj. George Herbert Scott, the R.34 flew from East Fortune in Scotland to Mineola, Long Island, in 108hr. Illustrating the influence of the prevailing westerlies, the return journey via Clifden took seventy-five hours. The enclosed airship afforded a more comfortable flight than the open Vimy. Crewman Lt J.C. Shotter noted: 'We saw a vast expanse of sea and fog. There is much more excitement in driving a taxicab.'

American aircraft designer Grover Loening was unimpressed by the 643ft-long airship: 'Close up one was astounded to see how the frame squeaked, bent and shivered with the cloth covering almost flapping in wind gusts. I was shocked at its flimsiness.'

Because they could travel longer distances with heavier pay loads, airships were regarded by both Alcock and Brown as the most economical means of air transport, pending the arrival of more efficient motive power. Deutsche Zeppelin Reederei of Germany inaugurated a seasonal transatlantic service in October 1928, using the giant dirigible *Graf Zeppelin*, which accommodated twenty passengers. But Loening's misgivings were well founded. The hydrogen-filled vessels eventually proved to be deathtraps. The R.34 was destroyed when it hit a Yorkshire hilltop the year after its Atlantic success; a foretaste of the disaster that killed Maj. Scott and most of those aboard the R.101 when it came down at Beauvais ten years later. The airship era ended when a hydrogen gas-fuelled inferno consumed the *Hindenburg* at Lakehurst, New Jersey, in May 1937.

Although shocked by the number of fatalities, Arthur Whitten Brown took a keen interest in the 1927 Atlantic attempts for hotelier Raymond Orteig's $25,000 prize for a non-stop flight between New York and Paris. No fewer than twenty-one aviators perished, including French war heroes Capt. Charles Nungesser and Capt. Francois Coli, Irishmen James Medcalf and Terence Tully, and Leslie Hamilton, Freddie Minchin and Princess Ludwig Loewenstein-Wertheim. Perhaps the most poignant loss was that of English naval commander H.C. McDonald, who later attempted to be first across in a light aeroplane. With a brisk 'So long' to a handful of spectators, he took off from Harbour Grace in his tiny open-cockpit de Havilland Gipsy Moth and was never seen again.

These tragedies were forgotten when Charles Lindbergh won the Orteig prize in his Ryan Aircraft Company NYP monoplane *Spirit of St Louis* on 21 May 1927. His remarkable thirty-three-hour epic flight from New York to Paris was the first solo crossing of the Atlantic. 'Alcock and Brown showed me the way,' he acknowledged. Three years later Erroll Boyd piloted his Bellanca monoplane named *Maple Leaf* from Harbour Grace to England, to become the first Canadian to fly the Atlantic. The former fighter pilot said: 'It's the realisation of a dream, to follow in the wingmarks of John Alcock, who taught me all those years ago in Eastchurch.'

Adulation for all-American hero Lindbergh so detracted from the achievement of Alcock and Brown that many later mistakenly credited him with the honour of the first non-stop crossing. Even in Britain, historian Henry Jones suggested in 1927 that Alcock's greatest contribution was training pilots for the war, rather than his Atlantic success.

Lindbergh was also inadvertently responsible for a film on the Vimy flight not going into production. Anthony Kilmister, OBE, a friend of the Brown family, recalled:

> I seem to remember that a film script was written when a book was published about the flight around the mid-fifties. There was talk of Kenneth More acting the part of Captain Alcock and Denholm Elliott playing uncle Teddy. But the Warner Brothers' film *The Spirit of St Louis* – about Lindbergh's solo flight – with James Stewart as the aviator came out at the same time, and that killed the idea of the Alcock and Brown film!

The first east–west Atlantic crossing by an aeroplane was achieved by the all-enclosed German Junkers W 33 monoplane *Bremen* in May 1928. Piloted by Capts James Fitzmaurice and Hermann Koehl, with passenger Baron Gunther von Huenefeld, it battled the Atlantic gales for thirty-six hours from Dublin's Baldonnel Airport to Greenly Island, Newfoundland. Landing a long way from its intended US destination, the *Bremen* repeated Alcock and Brown's nose-down landing on the crumbling ice.

Newfoundland and Ireland were united once more in May 1932, when Amelia Earhart landed her Lockheed Vega in Culmore, Derry, to complete the first solo Atlantic crossing by a woman. Jim Mollison concluded the ocean's solo conquest when he flew from Dublin's Portmarnock to St John, New Brunswick, in August 1932. Like many others, Arthur Whitten Brown was delighted six years later by the ocean's most unlikely pilgrim, 'Wrong way' Corrigan. Refused permission by US authorities for an Atlantic flight, the Irish-American landed in Baldonnel in an old Curtiss monoplane. Its door was fastened by baling wire, its compass a year older than Brown's Vimy. Claiming to be a victim of the same fog that had bedevilled Alcock and Brown, he enquired: 'I'm Douglas Corrigan. Just got in from New York; where am I?'

17

BROWN REMEMBERS ST JOHN'S

The happy days spent in St John's; the good company
at the Cochrane house; and the many friends left behind,
all form a golden memory which it is my privilege to possess.

Arthur Whitten Brown

The death of his pilot diminished Arthur Whitten Brown's life. According to Alcock's brother, Capt. E.S.J. Alcock, the shock permanently affected the battle-scarred Vimy navigator. He became more reserved and withdrawn. His sedentary work was a sharp contrast to the stimulation of Atlantic adventure and navigation. He told a journalist: 'I am now a business man pure and simple. I merely want to be known for what I am now – an engineer. That is the way I earn my bread and butter.'

Col Arthur Lynch described him at this time:

Sir Arthur Whitten Brown is small and slight, and except for the freshness of complexion of a temperate man he looks older than he is. His hair is already streaked with grey, his clean-cut intellectual features have taken the set cast of the thinking man, and his voice has the clean-cut utterance of the well-educated Yankee. In his quiet way, he has a fund of humour.

Brown's war wounds continued to trouble him, despite the fitting of a special surgical boot after an operation at a London hospital in 1921.

But in November that year he attended the unveiling of a tablet to Alcock and himself at Manchester town hall, where he and the pilot's father were presented with gold medals. He was less enthusiastic about such functions as the Vickers and Rolls-Royce tenth anniversary lunch at the Savoy in June 1929. He unveiled a plaque at Burry Port in 1930, to commemorate the arrival there in 1928 of Wilber Stultz and his passenger, Amelia Earhart.

In August 1930 Brown was delighted to greet a grizzled Louis Blériot and Amy Johnson at the *Daily Mail* lunch to celebrate Johnson's first solo flight by a woman from England to Australia. He was also happy to present sports prizes at Gowerton Intermediate School outside Swansea. Mrs Gwen Williams recalls: 'He was a very nice and friendly man. But his wife was really beautiful and, as young girls, we wondered why she had not married someone more handsome!'

In 1931 Brown made a return visit to New York on the *Carinthia* to introduce his 9-year-old son, also named Arthur, to his Brooklyn relatives. Despite having been a German prisoner of war only twenty years earlier, he attended a 1936 function organised by the Swansea British Legion for British, French and German veterans. Endorsing the radical reunion, he insisted: 'The gathering brings to fruition the hope expressed by the Prince of Wales for the inculcation of international amity. I believe we have set an example to the world.'

The Vimy veteran accepted some public honours, notably the insignia of the order of Sts Maurice and Lazarus from King Victor Emmanuel III of Italy, which he was to return on the outbreak of the Second World War. But he drew the line at the erection of a monument to commemorate the Atlantic flight. In 1939 Sir Alexander Duckham wrote to him about a proposal to erect a memorial in Clifden: 'To give such a monument to the Irish Free State would be considered by them as a friendly gesture from the old enemy, England.' Brown replied:

It is not modesty that dictates my attitude towards monuments. The publicity which would attend the fulfilment of your wishes is detrimental to me in my work and I want to avoid it. Your desire to honour Alcock and me is deeply appreciated, and it means more to me than any monument. It is not in my power to grant or to withhold from you what you so kindly term a privilege. I can only express my conviction that any monument should not involve living persons, and that in any case, twenty years is too short a time to warrant the erection of such a monument.

Despite his natural reticence, Brown was always willing to help others. Harold Hughes remembered:

My mother's cousin, Lewis Davies, worked at Metropolitan Vickers and he had shown Arthur Whitten Brown some of my structural drawings of World War 2 aircraft. Mr Brown invited me to his office in Swansea. He was dressed in an immaculate suit but his pleasant smile put me at my ease immediately. He told me he was quite impressed with the drawings and offered to get me an apprenticeship at Rolls-Royce or Bristol Engines. I was quite flattered at his offer but unfortunately, I had just volunteered to join the RAF. I always remember his encouragement.

The RAF provided a constant in Brown's life. He contributed generously to Air Cadet sports appeals and he rejoined at the outbreak of the Second World War, to train pilots in navigation and engineering. He became the first Commanding Officer of 215 (City of Swansea) Squadron of the Air Training Corps when it was formed in 1941. William George Sutton was impressed by his affability and enthusiasm when he welcomed the former Vimy navigator to a squadron inspection. Brown was also a battalion commander in the Home Guard, and was appointed Deputy Lieutenant of Glamorgan.

The Second World War twenty years later was a particular insult for a man of Arthur Whitten Brown's sensibilities. It rudely shattered his former idealistic hopes that aviation would promote world peace. Swansea's industries and port ensured that it was a prime German target. Brown was lucky to escape unscathed when a three-night blitz from 19 to 21 February killed many acquaintances and brought terror to the city. More than 600 people were killed or injured. Swansea was changed for ever; its centre was razed and almost 900 premises destroyed. Brown's father-in-law, Major David Kennedy became another air-raid victim when he was killed in London's High Street Kensington on 19 November 1940.

Arthur Brown junior cemented the RAF association when he joined 605 Squadron as a flight lieutenant. He regularly informed his frequently ill father of his adventures, including an incident in March 1941: 'I bent a 'Lizzie' [Westland Lysander] tail the other day – hit a bump on landing!'

But paternal pride was short-lived. Another flying tragedy marred Brown's life. Nine months after his son married he was reported missing in northern Holland. He had left on the morning of 6 June 1944 to carry out a patrol in support of the first stage of the D-Day invasion. It appeared that he and his navigator, Victor Brewis, were shot down after failing to douse their aeroplane's recognition lights. Brown responded to the news: 'We are trying to be optimistic. But I find the fact about the recognition light very distressing. My wife does not grasp the full significance of this and should you write again, please do not refer to it again.'

Brown's optimism was in vain. The Air Ministry informed him that the Germans had forwarded confirmation of his son's death and his burial in grave No. 1038, Hoorn Cemetery. The news came on 12 June, one week before the twenty-fifth anniversary of the Atlantic flight. The death of his only child was a body blow for Brown. The irony that his son had perished in the air was hardly lost on the man who had played such a key role in aviation's development.

Arthur Whitten Brown aged rapidly after his son's death. His hair receded, his face became more lined. He presented his medals to the RAF, and in September 1945 he offered the Vimy propeller that Vickers had given him to No. 19 Training School at Cranwell, Lincolnshire. He cautioned:

This is one of the two original props which actually crossed the Atlantic. One was kept by Mr P. Maxwell Muller, and the other given me by Vickers. The two props which are in the Science Museum are not the originals and therefore I would ask you to avoid publicity, except within the RAF.

In the summer of 1946 Brown flew the Atlantic for the second and final time. 'They have taken all the fun out of flying. This is like sitting in your own drawing-room,' he told a journalist. Although he had chaffed at the US delay in entering the First World War and had been one of the first to enlist in the British Army, he proclaimed a strong affinity with the USA:

America, that's home and always will be. I'm technically a British subject, but really at heart I'm an American. Why, I used to live on Herkimer Street in Brooklyn, just off Fulton Street. I have relatives there on Pierrepont Street now. I am proud of my American origin.

The Kilmister family were close friends of Sir Arthur and Lady Whitten Brown in Swansea. Anthony Kilmister, OBE, an author and charity campaigner, remembered:

My father and mother, Claude and Margaret, lunched with Sir Arthur and Lady Whitten Brown nearly every Saturday in the old Mackworth Hotel in Swansea and also met socially at other times. Sir Arthur, known to me as 'Uncle Teddy', was a very warm but shy character and 'Auntie Kay' was absolutely lovely. Together they made a very nice couple. As he had lost his own son, Arthur Junior, who was killed flying with his father's old squadron in 1944, Sir Arthur lavished a lot of affection on me. I even inherited Arthur Junior's toboggan. Uncle Teddy never forgot a present for my birthday on July 22, which was a day before his.

Although he was quite lame and rarely without his walking stick, he would also come to my Prep school's sports and speech days. The headmaster was delighted to welcome him and on a number of occasions asked him to address the assembled boys. But the hoped-for speech on the transatlantic flight never materialised. Instead, in his very slight American accent, he would encourage the boys to keep up their good work and never to slacken in their studies – which might not have been what they wanted to hear either!

I saw the propeller from the Vimy many times in his office in Wind Street, but that's the closest we ever got to the topic of his adventure with the Vimy. Uncle Teddy was often described as being shy. Perhaps having become fed up with so many previous interviews, he would close up like a clam whenever the subject of the Atlantic flight was mentioned.

Arthur Whitten Brown had a soft spot for both animals and a tipple. Anthony Kilmister recalled:

He encouraged their poodle to rest beside the clutch pedal when he drove along in his Daimler! I remember the car being flagged down on Victory night in 1945 by a policeman who said: 'You're not flying the Atlantic now Sir Arthur.' He had been driving it with excessive speed even for those pre-breathalyser days but Victory night was Victory night and there was no question of admonishment. I remember one year my mother and Auntie Kay went up to London for the Christmas Sales. I went for lunch with my father to Belgrave Court. Uncle Teddy served the remainder of their Christmas pudding over which he poured about half a bottle of brandy. He then lit it and the flames fairly exploded off the platter!

Brown's health gradually deteriorated, and Vickers allowed him to work restricted duties. But he still responded to requests for information on the transatlantic flight, about which he always retained fond memories. Shortly before he died he thanked the Newfoundland government's information bureau:

If Sir John Alcock were alive today, I know that he would be of one mind with me in remembering the generous hospitality afforded to us and to the devoted panel of riggers and mechanics who erected the Vickers Vimy and tuned its Rolls-Royce engines so as to make our success possible.

The happy days spent in St John's; the good company at the Cochrane house; and the many friends left behind, perhaps never to be met again, yet never forgotten; all form a golden memory unique in history which it is my privilege to possess. Among my most priceless treasures is a silver cup presented to me by the people of Newfoundland as a token of their goodwill. I see it each day; and each day it renews the bond between that historical island and myself.

The year 1948 brought the shocking assassinations of Gandhi and Count Bernadotte. After a holiday in Scotland, Brown declined an August invitation to visit Canada: 'I am not well enough to make the journey at present.' He and his wife were planning a cruise, when, on 4 October, he died at home at the age of 62. *The Times* reported the inquest findings:

A verdict that Sir Arthur Whitten Brown, the transatlantic flying pioneer, died from asphyxia due to an overdose of barbitone, otherwise veronal, accidentally self-administered, was returned by a jury at the inquest in Swansea yesterday. He was found dead in bed by Lady Whitten Brown on the morning of October 4 at their home at Belgrave Court, Swansea. Lady Whitten Brown told the Coroner that her husband had recently suffered a nervous and physical breakdown.

Lord Brabazon of Tara lamented: 'Alcock and Brown crossed the Atlantic eight years before Lindbergh, when equipment was a good deal more primitive and the feat all the more remarkable. Brown lived for many years in the west country unrecognised as the hero he really was.'

Anthony Kilmister, OBE, remembered:

The last time I saw Uncle Teddy, he was cheerful and upbeat. No doubt he had been distressed by the death of his son, but he had got over it and turned to other things. His death came as a shock. I was away at a Shrewsbury boarding school at the time and I think that my parents may have kept the news from me for a while to spare my feelings. I still have a First World War souvenir, wrapped in chamois leather inside a tin box which he gave me. It's a little mirror and with it a piece of cardboard on which he had written 'Found on the battlefield of Arras, 1917.' I also had his flying boots and the torch from the Vimy. I gave these to the Clifden Museum in 1994 on the 75th anniversary of the flight.

Arthur Whitten Brown's ashes were buried in the modest Kennedy grave in St Margaret's Church cemetery, Tylers Green, Penn. His widow, Kathleen, died four years later and was interred beside him. The area was already famous for its association with another transatlantic adventurer, William Penn. The founding father of Pennsylvania, home of Brown's maternal family, was buried in nearby Chalfont St Peter. For a person who loved peace and quiet, Arthur Whitten Brown could hardly have found a more appropriate resting place. An oasis of tranquillity and birdsong, the Buckinghamshire cemetery is surrounded by ancient beech woodlands and the unassuming Chiltern Hills. In the skies above, jet trails unite America and Europe and inscribe a constant tribute to the path he and John Alcock blazed across the celestial highway in June 1919.

Fellow Arras comrade Alec de Candole penned what could be the flier's most fitting epitaph:

> When the last long trek is over,
> And the last long trench filled in,
> I'll take a boat to Dover,
> Away from all the din;
> I'll take a trip to Mendip,
> I'll see the Wiltshire downs,
> And all my soul I'll then dip
> In peace no trouble drowns.

It was only after Brown's death that one of the most enduring legends of the first non-stop transatlantic flight surfaced. This was the story of his daring mid-air walk on the Vimy's wings, to clear the ice and snow which had blocked the engine air intakes and covered exterior instrument gauges. The ice, which also affected the aileron hinges, was encountered early on Sunday morning, 15 June 1919, when the pair attempted to climb above the clouds in search of a sun sighting. Practically every subsequent feature on the flight reiterated this story, which appeared in Graham Wallace's 1955 account, *The Flight of Alcock and Brown*, and was repeated by Alcock's younger brother in his 1969 book, *Our Transatlantic Flight*. According to Wallace, the handicapped Brown walked on the iced-up wings no fewer than six times, an heroic endeavour that stirred as many generations of schoolboys as the tales of Robert Falcon Scott's Antarctic valour.

An examination of the aeroplane in London's Science Museum will immediately cast doubt on this alleged feat. Only 3ft away from the cockpit, the propellers alone would inhibit anyone from climbing out. With his bulky flying suit and injured leg, Brown could neither have cleared the cockpit's protective sidescreen nor squeezed through the vertical struts in order to reach the engines. The fierce slipstream would also have plucked him off the wing.

There was no mention of any wing-walking in Brown's immediate post-flight interviews. The *Daily Mail* quoted John Alcock: 'My radiator shutter and the water temperature indicator were covered with ice for four or five hours. Brown had continually to [climb up] to chip off the ice with his knife.' As the water temperature gauges were on the instrument panel, this was either a slip of the tongue due to tiredness or an error on the reporter's part. The only gauge that Brown could have cleared by climbing up was the fuel overflow gauge, immediately behind the cockpit. This he could do by kneeling on his seat, as he recorded in his log book and in subsequent accounts of the flight.

The books by Wallace and Alcock's brother contain factual errors and discrepancies. The former was a writer of film scripts who did not sacrifice drama for accuracy; the younger Alcock apparently erred in his recall of what his brother had told him fifty years previously. Both writers referred to Brown clearing the fuel intake gauges and also the air intakes. There were no such gauges inside or outside the cockpit. The air intakes were situated between the banks of engine cylinders and not in view from the cockpit.

A significant feature of the wing-walking stories is that they were never mentioned in any contemporary accounts of the 1919 flight. They probably derived from Courtenay Edwards's article on Brown's death in 1948. The *Daily Mail* journalist recalled that Brown had told him two years previously on a flight to New York: 'When I came over with Alcock, I had to climb out on to the wing to chip ice off the oil-pressure gauges.' Brown was still depressed at this time over his son's death, his recall may not have been the best, but it is more likely that the journalist misquoted him after the two-year interval, and also confused the gauges. Edwards erred in the same report when he said that Brown's son had accompanied his father to the transatlantic flight's twenty-fifth anniversary luncheon. Brown junior had been killed ten days beforehand.

London Science Museum researcher Peter R. Mann made a comprehensive study of the wing-walking legend and attempted to replicate Brown's alleged feat. He also made an exhaustive examination of the navigator's log book and all the story's sources. The log made no mention of such episodes, and its regular entries cast grave doubt on the alleged times and altitudes of these exercises. Surmising that lack of technical knowledge may have confused journalists, Mann concluded his 6,000-word report: 'All sources other than Brown's *RAF and Civil Aviation Record* account can be rejected as inaccurate. Brown stood up in the cockpit … he almost certainly did not get out on to the wing.'

Although the fuel-overflow gauge was within easy reach when standing up, this itself was no mean feat, considering the navigator's war injuries and his exposure to the cold and violent slipstream. Brown himself referred to the exaggerated stories about the Vimy flight in a letter to a New York friend shortly before he died:

> After so many years, it is astonishing to read of many misrepresentations which, probably, were overlooked at the time, or were the results of over-enthusiasm. There are also many exaggerations regarding adventures and dangers of the transatlantic flight.

Brown's wing-walking was a journalistic invention. But, only a few years previously, he had in fact clambered out of a cockpit in mid-air. That was in even more terrifying circumstances, as his burning aeroplane plummeted to earth in the wartime crash that almost killed him. After his 2005 re-enactment Atlantic flight with Steve Fossett in a replica Vimy, navigator Mark Rebholz insisted:

> The wing-walking stories may be fiction. But nothing can detract from either Brown's courage in clearing that gauge in such discomfort, or the navigation with which he unerringly guided the Vimy across the ocean to land only miles from the fliers' original target. Like Alcock, he was a real hero.

18

MONUMENTS AND TRIBUTE FLIGHTS

◆◇◆

Ta a ngaisce greannta ar chlar na speire.
Their heroism adorns the expanses of the sky.

Ballinaboy monument inscription

◆◇◆

Alock and Brown's dreams of regular commercial Atlantic flight were finally realised by flying boats, rather than landplanes, which demanded expensive airport bases. Britain's Imperial Airways and Pan American Airways' Juan Trippe launched the first scheduled service in 1939 from New York to Marseilles via the Azores and Lisbon, and New York to Southampton via Botwood, Newfoundland and Foynes, Ireland. The first east–west Atlantic flight to cleave the water of Foynes was commanded by Capt. Kelly-Rogers, later Churchill's BOAC pilot and organiser of a monument to Alcock and Brown at Ballinaboy. The first direct Foynes–New York flight was flown by Charles Blair, husband of actress Maureen O'Hara.

Landplanes eventually superseded the flying boats. By 1950, with intermediate stops in Gander and Shannon, such carriers as Pan Am, TWA, Trans Canada Airlines, BOAC, and Air France made the Atlantic the world's number one route in terms of traffic and revenue. It had taken the common man a mere three decades to follow in the footsteps of the Vimy pioneers. Regular jet flights started in the late 1950s, after Sqn Ldr Callard's first 1951 crossing from Belfast's Aldergrove Airport to Gander in four hours and thirty-seven minutes in an English Electric Canberra bomber. Supersonic services soon followed Brian Trubshaw's 1974 record-breaking Concorde flight from Fairford to Bangor, Maine, in two hours and fifty-six minutes, a time that would have astonished Alcock and Brown (as would have Neil Armstrong's moon landing in 1969, only fifty years after their Atlantic flight).

Although Arthur Whitten Brown died prematurely, he outlived most of the other 1919 transatlantic aviators. Harry Hawker died in 1921 at the age of 32, after suffering a haemorrhage that caused him to crash near Hendon. His navigator, Mackenzie-Grieve, died in 1943 in Victoria, British Columbia, a year before 79-year-old Adm Mark Kerr. Air Cdre Herbert Brackley was appointed Director General of British South American Airways; he drowned at the age of 53 during a 1948 stopover in Rio de Janeiro. Poacher turned gamekeeper Freddie Raynham became an air accident investigator for Britain's Air Ministry. After touring the USA by caravan with his wife, the restless pioneer died in Colorado Springs in April 1954 aged 61.

Ernest Archdeacon was awarded the *Légion d'honneur* and became a member of the Chamber of Deputies before dying in 1955 at the age of 88. Henry Farman died three years later, aged 84, and is buried in Passy Cemetery, near air and motor race sponsor James Gordon Bennett. J.T.C. Moore-Brabazon played a leading role in the development of aerial photography. A successful tobogganist, he won the Curzon Cup three times on the Cresta Run, where he raced until he was over 70. Minister of Transport in Churchill's wartime cabinet, he was knighted in 1942 and was also awarded the French *Légion d'honneur*. Before he died in 1964, aged 80, Lord Brabazon of Tara insisted: 'The fun of being in at the beginning of any new development will remain with you all your life.'

Cdr Albert Read became Chief of Air Technical Training in Chicago. He died aged 80 in 1967, and his NC-4 flying boat is displayed at the National Museum of Naval Aviation in Pensacola, Florida. John Alcock's friend, Bob Dicker, passed away in 1979 at the age of 86. Brooklands pioneer Sir Edwin Alliott Verdon Roe died in January 1958, aged 80. Knighted five years after Arthur Whitten Brown's demise, Tommy Sopwith outlived all of the early aviators. A flypast of military aircraft over his Hampshire home celebrated his 100th birthday. The last of the great aviation pioneers died in 1989 at the age of 101.

Alcock and Brown are celebrated by many memorials. Following the 1921 Manchester town hall plaque, others were erected at Alcock's house at 6 Kingswood Road, Fallowfield, and at Brown's home, 6 Oswald Road, Chorlton-cum-Hardy. Fellow aviator James Mollison organised the 8ft-high plaster-cast sculpture by William McMillan of the helmeted aviators that Lord Brabazon of Tara helped to unveil at London's Heathrow Airport in 1954. A more abstract bronze tribute by Elisabeth Frink was erected at Manchester Airport in 1962. The original Vimy propeller presented to Percy Maxwell Muller is displayed in the Brooklands Museum. The second propeller was given to Arthur Whitten Brown and hung for many years on the wall of his office before he presented it to the RAF. Like the Vimy's radio, it is now missing (possibly lying unrecognised in some museum or staff mess), an undeserved fate for such a historical artefact.

St John's Airport commemorates Alcock and Brown with a plaque and a 1919 propeller. The city's Rooms Museum displays one of the wheels of Harry Hawker's Sopwith. The second is in Admiralty House Museum, Mount Pearl, whose exhibits include a ground screw used to anchor the Vimy. On the flight's fiftieth anniversary, in June 1969, a plaque by Hans Melis was erected at the junction of Blackmarsh Road and Cashin Avenue, St John's, close to the actual take-off site. The Vimy taxied from near the Hamilton Avenue and LeMarchant Road junction, then flew north-westwards before it turned and swept back over Hamilton Avenue to the Narrows and Signal Hill. Two local thoroughfares have been named Vimy and Vickers Avenue.

Among the 1969 audience were Leslie Curtis, Mrs Augustus Lester, daughter-in-law of Mr Lester, and Harry Symonds, who had witnessed the Vimy's take-off. Harry confirmed that the monument site was accurate:

The plane began here and taxied over Symonds' field, taking off from Driscolls, where A.E. Hickman's is now. It revved its motors right here, the blast was enough to knock you down. After she left the ground, she skimmed the Topsail trees up where Cook and Jones is now. She disappeared down the valley, and everybody started running that way, but then we saw the plane come into view again. She made a swerve where the Avalon Mall is and glided over the city, up over Cabot Tower.

Commemorative stamps were issued in many countries. On the fiftieth anniversary in 1969 Capt. Eugene Locke flew First Day Covers from Newfoundland to Ireland. Flt Lts W.N. Browne and A.J. Alcock MBE, John Alcock's nephew, marked the sixtieth anniversary by flying special First Day Covers in their Phantom jet from Newfoundland to England via Derrygimla bog. John Alcock's niece, Anne, unveiled a plaque on Ballinaboy Hill overlooking the landing site on the 75th anniversary of the flight. Among those present were Tony Kilmister, OBE, and Albert Millar, now the 83-year-old proprietor of Millar's Connemara Tweeds.

Clifden Station House Museum's proudest aviation exhibits are Brown's flying boots and torch, donated by Tony Kilmister. The feline mascot Lucky Jim can be seen in Manchester's Museum of Science and Industry, together with a camera carried on the flight and the aeroplane's clock. As well as portraits of the fliers, Hendon's RAF Museum houses Brown's Brandis sextant and suit, the Vimy's compass, the horseshoe from Alcock's seat and the Twinkletoes mascot. The fliers' faithful Vimy itself can be seen in London's Science Museum.

Connemara hosts the most evocative monument to Alcock and Brown, a 14ft-high limestone 'tail-fin'. This was erected in 1959 on Ballinaboy Hill, which their Vimy had overflown on its way to the nearby Marconi station, and across which Alannah Heather had raced forty years earlier to see the stranded aeroplane. Pointing towards the landing site 1.5 miles away, it was unveiled by Irish Taoiseach, Sean Lemass. The distinguished audience included the monument's organiser, pilot Capt. Kelly-Rogers OBE; Ireland's most neglected aviation hero, the first west–east Atlantic flier, Col James Fitzmaurice; and former navigator Paddy Saul. Also present were Alcock's brothers Albert and Capt. E.S.J. Alcock; the flier's nephew, A.J.H. Alcock and Frank H. Teague, the Marconi wireless operator who first told the world of the Vimy's success.

Among those who welcomed the monument was Harry Sullivan, whose measles attack had enabled him to witness the Vimy's arrival. The supermarket proprietor remembered:

> So many emigrants had taken weeks in boats to America that people could not credit that this flying machine had done the 1900 miles in sixteen hours. I wasn't allowed out to the bog, and I remember being very jealous of my brother, Billy, who saw the machine. But, even though it had frightened me, I was pleased to have been one of the few who had seen the plane before it landed.

The life of Errislannan witness Alannah Heather likewise spanned both the Vimy's arrival and its commemoration. Beside the townsland's unassuming Holy Trinity Church, the artist lamented the 1922 burning of the Marconi station by nationalists:

> And so it closed and 300 men, who cut turf for the fuelling of the station, were left unemployed. Now there is nothing to show that it was ever there except a few slabs of concrete. In September 1978 a BBC television crew of six arrived at the quay and took me up that rocky, worn-out track to show them where the 'plane had actually landed. I stood on a heather-covered hillock in my Connemara jersey, jeans and gumboots, and told them about that day sixty-odd years before. They filmed the lonely ruins of the Marconi Station, the empty bogland and the mountains, and broadcast it to the world. How little my brother and I had imagined this as we ran barefoot across the bog to the 'plane all those years ago.

In addition to the Alcock and Browne fly-over, two further commemorative flights were made from St John's to Ireland. Eugene Locke and Thomas Lee celebrated the fiftieth anniversary of the Vimy Atlantic crossing by flying a twin-engine Piper Navajo along Alcock and Brown's route in ten hours thirty-four minutes. In 1994 an Australian–American team led by Lang Kidby and Peter Macmillan built a replica open-cockpit Vimy. Cheers and tears from hundreds of spectators greeted the July 2005 arrival of the aeroplane, crewed by Steve Fossett and Mark Rebholz, as it completed its eighteen-hour re-enactment flight at Ballyconneely's golf club.

What was it like to fly as Alcock and Brown had? Rebholz, a 52-year-old commercial pilot, said:

> We were in cloud and darkness for about four-fifths of the flight. I barely got three sextant shots, all credit to Alcock and Brown for their great achievement. The 'plane also doesn't have trimming, it would have been so easy to lose control had we not paid constant attention.

Steve Fossett insisted:

> It was a unique opportunity to be an aviator like those of the early twentieth century, to face the same demands and the same trials. And we certainly learned the reality of early aeronautics, we had our hands full! We flew at about 1,500 feet with a slight tailwind, for most of the journey. The Vimy proved a difficult aeroplane to fly. She handled like a 1919 machine and we knew that anything could go wrong, just as it frequently did with those 'planes. It was hard physical work and a long flight. Like Alcock and Brown, I was relieved to see the Irish coast.

The first non-stop Atlantic fliers were also role models for Fossett's adventurous friend, Sir Richard Branson:

> In contrast to Lindbergh, Alcock and Brown were old fashioned stiff-upper-lip heroes, who piloted their unreliable twin engined bomber through appalling weather conditions only feet above the Atlantic. With no hope of survival should they lose an engine in flight or run out of fuel. Their epic landing in an Irish bog was even in my mind when Per Lindstrand and I briefly touched our balloon down in Northern Ireland during our 1987 crossing of the Atlantic.

Alcock and Brown would surely have appreciated the crossings made by Fossett and Branson, and also the microlight attempts of Brian Milton and Eppo Newman, who succeeded in 1990 via Scotland and Iceland. The most unusual tribute to the two pioneers was completed in August 2003. After its thirty-nine-hour flight from Cape Spear in Newfoundland, the scarlet TAM model aeroplane replicated Brown's accuracy by landing 100yd off-target underneath the Ballinaboy monument. It was the brainchild of Maynard Hill of Silver Spring, Maryland, and a team of volunteers that included Joe Foster, Beecher Butts, and Dave Brown. A visionary in the Northcliffe mould, the latter said: 'If a small model airplane can fly across the ocean, maybe some day jets will be able to carry cargo the same distance without a single human on board.' Maynard Hill reiterated: 'We chose the route as our tribute to the brave Alcock and Brown who blazed the non-stop Atlantic trail eight decades previously.'

Alcock and Brown made a unique contribution to the advancement of aviation. But, like many human discoveries, it cannot be denied that misuse of the aeroplane greatly increased the sum of human suffering. Arthur Whitten Brown lived through the aerial horror visited on the innocent populace of Coventry, Dresden, Hiroshima, and his adopted Swansea. His only child was a victim of war. Like many, he was shocked by the abuse of aviation for destruction, rather than for the realisation of his dreams of world unity. Just as later man would recoil from televised spectaculars of napalmed Vietnamese children or hapless Iraqis being carbonised by the latest American technology; 'collateral damage'.

John Alcock's pupil, pioneer Canadian aviator Erroll Boyd, condemned the killing of civilians by aeroplanes. Their use for bombing contributed to the great pioneer Santos-Dumont's suicide in 1930. Britain's first pilot, Lord Brabazon of Tara, regretted that the advances in mechanical sciences had been so rapid and overwhelming, as to have outpaced the political wisdom of mankind to use them for the best:

Flight, which was to knit the world together into a true internationalism, where to know all was to forgive all, has become the bogey and terror of the world from which we hide like rats. Thus do the triumphs of man's ingenuity get debased and prostituted.

As aggression, greed and ignored injustice continue to threaten planet Earth, it is tempting to be overwhelmed by the negative. But not on the heights of Ballinaboy Hill. Buoyed by the heady breezes wreathing the monument to Alcock and Brown; one can only feel a resurgence of pride in man's incredible progress. Achievement, like love, ennobles. Man stumbled before he walked. Parliament replaced civil war. Hollowed-out tree trunk led to steamboat. The Wrights realised the flying fantasies of Cayley. The courage and skill of the Vimy fliers routed those who scoffed at hopes of bridging the fearsome Atlantic. Their accomplishment restored self-belief and helped to dispel the post-First World War darkness. Almost a century later it continues to reverberate with positivity. Man conquered the air and the impassable oceans. He will also surely overcome his own insecurity and tribalism to make the world a safer and more civilised place.

Silhouetted against the vault of the sky, the resolute tailfin blends seamlessly with the primeval landscape of Europe's last western shores, as if reiterating that only in harmony with nature can man survive and develop. The monument directs not only to the landing site but also confidently to the future. As inspirational as any Romanesque ruin, its audacious anchorage is pervaded by a sense of timelessness and spirituality. A shrine to man's enterprise and the miracle of flight, the monument has become an energising focal point for visitors from all over the world. One can feel the presence of gods and the ghosts of aviators long gone. And, particularly of two men who did the allegedly impossible, not for money or transitory fame, but for enthusiasm, conviction and the challenge. The monument inscription renews one's pride of species: '*Ta a ngaisce greannta ar chlar na speire.* Their heroism adorns the expanses of the sky.'

Ballinaboy Hill is also a haven for wild birds. They dart unexpectedly from boggy hiding places or hover for unsuspecting prey. Larger species frolic with the elements and proclaim the unceasing wonder of flight. It was the study of these winged creatures that finally revealed the secret of flight and precipitated the scarcely credible transport revolution which modern man accepts so casually. High above the clouds and storms which bedevilled Alcock and Brown, jet trails betray the hundreds of aeroplanes which cross each day between Europe and America. Meals are served and earphones distributed as they fly over the landing site of the two men who first unlocked the door to direct Atlantic flight.

The fliers' presence is palpable as one stands by the monument and looks across the boulder-strewn wilderness to the Vimy's landing site. In the early morning, if one has the will to listen, one can hear the throaty sound of two slow-revving engines and see an off-white speck fly unsteadily in from the ocean. Crawling along the background ridge of hills, it gradually assumes the shape of a biplane before it circles low-lying Clifden. The aeroplane wheels around and heads for the hill. Growing ever larger, it yaws from side to side but maintains its determined approach.

Engine noise floods the sky. The machine's wings suddenly blot out the light as it sweeps overhead towards the Marconi station. Two men can be seen peering anxiously over the sides of the cockpit. Who are they? Where have they come from? One can hear the cries of the startled station crew as the aeroplane circles, then banks and turns into the western wind. And see them scramble across the bog as the Vimy slowly descends and is reunited with the ground. And imagine their wonder and incredulity as they finally understand the pilot's shouted words: 'We are Alcock and Brown. Yesterday we were in America.'

John Alcock was the first person to make that statement in Europe.

APPENDIX

CENTENARY BOARDWALK PROVIDES
EASIER ACCESS TO VIMY LANDING SITE

A haven for hares and sheep, as well as birds, remote Derrygimla bog is just as wild and unspoilt as it was when Alcock and Brown touched down here on the overcast Sunday morning of 15 June 1919.

However, the good news for centenary visitors is that Clifden Chamber of Commerce, Failte Ireland and Galway County Council have developed a safe new walking route with interactive displays, which allows easier access to the general landing area.

The trail includes audio-visual panels and 'Historioscopes', sited at strategic points along the 5km of the Marconi company's early 1900s paths and railway line. It additionally features many previously unseen historic photographs, from private sources and from the archives of the Bodleian Library and the Essex Record Office.

With the support of the National Parks and Wildlife Service, a major new extension is also being planned to the east of the present development. The new 1.5km walk will take visitors to an elevated point overlooking a spectacular view of the Twelve Bens mountains and Lough Fada.

This section was the location of the Marconi Station's huge aerial array, about which the walkway will inform visitors. The route will feature disabled access, walks from the earlier developments should also be upgraded to the same standard.

A First World War soldiers' blockhouse site coincides with the walk's highpoint. Observers here in June 1919 would have had a grandstand view of Alcock and Brown's circuits of the station, before they finally skirted the most easterly aerial near Lough Fada and made their landing.

For newcomers, the signposted Alcock and Brown landing site is on the left side of a crossroads 5km south of Clifden on the A341 road.

Opposite, Errislannan Road leads up to the evocative granite tail-fin monument, which points across the other-world landscape to the Derrygimla landing site.

The final welcome news is that historians Pat and Shane Joyce have established the long-awaited coordinates of the historic landing site: 53° 26' 26' N, 10° 00' 52' W.

BIBLIOGRAPHY

Alcock, John, and Brown, Arthur Whitten, *Our Transatlantic Flight* (William Kimber, London, 1969).

Allaz, Camille, *The History of Air Cargo and Airmail from the 18th Century* (Christopher Foyle Publishing, London, 2005).

Allen, Sir Peter, and Robson, Graham, *Transport Pioneers of the Twentieth Century* (Patrick Stephens, Cambridge, 1981).

Andrews, C.F., *Vickers Aircraft since 1908* (Putnam, London, 1969).

Barker, Ralph, *Great Mysteries of the Air* (Pan Books, London, 1968).

Bellamy, D., *The Wild Boglands: Bellamy's Ireland* (Country House, Dublin, 1986).

Boase, Wendy, *The Sky's the Limit. Women Pioneers in Aviation* (Osprey, London, 1979).

Blythe, Ronald, *The Age of Illusion. England 1919–1940* (Phoenix Press, London, 2001).

Boddy, William, *The History of Brooklands* (Grenville Publishing, London, 1979).

Brabazon of Tara, Lord, *The Brabazon Story* (William Heinemann Ltd, London, 1956).

Byrne, Liam, *History of Aviation in Ireland* (Blackwater Press, Dublin, 1980).

Cahill, Liam, *Forgotten Revolution: The Limerick Soviet 1919* (O'Brien Press, Dublin, 1990).

Chant, Christoper, *Aviation, an Illustrated History* (Orbis Publishing Ltd., London, 1978).

Clarke, George Herbert, editor, *A Treasury of War Poetry* (Houghton Mifflin Company, Boston, 1917).

Crouch, Tom D., and Jakab, Peter L., *The Wright Brothers and the Invention of the Aerial Age* (Smithsonian National Air and Space Museum, Washington, DC, 2003).

Croydon, Air Cdre Bill, CBE, *Early Birds. A Short History of How Flight Came to Sheppey* (Sheppey Heritage Trust, Sheerness).

Culbertson, Julie, and Randall, Tom, *Permanent Parisians* (Robson Books Ltd, London, 1991).

Dixon, Charles, *The Conquest of the Atlantic by Air* (Sampson, Low, Marston, London, 1931).

Ellis, F.H. and E.M., *Atlantic Air Conquest* (William Kimber, London, 1963).

Fairlie, Gerard, and Cayley, Elizabeth, *The Life of a Genius. Sir George Cayley, Pioneer of Modern Aviation* (Hodder & Stoughton Ltd, London, 1965).

Gallagher, Desmond, *Shooting Suns and Things. Transatlantic Fliers at Portmarnock* (Kingsford Press, Portmarnock, 1986).

Gardner, Helen, editor, *The New Oxford Book of Verse* (Clarendon Press, Oxford, 1972).

Hawker, H.G., and Mackenzie-Grieve, K., *Our Atlantic Attempt* (Methuen & Co, London, 1919).

Heather, Alannah, *Errislannan. Scenes from a Painter's Life* (Lilliput Press, Dublin, 1993).

Hitti, Philip K., *A Short History of the Arabs* (Macmillan, London, 1948).

Johnson, Paul, editor, *20th Century Britain. Economic, Social and Cultural Change* (Longman, London, 1994).

Koehl, Hermann Fitzmaurice, Maj. James, and von Huenefeld, Baron Guenther, *The Three Musketeers of the Air. Their Conquest of the Atlantic from East to West* (Putnam, New York, 1928).

Lewis, Cecil, *All My Yesterdays* (Element Books, Longmead, 1993).

—— *Sagittarius Rising* (Penguin Books, London, 1977).

Lindbergh, Charles, *The Spirit of St Louis* (Tandem Publishing, London, 1975).

Lovell, Mary S., *The Sound of Wings. The Biography of Amelia Earhart* (Arrow Books Ltd, London, 1990).

Lynch, Brendan, *Triumph of the Red Devil – The 1903 Irish Gordon Bennett Cup* (Portobello Publishing, Dublin, 2002).

Mackersey, Ian, *The Wright Brothers* (Time Warner, London, 2004).

Mason, Thomas Monck, *Aeronautica* (F.C. Westley, London, 1838).

O'Meara, Professor John, *The Voyage of Saint Brendan* (Colin Smythe, London, 1981).

Posthumus, Cyril, *Sir Henry Segrave* (B.T. Batsford Ltd, London, 1961).

Praeger, Robert Lloyd, *The Way That I Went* (Methuen, London, 1947).

Rhodes, Mary, *Sweethope Cottage and an Abandoned Box of Memories,* (Blackwell Print, 2011).

Saint-Exupery, Antoine de, *Night Flight* (Penguin Books, London, 2000).

Scott, J.D., *Vickers – A History* (Weidenfeld & Nicholson, London, 1962).

Severin, Tim, *The Brendan Voyage* (Hutchinson, London, 1978).

Skinner, Liam, and Cranitch, Tom, *Ireland and World Aviation* (Director Publications, Dublin, 1988).

Stevenson, R.L., *Poems* (Chatto & Windus, London, 1918).

Tobin, James, *To Conquer the Air. The Wright Brothers and the Great Race for Flight* (Free Press, New York, 2003).

Verne, Jules, *From the Earth to the Moon* (Ward Lock, London, 1924).

Wallace, Graham, *The Flight of Alcock and Brown* (Putnam, London, 1955).

Weldon, Niall G., *Pioneers in Flight: Aer Lingus and the Story of Aviation in Ireland* (Liffey Press, Dublin 2002).

Wells, H.G., *The War of the Worlds* (Pan Books, London, 1975).

Wordsworth, William, *The Excursion* (Macmillan & Co. Ltd, London, 1935).

Yeats, W.B., *Collected Poems* (Macmillan & Co. Ltd, London, 1961).

MEDIA

Irish Independent

The Irish Press

The Irish Times

Connacht Tribune

Daily Express

Daily Mail

Daily Sketch

The Despatch

Evening Standard

Manchester Guardian

Sunday Chronicle

Sunday Evening Telegram

The Times

Empire News

Matin

Le Journal

Deutche Tageszeitung

The Telegram, St John's

Daily News, St John's

The Evening World, New York

The New York Times

New York World

The New York World

The Aeroplane

Aeroplane Monthly

Badminton Magazine

The British Westinghouse Club News

Brooklands Gazette

Colliers Magazine

Flight

London Opinion

O.E.78., The Bulletin of the Irish
   Airmail Society

Punch

Royal Air Force and Civil Aviation Record

Vickers World

INDEX

You may also enjoy …

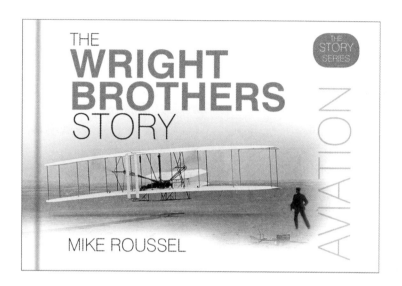

9780750970471

The creative and technological genius of the Wright brothers, Wilbur and Orville, led to the first powered and controlled flight. Packed with facts, figures and little-known details, *The Wright Brothers Story* charts their triumphs and tragedies as they set about making history together.

You may also enjoy …

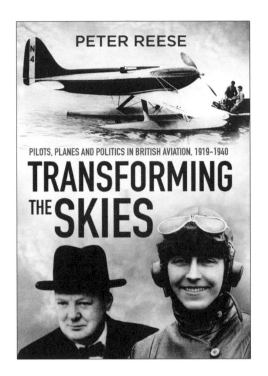

PETER REESE

PILOTS, PLANES AND POLITICS IN BRITISH AVIATION, 1919–1940

TRANSFORMING THE SKIES

9780750984102

In *Transforming the Skies*, Peter Reese charts the dramatic changes that swept aviation across the dynamic interwar period, revealing the transformative last-minute preparations for defence in a world where much depended on the contributions of some outstanding individuals.

You may also enjoy …

9780750983662

The Honourable Mrs Victor Bruce: record-breaking racing motorist; speedboat racer; pioneering aviator and businesswoman – remarkable achievements for a woman of the twenties and thirties. This is the story of a charismatic woman who defied the conventions of her time, and loved living life in the fast lane.

The History Press

The destination for history
www.thehistorypress.co.uk